D0643814

THE
PSYCHOTHERAPIST
AS HEALER

THE
PSYCHOTHERAPIST
AS HEALER

T. Byram Karasu, M.D.

JASON ARONSON INC.
Northvale, New Jersey
London

This book was set in 11 pt. ITC Berkeley by Alabama Book Composition of Deatsville, AL, and printed and bound by Book-mart Press, Inc. of North Bergen, NJ.

Library of Congress Cataloging-in-Publication Data

Karasu, Toksoz B.
     The psychotherapist as healer / T. Byram Karasu.
          p. cm.
     Includes bibliographical references and index.
     ISBN 0-7657-0302-5
     1. Psychotherapy—Philosophy.   2. Psychotherapists—Psychology.
     3. Psychotherapy—Case studies.   I. Title.

     RC437.5 .K373 2001
     616.89'14—dc21

                                                                    00-045345

Printed in the United States of America on acid-free paper. For information and catalog, write to Jason Aronson Inc., 230 Livingston Street, Northvale, NJ 07647-1726, or visit our website: www.aronson.com

Contents

Acknowledgments

First and foremost, I wish to express my utmost gratitude to some truly special members of my staff. I am especially indebted to Ms. Betty Meltzer for her invaluable literary assistance and unabated dedication to the realization of this book. I am most grateful to Mrs. Hilda Cuesta for her remarkable good humor and diligence in typing and retyping, and doing all the tedious secretarial tasks associated with this endeavor. I am also thankful to Mrs. Josephine Costa, whose incomparable competence and affectionate presence in running my office makes us all work at our best.

I am indebted once again to the exemplary staff of Jason Aronson, especially Judy Cohen, senior production editor, who guided every step of the publication process with impeccable skill and care. My great appreciation to David Kaplan for the excellence with which he thoughtfully and meticulously copyedited the final manuscript. Gratitude, as always, goes to Norma Pomerantz, director of author relations, for continuing to be her gracious and reassuring self. Lastly, my enduring thanks to Jason Aronson himself for his sage advice and exceptional vision.

Introduction:
The American Guru

The thing itself always escapes.

— J. Claude Evans

The first therapists were most likely gurus by some other name. They were healers of mind and body sanctioned by and reflecting their tribe, its values, and its belief systems. Guru, in the Hindu language, means weighty, a teacher in spiritual and philosophical matters, a guide for life experiences and dilemmas. They incorporated their healing knowledge—the sciences of the times—into each culture's philosophical religious systems.

With the progress of medical sciences, gurus relinquished their body healing practices, although in most cultures some sort of medical miracles are still sought with fervor. By and large, however, gurus have taken a separate and superior role to medicine; they applied forms of spiritual collaboration, such as praying, or more elaborate explications, such as the devotion to God to strengthen the immunological system, or used forms of transcending, such as a peaceful union with God or simply accepting the will of God.

In the West, the differentiation of medicine from religion paralleled the differentiation of philosophy from religion as well. Eastern religions and philosophy remained highly intertwined, if not one and the same. Western philosophy, especially existentialism, identified its demarcation lines with religion. It did that partly by negating it. Not only was God dead, but he had to be killed. There emerged pseudo-gurus of reason, truth, ethics, metaphysics, the principles of knowledge, and the conduct of human beings.

By the term *pseudo-guru*, I don't mean to imply that they weren't suffering from some grandiose delusions. They killed God in order to replace him. Their belief system was intended to undermine itself. They questioned their very own existence, and they wanted to be questioned. But they couldn't be gods or gurus in a real sense of the word, because they doubted. According to one story, kids would chase the philosopher Heidegger in the street by shouting after him "Either or! Either or!" God never doubts and cannot be doubted.

Against that background entered Freud, perhaps the first real Western guru. He didn't achieve that status by integrating religion and philosophy, as did his Eastern counterparts, but by explaining them. He didn't reject or negate them by confrontation, but by explanation. He said that religion is a mass neurosis, maybe a needed one, an antidote against the emptiness of existence.

Freud provided that most comprehensive and most elaborate theory of mind in man's history. For him, man was neither at the service of God nor in pursuit of existential truths, but at the mercy of his unconscious. Man created God to ease his own image, and God reciprocated. Man was his own creation. He was the master and the slave, the perpetrator and the victim, alone all by himself. Freud also thought that existential philosophy was simply an existential neurosis. He and only he (his theory) could help the neurotics, if they could only lie down for a while, give or take five years.

In Europe not many wanted to lie down on the couch,

whether philosophers or otherwise, unless they themselves were interested in being psychoanalysts. After World War II, when analysts came to New York through what is affectionately known as the Neurotic Exchange Program, they found very fertile ground. There were Freudians, neo-Freudians, Sullivanians, Jungians, Adlerians, Horneyans, Reichians, Kleinians, Kohutians, and more. In 1980, I counted twenty-six analytical schools in New York based on a systematic misunderstanding of Freud. How did I define a school of psychotherapy? By a single, but very rigid criterion: Not only did they have to have their own guru, but they also had to own a townhouse in Manhattan!

While psychotherapy grew like Topsy in New York, by the time it reached California it was growing topsy-turvy. Once it was discovered that the placebo is psychotherapy, psychotherapy came to mean whatever psychotherapists did. And the psychotherapist was whoever said, "I am a psychotherapist." [**Have we now become "over-the-encounter" therapists?**]

In the West, therapists' exalted immunity from religion and philosophy limited their maturation to the process of self-understanding, only to the detriment of their patients, insofar as the therapist can help a patient grow only as much as he himself has grown. This is why the formative process—*not* the training—becomes of paramount importance. One's advanced degrees and even training to some extent are forms of cultural or societal sanction that place the person in an earned position. Formal training is needed, says Jerome Frank, as the basis for the therapist's conviction of his effectiveness. Once legitimized by certified diplomas, the healer status is bestowed upon the individual by society and lends credence and authority to his or her esteemed status. For Frank (1974), a socially sanctioned role as help-giver constitutes one of the common features of all healing practices; it applies to the religious healing of primitive societies as well as to secular and scientific medicine, to the Eastern as well as Western guru.

Therapists (like any other skilled workers) can be limited by their select training and experience. They may hold allegiance to particular ideas and methods and are constrained by those with which they are most familiar, the ones they know and favor. Those clinicians who are excessively committed to the tenets of psychology, biology, or sociology may end up underplaying man's ethical and spiritual dimensions. By emphasizing techniques, they may make man impersonalized, compartmentalized, analyzed, calculated, and now managed—thereby diminished. No wonder psychotherapy became a misnomer. The therapist, however well trained, should *not* be too scientific about people or pathology. He or she must maintain a certain free margin, a sense of curiosity and credulity, or even ignorance, in order to regain his innocence.

The clinician needs to be concerned with what makes man unique, but also with what is universal—the anguish of isolation, alienation, and meaninglessness as well as existential guilt over forfeiting one's potential. Real pathology is "human diminution," says Abraham Maslow. Those who are too focused on self-enhancement may unwittingly advocate self-diminution instead of self-growth. One must transcend such self orientations in order to reach toward a universal consciousness. True therapy opts for such a higher state of consciousness, and in so doing, targets the spiritual center of man.

We pay too much attention to the training of therapists and not enough to their formation. The latter encompasses personal growth, broad education, and a life philosophy. It addresses the issue of one's being and becoming. On a less lofty level, the clinician also must take care of his or her own deficits and conflicts, so as not to inflict them on patients. This is the only profession that takes what it gives to others. The therapist must continually fertilize himself with broad curiosity and interests, while at the same time seeking informed simplicity. A friend in treatment asked the late Anatole Broyard how he could know that he was under the care of the right person. Broyard responded by asking: Does she read Dostoyevski?

The therapist must anchor himself—mind, body, and soul—

in intellectual endeavors, emotional intimacies, communal engagements, and, especially, by grounding his soul in the serenity of believing. That means finding one's authentic self, as all therapeutic techniques ultimately emanate from within the therapist. That is why the therapist is not what he does, but who he is, and there are no such things as schools of therapy, there are only psychotherapists.

Finally, one must recognize that this is not a field for spectacular successes. Rewording Freud: Every therapy is a relative failure. The ethical tranquillity of the therapist largely depends on his ability to live with optimum disillusionment. Then psychotherapy becomes not so much a profession as a way of being, a soulful and spiritual existence.

In the West, the healers are initiated from the broader field of psychology. It begins with a charismatic individual first, mastering a specific art of healing, which means bringing his/her training, sensitivity, perceptiveness, compassion, intelligence, and motivation to the clinical work and shaping these resources and skills. Such a healer has a confident self presentation, if not genuine self conviction, with thorough indoctrination in theories and techniques contained in their own narrow context.

Eventually, within the scope of these accepted (and often reified) doctrines, the healer begins with a vulnerable grandiosity to raise many of the questions that each healer mulls over with his or her colleagues, and even more so when alone. Such inquisitiveness eventually leads the person to explore the nuances of each dilemma by interweaving his or her own thoughts and experiences, with knowledge drawn from well-known healers and scholars of other schools.

As the healer searches for new answers and/or confirmation of old ones, he becomes someone who no longer needs to define identity and selfhood by strict adherence to established schools of thought. Rather, he begins to confront the fragility of preordained premises, and recognizes that time-honored tenets always reside somewhere between reality and fantasy, truth and myth. What follows is the ability to acknowledge both the seductions of entrenched theories as well as their conceptual constraints. Such an individual is metaphorically the "last therapist," by being one who "will dwell in that place which uncomfortably distances itself from the primacy of theory" (Karasu 1996, p. 135).

However, in spite of cumulative knowledge, deep insight, and even tolerance to not knowing, which may portend finality, the therapist generates newer queries. Their ostensible solutions lead to the creation of even more dilemmas, only to be rescued by escaping from one's specialty. This means viewing therapy-related issues in the larger context of life and having enlightenments emanate from common wisdom, philosophy, and spirituality. Even the presumed end points of all seekings are not fixed states and, in Jaspers's (1963) terms, a final terra firma is never found. In this regard, ranging from the tomes of the past to the philosophy of postdeconstruction, he posits a critical way of thinking—not only breaking down existing forms to find new meaning, but also transcending them.

In the revolution of this transcendent process, and the complex course of internal dialogues and reflections, the questions and answers become seamless. Ultimately, the therapist, master healer and philosopher merge; they thus become not merely complementary, they are *one*: The Healer.

ONE HUNDRED YEARS OF WONDERING

> A man came to a Zen master, and asked, "How are things?" The Master replied, "Just as they are."

In the psychotherapist's quest to know a patient, communication generally begins with the cautionary words, "I wonder..." This is primarily intended to express inquiry but, at the same time, not to be preemptive or suggestive. If the clinician is inquisitive as well as empathic, this stance can secure the open-ended nature of the patient's self-exploration. Occasionally, however, incessant searching on the part of the practitioner may also represent an underlying phenomenon of genuine doubt about his profession and himself. Unfortunately, this is usually inadequately addressed. Lacking in humility psychotherapists seem frequently wrong— but *never* uncertain.

Yet if you look back over the last one hundred years, you'll find that therapists have made different overwrought, overargued claims at different times, then recanted them with the same conviction, only to reclaim them again as a variation of the intellectual debris of the original misconception. How can one comprehend such a repeated pattern? [**Can it be that form follows failure?**] Theoreticians, of course, have an explanation of their ardent allegiances, as they do for everything: Psychotherapy, in order to work, requires the clinician's self-confidence about his or her power to heal. Such healing power is endowed upon those who believe in what they do, regardless of what that is. Therapists need their theories initially to ground themselves professionally, if not even personally. As the old saying goes, "You don't have to be right, you just have to be convincing." The power of persuasion, a major ingredient of psychotherapy, comes from such self-conviction, especially if it is buttressed by a shared belief system. But for psychotherapy to endure, it must not be insulated from the local and universal communities and their culture, religion, philosophy, and common wisdom.

In this book, a psychotherapist presents vignettes from the treatment of a younger therapist who is objectively more intelligent, better educated, and more broadly talented than himself, who also had prior orthodox analyses and two lengthy therapies: one with an eclectic therapist and one with a Kohutian. The therapist continues to wonder in a format of multiple internal dialogues. This symbolically represents the long and complex history of diverse thinking about pathology and treatment. It simultaneously attempts to bring forth a broader and more universal worldview, a collective voice to transcend the boundaries of the profession per se—an unforeseen and ultimate unity. Here the clinician's search for new experiential truths—through continued inquiry beyond the boundaries of the profession per se—serves to force the field from its cocoon, its many years beset by internecine conflict, isolation, and polarization. This quest is expressed through openness to others within and outside of the field. It begins with an impasse with the patient and looks at varied experts for help, and culminates in an inner voice not heard before. It is hoped that this resonant voice then becomes not an end in itself, but a new beginning.

In this context, the themes represent a major shift in the way the therapist views himself and other human beings, not just patients. Specifically, in Anderson's (1997) contemporary terms, the healer is no longer "a knower who is certain about what he or she knows (or thinks he or she knows)" but rather, "a not-knower . . . and regards knowledge as evolving" (p. 4). In short, each inner conversation embraces known and unknown territory that continually reaches toward new discovery. As such, these internal dialogues are designed to transcend the psychotherapist's century of wavering between mutual mythology and personal confidence, or its opposite, collective certainty and individual doubt, and reach a serenity of soulful and spiritual existence where everything and everyone is no longer "just as they were."

The Psychotherapist's Anthropological Epitaph: A Haphazard Philosopher

The practice of psychotherapy may make one a better therapist, but not necessarily a better person.

—Anonymous

MINING MINDS

"Hi!" A slightly overweight brunette with piercing brown eyes approached me. "My name is Carolyn. I recognized you from your book jacket photo on The Psychotherapist's Interventions. *I'm a therapist myself. I really liked your deficit/conflict-based classification of human troubles. I've been recommending that to all my practitioner colleagues. It's very useful. I don't remember the publisher having made a book party for you, because I never miss them."*

I replied, no, he didn't. This interchange occurred at a cocktail reception to celebrate the publication of a friend of mine's latest book. Carolyn buttonholed me for fifty minutes and intelligently differentiated the Kohutian view from that of Kernberg and suggested that I "should stop wasting your time trying to reconcile such discrepant perspectives, as polarization is needed for scientific enhancement." "Synthesis is a premature conclusion," she said, "keep analyzing." "Your book on deconstruction is also a search for the finite, thus boring and too serious. The infinite players are playful and interest-ing." As she kept explaining the contribution of each theoretician to the present-day therapist, I was getting depressed. Not only didn't my publisher throw a party for me, but this young woman could easily summarize my professional world while standing on one foot—mine.

Do you ever get the sense that you're in the wrong business? Is psychotherapy a business, an art, or a science? [**Any two therapists can tell each other all they know in fifty minutes, says a witty, disgruntled patient.**] We all start writing poems, and, failing at that, go on to write short stories and, failing at that, become novelists, says William Faulkner. If you fail that too, there is always the option of becoming a therapist. All the altruistic rhetoric aside, all the self-growth–related consolations notwith-standing, what kind of profession is this anyway? People come and complain about their parents, spouses, children, jobs, friends, bad luck, and ill fortunes; then they complain about you, how unhelpful you've been, in fact, how uncaring, insensitive, igno-rant, and impotent a person you are—and furthermore, you're only interested in taking their money. You're supposed to ac-knowledge, bear, and put into perspective all of these accusations. But at the end of the day, you begin to wonder.

"As far as I'm concerned," continued Carolyn, "understanding Lacan is a farce." Mercifully, a middle-aged man came by and touched her waist gently. Carolyn turned around, saw him with great delight, gave him a big hug, and they quickly and passionately engaged in talking to each other. Simultaneously, an older woman asked me whether I worked for the publisher. I said, "No." "Well, I'm an editor, what do you do?" she pursued. Having just barely recovered from Carolyn, I was just a little gun-shy about telling anybody what I do. Furthermore, the question never is satisfied with an answer of "I am a psychotherapist."

Mind you, people actually ask me to define what is it that I *do*, exactly, as a psychotherapist. This interchange doesn't occur in a lecture hall, but at a dinner table or cocktail party. So I used to say, "I do psychotherapy or—I heal minds." A finer shading may have been less pretentious. After all, I couldn't easily say that I work with lunatics *outside* of the asylum, some of whom are probably right here, at this very social event!

The self-conscious author Roy Blount, Jr. tells of similar discomfort at being a writer, suggesting, "If you were a member of Jesse James's band and people asked you what you were, you wouldn't say, 'Well, I am a desperado.' Instead you'd say something like, 'I work in banks or I have done some railroad work' (Charleton 1980, p. 46). So, if there is a quick-exit possibility, I tell those who ask that I'm in the refueling business, I do psychological attunement, or in these modern times, I may easily answer that I'm an emotional fitness expert. On other occasions, usually after a few drinks, using the archeological paradigm I refer to my trade as "mining minds," a pattern matcher or a guard at a museum of psychopathology.

"Well, I'm kind of a psychotherapist," I finally managed to utter. "Did you edit this book?" I tried to change the focus. "No," she replied, " I'm a kind of a therapist as well myself, you know, on the side. Do you practice imagery guided therapy?" "No, but you must," I said quickly. "Tell me, what is imagery guided therapy?" She was too willing to not only describe it, but also demonstrate the technique on me.

What has psychotherapy to say for itself? What is therapy really these days, anyway? [**Give me anything, as long as it is not psychotherapy.**] Everyone uses the term differently. It is mutually subversive. In the past, before the wholesale proliferation of schools, psychotherapy meant a diluted and adulterated version of psychoanalysis. It was divided into insight-oriented and *non*–insight-oriented (i.e., supportive), the latter being the contaminated and tarnished (no longer the "gold" of orthodox analysis). But now there are cognitive therapies, behavior modifications, primal screams, bioenergetics, encounter groups—you name it.

A mildly inebriated man came to my rescue. Apparently he was eavesdropping on our "interesting" conversation. "So, you two both are therapists, huh? OK, now do you know how many therapists it takes to change a light bulb?" The imagery therapist tried to brush him off to no avail, and ended up practicing her technique on him.

The emergence of so many modalities and separate schools has not only caused confusion, but also created serious credibility problems. With everyone on the psychotherapy bandwagon, it has understandably become the butt of numerous jokes, with more than a grain of truth. Some are endearing, while some are bordering on covert, and often overt, hostility. I heard someone define psychotherapy as "where the privileged devote themselves to the expensive, selfish, and impotent cultivation of subjectivity." Interpretation of the unconscious of the joke teller is a small consolation. Victor Raimy (1950) describes psychotherapy as an undefined technique applied to unspecific problems with unpredictable outcomes, for which rigorous training is required. Victor Borge, based on his uncle's chronic treatment with psychotherapy for innumerable ambiguous ailments, insisted that psychotherapy is "a cure for which there is no disease." Well, reputations, especially bad ones, are hard to live down. As to the proliferation issue, the psychoanalyst Richard Chessick addresses its heterogeneity when he says that there are as many therapies as there are therapists. And I say there are as many therapies as there are patients. The psychologist Edward Boring beats us both when he says that there are more therapists than people in this country. [**Do jokes grow best on the graves of old anxiety?**]

LIFE OF THE PARTY

Therapists are rarely fun people to have at a party. Their obsessive interest in the idea of normality and their own excessive self-awareness put them in danger of becoming nonpersons and only living vicariously. Their nonspontaneity and reticence to self-revelation—a common source of discourse—leaves them disengaged. Anthony Storr (1979) says, "Since therapists are, or ought to be, experts at 'drawing people out,' some of their social encounters may consist of a monologue on the part of the person with whom they are talking" (p. 176).

We therapists also have our own complaints. For example; how do you handle strangers who, in an informal setting or social gathering, approach you and ask advice once they've learned that you're a psychotherapist? Do you gently urge them to consult someone and politely give them a colleague's name? Do you give them your phone number, and welcome the opportunity, just in case? In the ambivalent interim, do you try to answer their questions as well as the current circumstances permit? Or do you adroitly attempt to change the subject or dodge any professional engagement, even if it may mean actively avoiding them? It's like the story of Proteus who had the power to assume any shape he pleased as well as the power of prophecy, which he was reluctant to exercise. When mortals wished to consult him, he would change his form with bewildering rapidity. Unless they clung to him through all his changes, they could obtain no answers to their pressing questions about the future.

I was bored and boring. As I was inconspicuously trying to head toward the door, Carolyn caught up with me. "Already? Listen, I was wondering whether you know anything about boredom." (Do I know!) "Do you think it's a form of depression or ADD? A friend of mine is fine about everything else, I mean career, education, looks, but he suffers from boredom." I needed some clarification: "Does your boyfriend himself suffer from the boredom? Or do you suffer from his boredom?" [The therapist's ear is never innocent.]

IF IT ISN'T WORTH PAYING WELL, IT ISN'T WORTH PAYING

Carolyn laughed loudly: "Listen, do you accept new patients? If not, I want you to at least do a consultation of my boyfriend." As I was muttering, "I'll be happy if he . . ." she said, "Here he is. Dr. Karasu, this is my B, short for Beau. B, Dr. Karasu is an expert on boredom. I want you to please make an appointment and go to see him. I'll leave you two now to work it out."

B was handsome, sober, and friendly. The first thing he asked was, "How much do you charge for a session?" "Three hundred dollars," I said. "You must be kidding," he replied. "Why are you so expensive? That's the going rate for call girls." "Is that first-hand knowledge?" I asked. "No, no, I wouldn't pay women to sleep with me," he denied. "Well, what would you pay a woman for then?" I asked as I tried to battle my boredom with aggression. "For nothing," he answered, "definitely not for talking to her." "How about listening to you?" I questioned, and felt bad. I'd better leave this party before someone gets hurt, I thought. As I said goodnight to him, he asked for my card. I felt worse.

Freud (1913) made the early observation that "money matters are treated by civilized people in the same way as sexual matters—with the same inconsistency, prudishness, and hypocrisy" (p. 131). Since then, an unconscious equation between sex and money has been grist for the analytic mill, at least in dealing with one's patients. The general belief is that a most revealing window of intrapsychic life can be peered into, using the handling of money as a mirror of inner conflicts. The negotiation and exchange of financial currency—spending or saving, hoarding or squandering, and the complex interplay of need and greed, or more metaphorically, the fundamental acts of giving and receiving as basic expressions of human commerce—become a symbolic measure of the capacity for love, sense of worth, and of the value placed on self and others.

From the standpoint of all medicine, Ferenczi (1928) observed that even the most prosperous individual spends money on doctors most unwillingly. Something in us seems to make us regard medical aid, which in fact we all first received from our mothers in infancy, as something to which we are automatically entitled. The therapist seems to be the mother a priori. Ferenczi, as psychiatrist, further contended that at the end of each month, when our patients are presented with their bill, their resistance is stimulated into producing their concealed or unconscious hatred, mistrust, and suspicion all over again.

At the same time, psychotherapists have themselves been chronically criticized for their preoccupation with money, not merely with having a professional penchant for exploring its meaning. Is it because the "purchase" of psychotherapy is like no other commercial transaction? You usually have no idea what you're getting—and there are no written warrantees. Phillips's (1997) apt portrayal of the currency of psychoanalysis is as follows:

> It is one of the paradoxes of . . . analysis that the patient agrees to buy something that no one can really describe. Psychoanalysis has its history, its theory, its rules. . . . But what is going to be said and what is going to be heard—and the consequences of all that ritualized speaking and listening and silence—are forever beyond anticipation. What the analyst and patient will make of each other is always an unknown quantity. In this sense psychoanalysis is both the exemplary and the parodic commodity: the kind of investment no rational person would ever make. You pay money for an indefinite period to somebody you know very little about; this person, who doesn't say very much, has no idea what the return on your money will be, but knows it will be painful whatever else it is. [p. 28]

So, how do you respond to a patient who complains that therapists are too well paid, and even directly inquire, "Why are *you* so expensive?" A few years ago a patient asked me this question in a stern manner of thinly disguised resentment. After all, there's no big overhead, no expensive equipment, no staff salary, no material, no storage. For centuries man has been pulling strings, to which nothing is attached. What is it that you and other therapists do to justify your fee?! You're sitting there in a comfortable chair in your own home/office, listening (attentively, yes), occasionally making some statements (interesting and thoughtful, yes)—but that's it. Why would such a distorted conversation be translated into $300 an hour? One patient retorted, "You must be giving brand-name psychotherapy. Can I get a cheaper, generic version of it?" I hardly contained myself from telling a story that Dr. Leopold Bellak told me:

> A general's car broke down and army mechanics were called to fix it. When they were unable to repair the car, they turned for help to an old village smith. The smith took a look at the car, rattled it a little and then banged it sharply. Immediately, the car started up. The general asked, "What do I owe you?" The village smith replied, "A hundred bucks." "A hundred bucks for one bang?" asked the shocked general. "No," replied the smith, "one buck for the bang, ninety-nine for knowing *where* to bang."

Incidentally, the patient's reaction to the therapist—ambivalence, or in more severe psychopathology, the expression of primitive, excessive, and unintegrated love and hate—is no measure of the durability of the relationship. In fact, I would say that it's the one criterion that I count on the least. Theodor Reik (1952) elegantly stated the transferential, thus unreliable, nature of his patient's distorted and displaced responses to him:

> I have been thanked for successful business transactions, for winning a law suit, for conquering a beloved woman, for making a technical discovery, for good luck at poker—all achievements of which I was wholly innocent. But I have also been accused of causing the outbreak of World Wars I and II, losses on the New York Stock Exchange, an attack of measles in a child a thousand miles away, defeat in a tennis game, the loss of a husband or wife—all happenings of which I was equally innocent. I have been blessed and cursed a thousand

times, killed and kissed in thought, annihilated and royally rewarded in fantasy. [p. 111]

Some patients exalt the therapist and wouldn't mind spending a large portion of their meager income on therapy. Others tend to resent paying the therapist, no matter how wealthy they are—especially when it's for something they deny having bargained for, such as having to explore their innermost feelings. Such a patient of mine defined the psychiatrist as a doctor some people go to slightly cracked and leave completely broke. Therefore, I have come to understand and accept the fact that I will be both praised and resented for my help by all who receive my treatment, and that any financial arrangement can bring out the patient's mixed emotions. Sandor Ferenczi (1928) tells of an early encounter with one of his patients: "'Doctor, if you help me, I'll give you every penny I possess!' 'I shall be satisfied with thirty kronen an hour,' the physician replied. 'But, isn't that rather excessive?' the patient unexpectedly remarked" (pp. 92–93). Well, we now know that the patient's reaction is not really so unexpected. Although this verbal exchange explicitly revolves around money, it symbolizes the larger unconscious issue of the nature of the ambivalent patient–therapist relationship. In this sense, money *does* matter.

Patients in treatment may be justly reminded of the care their mothers provided. Unconsciously expecting such nonreciprocated succor from the therapist, it is only those who are extremely demanding, with an accentuated sense of entitlement, who deserve the most attention, as they are looking for a mother they never had. If the therapist has grown out of his need for reciprocation and does not make too much of the money issue, so will the patient. [**Sooner or later, all archaic reactions exhaust themselves in the field of substitution.**]

2

Do Not Seek to Follow
the Footsteps of the Wise;
Seek Only What They Sought

THEORY: JUST SAY "NO"!

Only small fish swim in schools.

—Isaac Bashevis Singer

The morning following the book party I got a call. "Hi, this is Carolyn. We met last night. My boyfriend is not interested in therapy, but I wondered whether I could be your patient. The fee is OK with me." I said, "You know, we had a rather contaminating encounter with you and your boyfriend at that party, I'm not sure whether it would be feasible to . . ." She stopped me. "Of course, well let's just meet and see."

I saw her the following week for an hour and a half, as I always do for the initial interview. Carolyn gave me a quick anamnesis: She was 38 years old, never married, living alone in Greenwich Village, working half time in a mental health center plus privately practicing psychotherapy for fifteen to twenty hours a week. She came to the field from "a detour." First she wanted to be a teacher, a writer as her father is, got a Ph.D. in English from an Ivy League school, then got a master's degree in social work and also simultaneously attended a psychoanalytical school. She plays piano and viola, writes lyrics for a number of musicians, and acts occasionally in off-Broadway shows. Her parents live in New Jersey. Her father has retired early from his college professorship after a harassment complaint. He writes scripts for soap operas and makes good money. He is very energetic—a "hypomanic" man, very interesting but drinks too much and embarrasses himself.

The mother, though a college graduate, never had a job. She had a full-time one to manage her husband and also the kids: Carolyn and her four-year-younger brother. Her mother is the opposite of the father—passive, compliant, submissive, self-effacing, and chronically depressed. "Together they make one manic-depressive disorder." They also make an excellent duet, he playing the piano, she the violin. Her brother grew up under the mother's skirt to avoid the father. In his high-school years, he was into heavy pot smoking. He dropped out of college, became a total pothead, and moved to Los Angeles where he lives with a woman who is a musician. They both make their living by writing jingles for advertisers and also performing in a small band for weddings and parties. Carolyn had very little contact with him since her adolescent years. She also smoked some marijuana, was "promiscuous, but a very good student, always getting honors, like valedictorian, dean's lists, magna cum laude, you name it." I asked her what she got from her analyses and two other treatments, and what does she expect now?

"I found out that my family was borderlinegenic, neurosesgenic, and I had to have a parentectomy to gain my sanity. I figured out some of my conflicts and made headway to remedy them. Now what I'm interested in is to continue my search for the meaning of my life, what to do personally and professionally." I asked why she didn't go back to one of her previous therapists. She replied, "They ran out of either gas or patience with me. I wouldn't go back to any one of them and most likely they wouldn't take me either. Furthermore, the one who

gets there faster is the one who changes the horses." "What is 'there'?"
I questioned. She said, "That's why I'm here."
I said, "Fine, saddle me up."

> *Carolyn:* May I ask a silly question? I know you integrate various theoretical approaches, but in your practice do you have a basic orientation? I mean, are you primarily Freudian, Jungian, or something else?
>
> *Me:* All of them and none of them.
>
> **[The Healer is a reflection of his limitations.]**
>
> [I register that she's wondering whether I'm qualified to help her.]
>
> *Carolyn:* So, you're a jack of all trades.
>
> *Me:* And the master of none.
>
> *Carolyn:* Oh, I'm sorry, I didn't mean that.
>
> *Me:* But I did mean that.
>
> *Carolyn:* Hmm.

All schools believe that the therapist needs to be dedicated to a convincing theory, a theory that creates a more fitting "home" for his patients to be in, whose abstractions are apart from actual experience, and formed (and forming) at the interface between them. Wright (1991) stated, "If there were no theory behind it, the psychotherapy session would be a very strange meeting. It would be oppressive (because of its lack of mutuality), evasive (because it does not have a declarable objective), seductive (because it deliberately creates false hopes), impolite (because it assiduously avoids protecting the patient), [and] pretentious (because the therapist acts as though he knows more than he does)" (p. 437).

Most schools recommend that the therapist should stick with a particular school of psychotherapy and strictly adhere to its theoretical tenets. Although the theory can be either a catalyst or an impediment, it is somehow reassuring to remain within the structure of an established school that is presumably tried and true. Much comfort can come from preformed rules and techniques, just ready and waiting to be followed. After all, improvisations generate anxiety and are conducive to making more mistakes. So it is easy to cling to a single school, and what's more, it is safe to be surrounded by the confidence, support, and sanction of others.

Interestingly enough, these theories of mind do not always address the complex problems of daily practice. Many renowned thinkers have elegant, complex, and highly elaborate theories that ostensibly attempt to explain the human mind and its operating principles as well as strive for relevance in the clinical setting. Yet, as Michels (1988) says, the information, knowledge, and wisdom that a practitioner needs largely exist underground, transmitted through supervision, case conferences, and collegial agreement as a kind of professional folklore. Such folklore of practice is not completely unrelated to the theories of mind; in fact, it often uses the same terms and theories. But it has no cohesive conceptual base of its own, and when cornered, quickly falls back to the already reified theories of mind. Since these are often overrated and inherently limited in actual application to the patient, the gap between theory and practice remains.

Thus I thought that perhaps I can close that gap by an integrative paradigm possible at the level of clinical strategies, that is, making its nature content dependent. Actually I went one step further in this pluralistic modus operandi. [**Can we call this dogmatic relativism?**] I tried open-mindedly to learn from alternative types of therapy, including forms of Eastern healing as well as our own fringe schools. Unfortunately, I found to be true the old saying, that "If you have an open mind, people will throw all kinds of junk in it." Yes, I chewed lots of sugar cane, but I got some sugar, too. I delved into a panoply of Western schools, including some far-out, jazzed-up analyses and quadriphonic Freudian spinoffs that comprise California humanism, with their anti-intellectual motto, "Where ego was, there shall id be." I tried to take Fritz Perls's (1969) gestaltist advice, "Lose your mind, come to your senses." I even found comfort in William Coffin's fifth position takeoff of transactional analysis (which added to the four life positions of Harris's [1967] famous *I'm OK—You're OK)*, to wit, "I'm not OK, you're not OK, and that's OK."

From Tibetan meditation, I trained myself to hear the space between sounds. From Japanese Aikido, I learned the management of rapprochement by finding out how to feed pigeons in the temple's courtyard: If you walk toward the pigeons even with grains in your hand, they'll run away, but if you stand still, they'll come and eat in your hand. I also found that, although at the theoretical level of understanding and formulations, schools of thought differ, in fact most schools, at the level of practice, are indistinguishable. [**Are we heading in the direction of therapeutic atheism?**] As Andre Green (1977) has noted, "If we limit ourselves to the clinical data, we'll find large areas of common experience. Concerning technique, it is probable that we'll disagree. If we speak about theory, it is almost certain that we'll part ways. In short, we can share our perceptions but not our conceptions perhaps because we nurture different preconceptions" (pp. 15–16). Of course, such preconceptions are put in sharper distinction in practice when different outcomes are targeted. Past discussions have tended to concentrate on sequences that have a dramatic and time-limited outcome, such as Freudian catharsis or Reichian orgasm. Similarly, analysts tend to use symptoms as a starting point, whereas behaviorists view them as ends in themselves.

Schools were designed to differ. Thus ego psychology focuses on the adaptive function of ego to competing drives, rather than on the conflict between the forces per se. Jacobson (1964), for one, argued that infantile deprivation or overstimulation leads to arrests in ego development, hampering the person's ability to master the inner world by the use of appropriate defenses. Hartmann's (1939) pioneering work introduced a significant emphasis on the adaptive function of the ego to the environment as well. Thus, the basic thrust is not on conflict and symptom formation, but on success or failure of the ego's capacity to cope and adapt, on the nature of the ego's assets and defects as well as environmental deficiencies. Here cure requires the development of ego strength and adaptation to both one's inner world and external reality, primarily through a nontransferential relationship, a therapeutic alliance.

For Kohut, who is the originator of the school of self psychology, the most fundamental issue is the individual's need to organize his or her psyche into a cohesive configuration. This requires empathic reception from important individuals, so-called selfobjects. [**Is this what Wright means by "the maternal face" of theory?**] The remaining conflictual elements, that is, gross sexual and aggressive drive manifestations, are only the breakdown products of empathic failures. Thus the cure is for the therapist to provide an empathic and attuned atmosphere to foster development of a coherent self and object representation. This means to facilitate not insight, but transmuting internalization, in order to crystallize the self. Here the therapist serves as a contemporary selfobject for the patient, not merely a transferential figure from the patient's past.

Object relations theory asserts that the individual carries with him or her certain internal dramas, not just instincts. The object relationship school did not dispense completely with the drive theory, especially the libido concept, but emphasized its role vis-à-vis the relationship. [**Isn't the oedipal complex an object relations theory?**] Fairbairn (1954) put it plainly when he said that the libido is not pleasure seeking, but object seeking. The instinctual energy's aim is not simply to relieve tension, but to satisfy the basic human need to relate to others. Thus the "cure" is related to freeing ourselves not from the conflicts of our instincts, but from the constraints of internalized object relations. And, in accordance with this theoretical stance, the therapist moves away from analytical neutrality to act in such a manner as to be a good object for internalization.

While schools, including the school of symbolism, harbor an all-encompassing illusion of autonomy, one must simply realize that one can't relate to every patient the same way, nor is a single theory suitable for understanding and treating every type of pathology. As Jung (1933) said, "The shoe that fits one person pinches another" (p. 60); no size fits all. Based on the degree of consolidation of the patient's psychic apparatus, the therapist has to modulate his or her activities to establish and maintain a specific type of relationship with a particular person. He or she needs to recognize that the nature of the patient–therapist interplay is not static, but changes not only during the course of treatment, but from session to session, or even from moment to moment in psychotherapy. The clinician thus must be capable and informed enough to shift paradigms to meet the patient, wherever he is. Therapeutic monogamy is disloyalty to one's patient. With these shifting paradigms, the clinician synchronizes himself with the patient, not unlike teeth of a cogwheel. As the therapist becomes a presence in the patient's psychic life, technique evolves from that presence.

Finally, one can even take a cynical, or worse, nihilistic posture, and demolish all approaches and demoralize their adherents. Shane (1987) does this with a satirical bent:

> It is well known to those who do not hold that particular theory that, for example, all Kleinians are crazy and full of rage, all self psychologists cover their fear of aggression with the syrup of empathy, all classical analysts mask their fear of the primitive with a rigid insistence on mature responsibility, and all developmentalists dignify the banalities of the nursery out of a timid need to avoid oedipal passions. Moreover, all of these can agree on one proposition: the mixed-model theorists are either obsessively, phobically, or stupidly incapable of commitment, and, confusing apples with oranges, end up with a sloppy, inelegant fruit salad. [p. 201]

Nonetheless we need to understand that all this nihilism, cynicism, honesty, and dead seriousness plus the "linguistic

soliloquism, literary skepticism, hermeneutic circularity, all encourage a healthy profusion of frameworks and a deeper understanding dimensionality to cope with the constant, bullying need
for closure" (Friedman 1988, p. 466). The mind cannot tolerate
the open-ended disorder of not knowing. Furthermore, the mind,
as Kant says, has an innate predetermined framework. It organizes
information in an a priori fashion. Bias is an essential property of
mind. [**The therapist's only task is to grasp the raw data of
experience, for the preconceptual bars provide false security and
real limitations.**]

PERSON-NEAR EXPERIENCE: NO SIZE FITS ALL

The psychological frames that are usually used "trim a life to fit
the frame," according to Hillman (1996, p. 5). Here is a good story
about how we perceive things through such frames, our theoretical lenses.

> A behavior psychologist was sitting on the bench in the park
> observing the relation between a blind man and his dog, who
> were coming toward him. When they got very close to him, he
> coughed a couple of times to signal them, but the dog came to
> him, sniffed him, and lifted his leg and peed on the man's foot.
> The behaviorist kept observing without too much protest
> because it was obvious that the blind man understood what
> happened and apologetically blushed. But then the blind man
> pulled a dog biscuit from his pocket and offered it to the dog.
> That was the last straw. The behaviorist said indignantly,
> "Hell, don't you think you are positively reinforcing an
> undesirable behavior." The blind man said, "No, I am trying to
> find out where his head is so that I can kick his ass."

Kohut talks about experience-near theory, but no theory is
truly experience near, since it is impossible to approach data

without some preconceptions. Given that limitation, the marrow of the work in psychotherapy can be defined in three overlapping bases: first, psychotherapy's primary goal, that of remedying deficits and resolving conflicts; second, the nature of the patient–therapist relationship, which encompasses the empathic presence of the therapist, the working alliance, and transferential relations between the therapist and the patient; and third, the primary technique, which is to establish and maintain their interpersonal relationship. It has been said that the human relationship per se is never sufficient, and that the technique alone is not feasible. But in fact, technique and relationship are inextricable; or stated otherwise, one's technique is always embedded in one's relational predisposition. One's secondary techniques could be almost anything. That is why there are more schools of therapies than brands of breakfast cereal.

As the practice of psychotherapy is based on theoretical paradigms— admittedly an overused concept (Richard Darman, mocking the idea, says, "Brother, can you paradigm!")—we need a paradigm that can combine or transcend diverse perspectives of psychopathology and treatment. Examples are the integration of drive, ego, object relations, and self psychology approaches, and/or the synthesis of conflict and deficit models. (This doesn't mean that this very assertion itself will be exempt from some form of fallacy, or be immune from inherently self-limiting conjectures.)

Of course, there are those rare masters; one is Milton Erickson, who has been described as a psychotherapeutic Peter Pan, someone who could operate without any paradigmatic constraint, and would do anything, including cornering and conning the patient into changing. Haley (1973) describes one of his teachings in his book of tribute, *Uncommon Therapy*:

> *Interviewer*: Suppose someone called you and said there was a kid, nineteen or twenty years old, who has been a very good boy, but all of a sudden this week he started walking around

the neighborhood carrying a large cross. The neighbors are upset and the family's upset, and would you do something about it. How would you think about that as a problem?

Erickson: Well, if the kid came in to see me, the first thing I would do would be to want to examine the cross. And I would want to improve it in a very minor way. As soon as I got the slightest minor change in it, the way would be open for a larger change. And pretty soon I could deal with the advantages of a different cross—he ought to have at least two. He ought to have at least three so he could make a choice each day of which one. It's pretty hard to express a psychotic pattern of behavior over an ever increasing number of crosses. [pp. 290–291]

Such an unusual encounter cannot be fitted to any theory or paradigm—it is just Erickson genuinely being himself. One cannot decipher a blueprint of a generic technique in this encounter. The marrow, the bones, and the meat of Erickson's work, or for that matter, anyone's, emanates from the person's unarticulatable, undissectable essence of himself. [**One cannot articulate the whole into pieces without damage to the whole, says Cumming (1992) in contrasting the philosophies of Husserl vs. Heidegger.**]

THEORETICAL MONOGAMY IS BETRAYAL OF ONE'S PATIENT

Carolyn came to session with such a tight and short skirt that she couldn't sit on the chair. So she pulled her skirt up even more in an exaggerated fashion and spread her legs wide open.

> *Carolyn:* (Ironic smile) You must remember the scene in the film *Basic Instinct* where Sharon Stone is interviewed in a police station.

Me: I remember more than I have seen.
    [The Healer moves toward the heat.]
    [In the past I might have replied:
    "I wonder whether you want to throw me off balance, as she did the cops."
    Or
    "Any more thoughts on that?"
    Or
    "Do you feel you'll be interrogated by me?"
    Or
    "Do you wonder whether I am seduceable?"]
Carolyn: (Pulled her legs together) That's unusual! My last therapist was also an older man who interpreted every behavior of mine as a scheme to seduce him, as I might have liked to seduce my father. Three years and four hundred such interpretations later . . .

Our theories, at times, take on a religious fervor. Such predetermined ends generate an overdetermined concept. This "dogma eat dogma" began with Freud, who couldn't tolerate even minor dissensions. What he wrote was final and perfect, and it could not be improved upon. The swiftness of his revenges were so well known that he didn't even have to warn anyone of the potential calamities, should they tamper with his gospel. He could have as well repeated after the Revelations. "If anyone adds anything to this book, God will strike him with the plagues that are written in this book. If anyone takes away any words from this book, God will take away his portion of the Tree of Life and the Holy City that are described in this book."

The best example of the theoretical monogamy that promotes overdetermined concepts is the Oedipus complex. One can say that psychoanalysis has originated and pivoted around it. The oedipal conflict, the prototypic pathology, is supposed to be a nodal point in the consolidation of the superego and ego ideal. As the child identifies with the same-sex object, fear of punishment transforms into guilt, and idealization of the opposite sex transforms envy and jealousy into an ego ideal. This is the perfect patient of orthodox analysts.

In fact, if you carefully read the details of Sophocles's *Oedipus Rex*, you'll see that the portrait of Oedipus has great resemblance to an abused child. Arnold Cooper (personal communication, 1998) has noted this discrepancy in his rereading of the classic myth. He suggests that the significance of the change in point of view is made clear in the content of Sophocles's play. He believes that Freud, contrary to his usual practice, saw the meaning of the work in its surface. He thought it was a perfect fit when he came to the conclusion that if Oedipus murdered his father and slept with his mother, then ipso facto he must have wished to do so.

Although Odysseus is the one who is known as being "the man of many turns," *polytropos*, Oedipus had its own share of twists. Closer scrutiny of Oedipus reveals pertinent elements of this perfect fit that can be interpreted in many different and maybe more authentic ways. For example, Oedipus's parents decide, because of the prediction of the gods, to kill Oedipus; his father puts a thong through his ankles and his mother, Clytemnestra, actually hands him to a shepherd to be killed. From this very early childhood scenario is garnered the crucial findings that *Oedipus is an abused, abandoned, and adopted child who never, until near the end of the play, knows who his biological parents are.* It is also not surprising to realize that he is a severely impulse-ridden character. For starters, he almost automatically tries to kill every older man who crosses his path—Laius, Tiresias, the old shepherd, and Creon his uncle. Furthermore, he is unable to withhold or delay need gratification; emotion prevails over reason and he thus unthinkingly marries an older woman, despite knowing the prophecy that he would at some time sleep with his mother.

The critical point is that while Oedipus may well have had an Oedipus complex, we might better understand it in terms of his *preoedipal* history of abandonment and attempted infanticide. It is further revealed in its deleterious effects on his development of impulse control, capacity for object relations, self-esteem regulation, and self representation. I thus believe that the castration anxiety–related fear is mythological overshooting. I agree with Cooper, that castration anxiety is so close to consciousness because it is the least frightening, thus least repressed, of the body fears. More significantly, it represents compromise formations arising out of, as well as hiding within, the prior preemptive fears, which are of even greater threat. Thus the oedipal conflict, however potent, has preoedipal origins that are both more primitive as well as more powerful. Freud's perfect example of psychopathology, the Oedipus complex, turns out to be not just an oedipal conflict, but also an oedipal deficit, in fact, a preoedipal deficit, warping of the childhood nucleus.

Different theories run up against the same common problems, having both assets and limitations. For example, psychodynamic psychotherapy's introspective approach may help the depressed patient to search inward for self-understanding and sense of self as an adaptive alternative to pathological reliance on external sources of self-esteem; it may also strengthen general ego capacities needed for structural change. Yet its regressive transference can foster the very idealization and ungratified demands for love from others that often exacerbate the depressed picture per se, and may itself create inertia, or worse, despair which compounds the already depressive scenario. It is like saying, "Your situation is your misfortune." And how real are those remembered misfortunes anyway? Did they actually occur, or are they some distorted mix of memory and fantasy? Mark Twain once said, "My life has been full of misfortunes, most of which never happened."

In contrast, cognitive therapy allows the therapist to directly intervene in offering new logical thought patterns. Yet its aims may be too restricted, superficial, or temporary, stressing symptoms over unconscious problems of the past. It has been criticized for its critical overreliance on the patient's impaired cognition at the expense of affect, and also further diminishing the patient in the process. John Rush tells the following anecdote: When the cognitive-behavioral therapist confronts a patient with his or her dysfunctional thoughts, the depressed patient says, "I came here because I cannot be happy, and now you are saying that I cannot think straight either!" And interpersonal therapy can target in on recent marital disputes, role transitions, social deficits, or abnormal grief reactions. But its emphasis on the socioenvironmental context and social bonds, especially the spousal role, may overlook individual deep dynamics of loss. When one or another aspect is ignored, ubiquitous claims of therapeutic success from divergent treatments for depression soon lose their potency.

Both interpersonal therapy and cognitive-behavior therapy forget that marriage is also a developmental process. Regardless of the variety of real events that may precipitate depression, interpersonal therapy seems to be seeking solutions from significant others; cognitive-behavioral therapy seeks solutions from a straight-thinking therapist; and psychoanalytic psychotherapy tends to seek solutions from within. As one observer colorfully put it, the interpersonal therapist is like a travel guide who will give lots of information about the trip; the cognitive-behavioral therapist is like a travel companion who will come along on the trip; and the analyst is like a travel agent—he'll point the way; he will not give lots of information and definitely will never take you there; in fact, it is quite likely that, as with most travel agents, he himself may never have been there.

One can construct facts to explain one's theories. In fact, most therapists search patient testimonials for their autobiographical theories, rather than formulating a theory for that specific individual. Theory is a systematic sense of worldview, which interferes with creative adaptation. Many theorists have tried to loosen the therapist's tenacious attachment to his preferred theoretical viewpoints. These have ranged from recommending an attitude of irony (Schafer 1970), to demonstrating how useful *not knowing* can be (Havens 1986), to actively advising the clinician to continuously reopen all conceptual closures (Schwaber 1986). This "loosening" is also intended to encourage

therapists to be more eclectic and to integrate various orientations. However, not everyone is in agreement on doing so. For
example, Chessick (1989) notes its difficulty when he observes
that

> theoretical orientations are being used that directly conflict
> with one another and cannot be thought of as complementary
> because their basic premises, both their epistemological foun-
> dations . . . and their basic assumptions about human na-
> ture and its motivations . . . directly collide. This forces a
> radical discontinuity as we shift from channel to channel in
> our receiving instrument, rather than allowing us, as we
> would all prefer, to slide back and forth between theoretically
> consistent positions—or at least complementary positions
> that are consistent with one another. [p. 44]

All theories can include completely unproven assumptions,
even though they may be scientifically sound or at least plausible.
They can be compelling, even persuasive, especially if they are
susceptible to social support and professional sanction. The
theories have a fated fragility, in that they must forever straddle an
unsettled status that resides somewhere between myth and truth.
Yet viewing theories as a form of credible fiction is what scientific
openness entails. But "our interest is not in whether the theory is
true or false, or even whether it can be tested or falsified, but
rather in what difference it makes to a practitioner" (Michels
1988, p. 9), and ultimately, in the difference it makes for the
patient. That is, the theory must be always formed, and forming,
at the interface between the therapist and the patient.

Theories proliferate in order to fill gaps in knowledge. For
the same reason, psychoanalysis has to be rediscovered over and
over again, says Lacan (1977). Science advances by the perpetual
replacement of theories, in whole or in part, in the ongoing
exchange of falsified premises for presumably truer ones. A
scientific stance also avoids remaining on the opposite sides of the

dangerous coins of reductionistic dogmatism and skeptical nihilism. Somewhere in between are a panoply of potential truths. These myriad relative and partial truths are the pearls of different size, shape, and color. Our goal as clinicians is to find how to thread them together in such a way as to make a fitting necklace for a specific individual. [**It isn't pearls that make the necklace; it's the thread, said Gustave Flaubert.**]

NO-FAULT THEORY: THE THEORY OF EMPATHY EXONERATES THE PATIENT; THE THEORY OF CONFLICT EXONERATES THE THERAPIST

> *Carolyn:* I want to stop this litany against my parents, about their malign neglect and interest. Enough already. I'm a 38-year-old adult. I cannot keep blaming them for my present problems. I even feel guilty for doing that. I didn't want my last therapist talking about my parents' imprinting role in the development of my character. His theory was that my mother actually passively enabled my father, a kind of reciprocal pathology.
>
> *Me:* You know, theory means contemplation.
> **[The Healer is underdetermined.]**
> [In the past I might have asked for more details, recruited affect, explored her reaction to the therapist's theory and the therapist himself, wondered about her "guilt"—was she a coconspirator?—and more.]
>
> *Carolyn:* Contemplation? Well, he was very sure. He gave me two papers on the subject to read. They were both published in prestigious journals. If this is simply his thoughts, I wouldn't be in such a rage against my parents. I have not seen them or talked to them in the last year and a half. God . . . I miss them. They keep writing letters, leaving messages on my answering machine. They don't understand why I'm so hostile and

unresponsive. Are you saying that his theories are contemplations and not based on any facts?

Me: Facts of his seeing.

[**The Healer melts down the "hard facts."**]

In his acorn theory, Hillman (1996) reverses the classical evolutionary principle that ontogeny recapitulates phylogeny. For him the child is responsible for choosing his parents, thus exonerating the parents. Most other theories exonerate the child while holding the parents responsible for his troubles.

Each therapist ultimately develops a concept of psychopathology that solidifies his or her own stand about the etiology of illness, which has implications for its cause and cure. For example, if you conceptualize your patient's psychopathology as an end result of empathic failures by significant others in his or her early life, you basically limit the person's own responsibility in the etiology of illness. Consequently, a heavier weight falls on the therapist to undo that past failure. However, if you theorize a patient's psychopathology as an end result of the individual's internal conflicts, you are more apt to enlist the patient's part in the creation (and dissolution) of his or her problems. Then the onus of responsibility with regard to treatment can better shift from the therapist to the patient. That is why Kemper (1988) suggests that the theory of empathic failure exonerates the patient, whereas the theory of conflict exonerates the therapist.

Why are our theories primarily geared toward exonerating—or implicating—therapists or patients or family members? There seems to be a special penchant to place the etiological blame on schizophrenogenic mothers or depressed fathers in the mental disturbances of their children. [**"Keep my mother out of this,"** said one of my patients.] And any unempathic significant figure of early infancy is also implicated.

Other theorists use sweeping philosophical typologies that call for a fundamental division into two separate psychologies of man. For example, either you can hold allegiance to the conflict-based theory of Freud, thus adhering to a psychology of "guilty man" who is suffering from sexual repression derived from forbidden oedipal desires, or you can believe in the deficit-based theory of Kohut and propose a psychology of "tragic man" who is suffering from a fragmented or missing self that has derived from preoedipal lack of empathy. I think that such romantic intensification of basic belief systems is antiquated as well as unrealistic. Man, in real life, is both guilty *and* tragic, or neither, a complex product of evolving dynamics and changing times.

Why such reductionistic constructions? Couldn't there be a no-fault paradigm—including no-fault diagnosis, no-fault theory? As Lacan (1977) pointed out, it was not simply an old man's irony that prompted Freud, at the end of his life, to compare the constructions of the analyst to the delusions of his patient. Rather, a therapist's constructions as well as a patient's delusions, share a fundamental similarity; like myths, both are attempts at explanation and cure. What's more, whether a therapist's favored theory represents reality or reverie, is proven or unproven, if he or she relies too heavily on one theoretical paradigm, it can overwhelm one's own thinking as well as constrict the approach to patients. Thus the therapist gets reduced professionally and the patient gets diminished as a human being. In this regard, Levenson (1983) has suggested that in the perpetuation of such a self-congratulatory attitude, "The danger is that the theory becomes an ideological indoctrination *sui generis* and the patient becomes a disciple" (pp. 89–90).

At the potential risk of being called pluralistic (alas, another label), if not skeptical, I support Druck's (1989) stated position that there is much to learn from all theories, and all of them are only partially right. He further states:

> The appropriate question is not which theory is right? but rather, to what clinical issues can the therapist become more sensitive by understanding a given model? Much of the polarization among psychotherapists is a result of an empha-

sis on one factor and a relative neglect of others. Since patients can be understood from a number of points of view, a discussion of differences in emphasis is more helpful to the clinician than a debate about ultimate truth. [p. ix]

["We can no more test Freudian hypotheses 'on the couch' than we can adjudicate between rival hypotheses of Newton and Einstein by going to sleep under an apple tree," said Eysenck (1959, pp. 228–229).]

Theories are attempts at making sense of things. The ordering tendency of the mind searches for remedies for the phenomena of discontinuity, infinity, randomness, nameless dread, chaos, and meaninglessness. But bearing it all is more a grounding than the hollowness of the search for a remedy in the mind.

As each true artist melts down and reforges all past aesthetic laws, so does each man. The required nascent energy originates from the soul's moving toward the heat, and leaning toward it wholeheartedly.

The enlightened man is underdetermined. He maintains a certain free margin, and sense of curiosity and credulity. He doesn't presume to have arrived, he has no claims, no piety; he is a puzzled perpetual learner—not a studied pose, but genuine reflector on his limitations.

3

Only Not Knowing Portends Finality

HOTHOUSE PSYCHOTHERAPY: RESEARCH IN PSYCHOTHERAPY HAS NO ECOLOGICAL VALIDITY

Everyone has won, [but none gets] prizes.

—Variation of Lewis Carroll

Carolyn: Did you find that your eclectic, oh I'm sorry, pluralistic approach was effective? Because I don't know much about it. Is that the right name? Do you or others study that? Are there any outcome data?

Me: No.

Carolyn: No, to what?

Me: To all three questions.

Carolyn: That means that what you practice isn't called a pluralistic approach. Whatever it's called, its effectiveness is not studied; and there are no outcome data?

Me: Yes.

Carolyn: Are there other people besides yourself who practice your brand of psychotherapy?

Me: I don't know.

Carolyn: Well, don't you feel a little bit lonely and rather handicapped that you don't have companions in your journey, that by yourself the process of proving that what you do is worthwhile or utterly worthless will be extremely slow, if ever forthcoming?

Me: Down to Gehenna or up to the throne, he travels the fastest who travels alone.

Carolyn: You like Kipling? I presume you're reassuring me that I'll either get better or worse, but it'll be fast.

Me: There are many possibilities.

[**The Healer sees no fixed states.**]

After hearing my project to study the efficacy of psychotherapy on behalf of the American Psychiatric Association (APA) Daniel X. Freedman, with his mischievous smile, told me that once he was invited to give a grand rounds for forty-five minutes in a prestigious school. He was asked, "Could you talk about the efficacy of psychotherapy?" He said, "Sure, but what will I talk about for the other forty-four minutes?" His one minute, I hope, would have been to state that science requires that the person state not only what he believes, but also how he arrives at it.

To fit to such scientific criteria, psychotherapy and psychotherapy research have been mutually subversive. How can you generalize findings of diverse efficacy studies based on different theories? How does one go about combining the research of therapies with conflicting conceptual paradigms? [**Is nonscientific evidence accretionary?**] Why aggregate the results of these studies to begin with? The metaphorical answer is that, even if you teach an elephant to play the violin, you still need a string quartet of elephants to prove it. In any event, the first such aggregation was pioneered by Eysenck's "proving" that psychotherapy is not effective. Over a decade later, Smith and associates (1981) collected all the negative studies, reanalyzed the data, and this time proved that psychotherapy *is* effective. [**Is psychotherapy research like wine—the longer it ages, the better it gets?**] Luborsky and colleagues (1975), who had reviewed much of the psychotherapy outcome literature of the time, like *Alice in Wonderland*, classically concluded with the dodo verdict, that "Everyone has won and all must have prizes" (p. 995).

The reason for such a marked discrepancy in their respective results is partly related to the ill-defined subject of the study, which lends itself to a highly complex inferential process. It primarily reflects the fact that nonsystematic research investigations tend to be simply biased in their separate standards of selection and review. Even using Luborsky's special procedure for selection criteria (i.e., the "box score"), proved to be only relatively successful. What's more, it was definitely not immune from its own biases. Knowing this, Smith and Glass (1977) came up with a totally new methodology—meta-analysis—elevating research onto a higher level of insecurity. The integration of data from diverse studies is fraught with difficulties, and meta-analysis is no more than an attempt to apply to that task the judgmental, analytical, and computational skills of the empirical researcher.

As in all empirical research, however, the outcomes obtained are a function of the assumptions, resources, and skills applied by the investigators. Nonetheless, the study points clearly to three broad conclusions: first, the average impact of psychological treatments in recently published comparative outcome research approaches is a standard deviation unit; second, the modest differences between treatment methods are largely independent of other factors influencing outcome; and third, contemporary outcome research is not representative of clinical practice.

Despite appearances of having moved closer to the "temple of Truth," one must emphasize that this is a purely *quantitative* method of reviewing the literature, simply a statistical technique. A crucial aspect was to standardize the various outcome measures so that they could be displayed on a common scale of overall well-being. To the extent that all instruments are estimating that same construct, they would be comparable on a general level. It is like oranges and apples: they cannot be added or aggregated in the qualities of their taste, color, or shape, but they *can* be looked at through their common denominator of number of calories. This approach even leads researchers themselves to wonder whether their methodology is replicable, thus reliable. Maybe yes, but is it valid? Does it measure what it purports to measure? Do dozens of inconsistently-designed research investigations add up to a single valid and conclusive study? Beyond this, the American Psychiatric Association Commission on Psychotherapies (1982) has aptly pointed out that validity is a highly relative concept. The question is always, "Valid for what?" There are as yet no convincing answers to these queries and dilemmas. Thus, the perennial controversy over whether psychotherapy is effective will undoubtedly continue. [**Will it continue with rhetorical disinterestedness?**]

Incidentally (or not so incidentally), if psychotherapy is indeed effective, to what have these researchers attributed this finding? Statistically, what was the largest correlation with "effect size"? The answer was—believe it or not—the reactivity of the outcome indicator! This means that the more easily the outcome measure is faked, the larger the effects, as Hans Strupp has sardonically said. You know, maybe we should even eliminate this pressure for controlled trials altogether. Albert Einstein was the first to admit that "not everything that counts can be counted, and not everything that can be counted counts."

After all, knowledge is obtained in a variety of ways, other than the strict scientific method of controlled research in analogue context. Furthermore, there is no single approach that would be suitable for dealing with every hypothesis. What is best in any given situation may be determined by both theoretical and empirical considerations. In psychotherapy especially, inexperienced as well as experienced clinicians soon recognize that there is a gap between theory and practice. Even the experts have differed in their views of the role of the scientific method in the search for proven facts of everyday life. Einstein, for one, exalted the theoretical route to truth expressed in mathematical equations, which could subsequently be tested by actual experiences of the physical world.

In contrast, Freud (1916–1917) felt that direct inferences could better come from the reality of the human laboratory of clinical practice. In the latter paradigm, N = 1 designs are useful as a source of new ideas. Indeed much of the present information about the world has resulted from such singular and often anecdotal observations, not to mention the added ingredient of serendipity. [**Science issues only interim reports.**]

STUDY OF THE NORMLESS

> Only the poet knows the facts of sciences because he takes them as signs.
>
> —Ralph Waldo Emerson

Carolyn: Am I in a protocol of some sort? I mean, will my treatment be taped or studied in some other fashion? I looked up your previous work. You've been studying the psychotherapy process, published many papers, and even a book on the methodology of research. I don't mind if that's the case, but I wouldn't want to be in the control group and get a placebo psychotherapy.

Me: We'll be studying each other and all others.

[**For the Healer all relations are transpersonal.**]

[I do *not* ask whether she worries about being made a guinea pig; *not* whether she is ambivalent about being in therapy with an ex-researcher.]

Can a therapist practice psychotherapy and, at the same time, scientifically study what he does? [**Can he then be called the** "as-if" therapist?] First of all, research requires exclusionary criteria, which are designed to minimize false positives. Clinicians, on the other hand, need to minimize false negatives, because a single loss is a human loss, not just a statistical matter. The following anecdote highlights this: There was a man who claimed that he could make people disappear. So a panel was set up to investigate the truth of the claim, with a statistician among its members. The man brought in a hundred people, put them in a room, and then, as promised, only ninety-nine came out. Everyone was impressed, of course, except the statistician, who said, "One percent is not significant."

The conduct of psychotherapy is difficult enough as is, but to expect a rigorous design to be superimposed on practice is almost impossible. Furthermore, the rigor of design is one thing, its execution is another. As some researchers have pointed out, the concentration of outcome research at the analogue end of the clinical–analogue continuum places severe limitations on its generalizibility to everyday practice.

First, how do you establish a credible control group? The control group in psychotherapy means, at most, that the patient has not received treatment by a professional. It does *not* mean that he did not receive psychotherapeutic help from family members, friends, ministers, rabbis, or cab drivers. [**Can "unintentional psychotherapy" be a new school?**] Thus, zero level of treatment is unattainable. Second, to carry out an experiment, outside variables must be kept constant. How do you keep two to three hours a week of psychotherapy sessions constant, never mind the 165 or 166 hours per week of the patient's experience outside of the sessions? Third, what are you going to use as a placebo, especially if there is no certainty about what the active ingredients of psychotherapy are? It has been said by many that there may not be such a thing as a psychologically inert condition, and any reliable placebo will not remain theoretically inert, as *someone* will have an explanation of therapeutic activity.

The outcome measure issue is no less complicated. Which biological markers will you use to measure subjective experiences? Who sets the goal of treatment—the patient, the therapist, the family, the insurance company, or the IRS? Especially difficult is to compare therapeutic approaches based on different assumptions. In assessing criteria for change or cure, for example, how do you aggregate symptom-oriented behavior therapy with personality-oriented analytic psychotherapy? What methodological lens does one use?

With all of these difficulties and more, psychotherapists are expected to maintain an effective practice, to do credible research, and in these trying times, to write grants, no less. Well, the therapist isn't God, although some come close to such a delusional state. Incidentally, even God is apparently having problems with the funding agencies! I heard this little vignette recently: When God applied for a grant, they turned him down, citing the following critique:

1. Although he meets the criteria for creativity, that was a long time ago; he has created nothing since.
2. Although he has written a good book, he has no publications in refereed journals.
3. Despite showing great promise, the original work has never been duplicated.

London (1964) argues that psychotherapists have both a scientific and a moralistic function. The scientific function is that of manipulator of behavior; the moralistic function is that of secular priesthood. Anyway, these secular and nonsecular aspirations aside, I believe if you do just good work, the way that Horney (1987) described, that is, with wholeheartedness, comprehensiveness, and productivity, you are not only a good therapist, but also a good-enough researcher.

He can be good enough, maybe, but in reality the therapist

cannot really be a rigorous researcher, because the latter requires a high degree of clinical detachment. Laing (1960) claimed that science means knowledge adequate to its subject. He has written about the destructiveness of such detachment, satirically calling it the absence of the therapist's presence, or worse, the presence of the therapist's absence. Any other agenda besides being there for the patient, even an agenda as noble as that of the scientific one, contaminates the process of psychotherapy. Even Freud, the first psychotherapy researcher, admitted that "cases which are devoted from the first to scientific purposes and are treated accordingly suffer in their outcome; while the most successful cases are those in which one proceeds, as it were, without any purpose in view, allows oneself to be taken by surprise by any turn in them, and always meets them with an open mind, free from any presuppositions" (1912b, p. 114). [**In fact, the therapist must be surprised by nothing and be surprised by everything.**]

OUT OF THE ONE, MANY

> For psychotherapy, everything is going for it, except credibility.
> —Morris Parloff

It has been said that psychotherapy is a subjective study of subjectivity, unsuccessfully struggling to become an objective study of subjectivity. Therefore, the science of psychotherapy stands apart because it has both too few, or too many, answers. Since its unresolved dilemmas and problems cannot be solved at all or can be solved in too many alternative ways with competing and equally persuasive theoretical conceptualizations, there is a point where none of these has the power to exclude the others. In fact, they have fed on each other in order to proliferate, that is, from the classic "talking cure" (Freud's psychoanalysis), a screaming cure (Janov's primal therapy), a reasoning cure (Ellis's rational therapy), a realism cure (Glasser's reality therapy), a decision cure (Greenwald's direct decision therapy), an orgasm cure (Reich's orgone therapy), a meaning cure (Frankl's logotherapy), a relaxation cure (Wolpe's reciprocal inhibition therapy), to a profound rest cure (transcendental meditation). There are few sources for all these tributaries. ["**Out of the one, many**" reverses the United States motto "*E pluribus unum*," as Wilson (1998) points out.]

We know that psychotherapy practices are not uniform and that mental health itself is a fuzzy concept. We deal with the meaning of such elusive notions as ego strength and maturity, self-actualization, and maximizing one's potential. Furthermore, there is a multiplicity of silent influences. Given these limitations, I was about to conclude that it made no sense to talk about psychotherapy's effectiveness.

However, I reminded myself of how complex the research on body or mind is, whether on backache, tennis elbow, sty, headache, or cancer. Given the highly complicated methodological problems that inhere in these scientific efforts, I don't blame researchers for seeking solutions to soluble problems. Obviously, the more narrowly one defines and limits the parameters of an experiment, the more exacting the research, but then the less generalization is possible. By following lines of least resistance, psychotherapy researchers have even created a new category of science: substitute research. It's like the story of the drunk who dropped a ring on the street at night. As he was looking for it under a lamppost, a passerby stopped and helped, but to no avail. "Are you sure you dropped it here?" the passerby asked. "No," the drunk replied. "I dropped it down the street but the lighting is better here." So there are Ph.D candidates who are continually studying college students. After all, they are the most accessible— and willing—captive subjects. Morris Parloff thus insisted that the only conclusion that can be drawn from all these studies is that there is a major epidemic of snake phobia on American college campuses. In the pioneering meta-analysis of psychotherapy research, the statistical finding was that the average effect of psychotherapy over control conditions is about 0.90 standard deviation units immediately after therapy, but falls to around 0.5 units two years later. On this basis, Smith and associates came to the concise conclusion that the benefits of psychotherapy are not permanent. They were quick to admit at the heels of this decisive statement, however, that in matters of life as well as psychotherapy research, there is mighty little that is *not* temporary in the real world.

I guess one may also assert that all schools of psychotherapy are equally *ineffective*. The whole positive outcome result may not be more than global regression to the mean. Regression to the mean is an expected effect when extreme groups are selected for study, such as patients high on anxiety or low on self-esteem. This reflects the dubious finding that the more an initial set of observations deviates above or below the mean of the population distribution, the more a second set observations will move in the direction of the mean, even in the absence of any true change.

Parloff admitted, after 25 years of psychotherapy research, that unequivocal conclusions about causal connections may never be possible. This is because psychotherapy is not a simple stimulus that produces a simple response; it is a highly complex set of interactions between two or more people, extending over a period of time. Thereupon, he arrived at the only conceivable conclusion for the practitioner—contemporary outcome research is not representative of actual practice.

WOUNDED HEALER

> *Carolyn:* I wonder how you decided to become a therapist. You know I entered from the backdoor. I had a potentially very exciting profession. But I felt that if I truly engage into academia, I'll never have the time or energy to deal with myself—as if I were walking around with a

secret past, a lie that was lurking behind every act of mine, personal or intellectual. I presume I could have become a novelist, used my childhood, my pain as a source of inspiration, developed and embellished characters from my family, found solace by writing. But I thought that would be a perpetuation of lies with more interesting lies. And especially if I were to succeed as a writer, that would have sealed my past, never to be reached again. I didn't want to forfeit myself for my career. But within a month of my analysis, I decided I was too damaged to become a good therapist. I wasn't even sure whether I could even be a good patient, and if I can't help myself, how could I help others?

Me: The candle is not there to illuminate itself.

Carolyn: But where does the candle come from? What is it made of, and furthermore, I'm keenly aware that there are candles and there are candles. If honesty self-reflected, what this sickly candle could eliminate by itself is hardly visible, teetering at the edge of burning off.

Me: There is also a non–self-reflective awareness and self sameness that illuminates just by reflection.

Carolyn: Well, you have greater faith in me than I have in myself. Were you equally in doubt when you began? Did you come to the field from your personal traumatic experiences? I know I shouldn't be asking that, but I'm searching for a kind of self sameness with you to assure myself that if . . .

All variables being equal, therapist variables may turn out to be the most significant, but still with limited intrinsic impact. For example, psychotherapy-responsive depression is an inherently self-correcting condition. All the therapist may be doing is just speeding up this natural self-healing process. In fact, throughout history human beings have found various ways of facilitating or accelerating this process—some intuitive, some scientific, some random, some systematic. The establishment of a "school" at best represents the sanction of an internally cohesive theory of pathology and treatment. Yet all schools coalesce around the significance of the therapist–patient relationship. The patient part is understood, insofar as the healthier the patient at the onset, the better the outcome. It seems even more remarkable that the therapist has emerged as a most significant and relatively controllable variable, even though there is no evidence for it. Shamans, says Frank (1974), are drawn from the ranks of cured patients, inheritors of domesticated pathology, and the connoisseurs of domesticatible pathology. It takes one to treat one. It may be that the best therapists are like the early shamans, who recovered from the worst pathologies with the least handicaps. [**Only the deepest wounds that leave no visible scars make a healer out of the wounded.**]

LIMITATIONS IN SCIENCE INVITE AN OFFERING OF FAITH

Helmuth Kaiser said that psychoanalysis may not cure patients, but it sure does make psychoanalysts out of them. In fact, he decided to become an analyst himself. One of the most vexing dilemmas of the field still remains—to what extent psychotherapy can be considered a precise science, defined by such criteria as measurability, replicability, and empirical validation, versus its imprecise status as a form of art. Not enough effort has been made to generate the study of a psychological system applicable to our knowledge of therapy, with accuracy, precision, or adherence to an established standard. This is because psychotherapy cannot always be dealt with in accordance with the "facts." There are no material objects independent of mental concepts, ideas, and belief systems, and there is no actual existence of observable reality uninfluenced by emotions.

In this unscientific scenario, psychotherapy doesn't deal with anything that actually exists, as distinguished from something *thought* or *felt* to be. Thus psychotherapy inevitably rejects, or at least revises, "real" occurrences themselves, by subjecting to scrutiny their *meaning* to the individual. In short, it has no reality external to the mind. So, if the therapist deals only with observed objects and external events and nothing else, then he or she will not be practicing psychotherapy. On the other hand, if the therapist deals with subjective matters that are internal to the mind, then he or she will not be objective or scientific.

Of course, objectivity is not the only road to the truth. In applying the scientific method, the totality of principles should be considered, which includes rules of concept formation as well as the nature of observations and their validation. One can easily observe, identify, describe, and even measure a physical phenomenon, and then provide a theoretical explanation. Here "scientific" means acquiring knowledge gained by a systematic and operational approach to inherently unsystematic and intangible thoughts, fantasies, dreams, and wishes—life stories recalled and recounted in the presence of another.

On the one hand, psychotherapy could continue to be the deliberate study of intersubjective phenomena and of the therapy process, to identify the mental activities that form this complex entity. On the other hand, we can live with the idea that knowledge in psychotherapy has nothing to do with any form of science or systems, and psychotherapists should stop all these attempts at looking for concrete elements and definitive explanations, intersubjective or not. Rather, we as clinicians should accept psychotherapy as a sediment of knowledge, similar to what Lord Halifax said about education—it is what remains after you have forgotten all that you have been taught. This sedimentation of knowledge is such an ephemeral phenomenon, that it will always escape us any time we think we have found it. [**The horizon disappears as one draws closer.**]

The presumed end points of all seekings are not fixed states. Attempts at articulation of the intersubjective experience is like trying to decipher a melody from the grooves of a record.

The relations between people are not linear, but omnidirectional, formless, and discontinuous; not just interpersonal, but transpersonal; not prescriptive, but over-the-encounter and improvisational. They are timeless and spaceless. We couldn't know, even if we knew.

4

The One Who Knows Everything
Knows Nothing Else

WEDDING OF DOUBTS: ONLY CO-AUTHORED
TRUTHS ARE REAL

> *Carolyn:* Is it possible that my mother's passivity wasn't a
> malign coconspirator's enabling behavior, but that's how
> she was? In fact, she was passive about everything.
> "Mom, would you like me to get you something to
> drink?" She would answer, "If you like." I'm just making
> this up, but about any subject she'd never take an active
> stand. "Let's do this or that, do this or that" is not in the
> repertoire of this intelligent and talented woman. "Mom,
> get ready, we're going to the movies." She'd get ready
> without asking which movie. So it makes sense to me
> that she took the same attitude in my relation with my
> father. It was her character, a pattern of behavior, not
> specifically designed to set me up, would you say?
>
> *Me:* Possibly. [**For the Healer the truth is the appropriation
> of compassionate resonance.**]
>
> [*Not* "You want me to validate your conclusion."

Or worse,
"I wonder whether you're setting me up."]
Carolyn: Theory for two, tea for two, oh never mind. My free
associations aren't all that, you know . . .

The story of William Butler Yeats about the mind of the poet
is equally applicable to that of the psychotherapist. Yeats tells of
Icelandic peasants who found a skull in a cemetery and suspected
it might be that of the poet Egill. Its great dimension made them
feel certain it was, but to be absolutely sure they placed it on a wall
and struck it with hard blows of a hammer. When it did not break,
they were convinced that it was in truth the skull of the poet and
worthy of every honor. The therapist's stubborn preconceptions
and dogma far exceeds that of poets. For example, when it comes
to reconciling the difference between what the patient thinks is
the problem and what the therapist believes it to be, the therapist
rarely considers first entering into the patient's paradigm. As Carl
Rogers (1961) has suggested, in a very significant sense the client
and the therapist never know what the problem is until it is well
on its way to resolution. I agree, but thick-skulled therapists
would never concede it.

There is no absolute truth and reality anywhere else, so it
should be no surprise that the same goes for psychology and its
therapeutic formulation. The truth in therapy is a consensual
process between therapist and patient as the treatment evolves.
I'm not even sure whether there is any truth to this statement
either. We have to sober up on the concepts of truth and reality.
According to the parables of Gaul, the reality is incomplete, if
viewed from any point of view, and it is incoherent, if viewed from
all points of view.

A half-century ago Freud said that the relationship between
therapist and patient rests on the love of truth as its foundation,
that is, on acknowledgment of reality. Since change is a basic
characteristic of reality, however, there may be no finite truth.
Independent of its exactness, the truth, and the reality, in order to

be received by the patient a particular insight must meet certain criteria: it should have consistency, continuity, and synchronicity. It has to be logically sound; it needs to be maintained within the theoretical framework of the therapy, and last but not least, it should represent a microcosmic version of the mutual belief system between therapist and patient. The value of insight may reside in its form, aesthetic nature, and consensuality—not in its content, not in its rightness or wrongness, especially what the therapist may consider as such.

In Act III of George Bernard Shaw's *Major Barbara*, Undershaft says: "What! No capacity for business, no knowledge of law, no sympathy with art, no pretension of philosophy; only a simple knowledge of the secret of what puzzled all the philosophers, baffled all the lawyers . . . : the secret of right and wrong. Why, man you are a genius, and master of masters, a god!" This ironic praise is equally suited for therapists who pass judgment on the rightness or wrongness or truthfulness or untruthfulness of matters, including insight.

Ferenczi (1928) stated "Nothing is more harmful . . . than a school-masterish, or even an authoritative, attitude on the physician's part. Anything we say to the patient should be put to him in the form of a tentative suggestion and not of a confidently held opinion, not only to avoid irritating him, but because there is always the possibility that we may be mistaken" (p. 94). This position of doubt, nonetheless, may have its own drawbacks. In his cross-cultural study of persuasion and healing, Frank (1974) noted that interpretation is not merely the chief means by which the psychotherapist demonstrates his understanding of the patient, but perhaps equally important, it expresses his special expertise and command of the field. Skillful strategies arouse and maintain the patient's confidence in the clinician as a master of a special healing art, thereby enhancing the patient's hopes for help. The ability to make interpretations also reassures the therapist about his own competence. Alas, this is why those who are young and inexperienced—or old and insecure—are frequently tempted to display their savvy. This results in prematurely offering too rigid or too many interpretations and explanations. Frank (1987) says; "Comparison of psychotherapy with hermeneutics suggests, rather, that the criterion of the 'truth' of a psychotherapeutic interpretation, as of a religious text, is its plausibility—that is, the 'truest' interpretation would be one that is most satisfying or makes the most sense to persons whose judgment one accepts. In psychotherapy, the ultimate judge of an interpretation's truth is the patient" (p. 297). In short, the power of an interpretation to carry conviction to the patient depends on many factors, among them its ability to make sense out of the material the patient has offered, the patient's confidence in the therapist, and, ultimately, its fruitfulness, the beneficial consequences of the interpretation for the patient's ability to function and sense of well-being.

FEELING UNDERSTOOD PROMOTES THE LEARNING TO UNDERSTAND

> *Carolyn:* I must be boring you with this. I think I talked about it, I don't know, at least a dozen times. I feel like I keep repeating myself again and again. OK, one more time, but for the last time, I seem to need more than one man. Boring, right?
>
> *Me:* This is the first time I'm hearing it.
> [**The Healer loves the other.**]
> [*Not* to reassure:
> Of course not.
> Or to explain it:
> "Each time you visit the subject, we may see in from a different and previously neglected angle."
> Or to interpret it:
> "Somehow you think you must entertain me."
> Or
> "I wonder whether you feel that there has not been any

progress in treatment and my interventions brought us only to a boring impasse."]

Carolyn: (Laughs) It's interesting that you said that, as I was telling you that "I seem to need more than one man." Actually I felt as if I was telling it for the first time myself, with full knowledge that that wasn't the case. Isn't that strange? I am definitely not bored at all. I told the same stories or variations to three different therapists, and only the analyst I saw four times a week interpreted my repetition as my unconscious intention to bore him, almost exclusively. I think weeks would go on and we would talk about nothing else but my design to bring the treatment to a boring impasse. Others would listen and comment, each time a little differently, mostly empathically, at times searchingly, but there was not a steady dose of the same stand. So I guess it got imprinted in my mind that whenever I need to repeat a story I wonder whether I'm boring you. Your response makes me feel understood. I want to learn now.

The frequency of contact between patient and therapist was originally conceptualized to accommodate the intensity of the transference. If the treatment is transference based, then it requires frequent contact as sessions build on each other conceivably ad infinitum. The past and present are relived within the transference.

However, if the treatment is primarily non–transference based, then it is a reporting process and requires no specific frequency, as the sessions could conceivably have a life of their own relatively independent of each other. To patients' question as to how often the sessions should be is Bugental's (1987) response: You go to the beach, dig a hole, come back the next week, dig the same hole. But if you go back to the beach every day, begin where you left off, you dig a deeper hole. The real issue is not as much how frequently you meet with a patient, but what you *do* when you're together in a session, and what kind of relationship would set the optimum stage for transmuting identification and internalization to occur. [**This is getting into the thick of thin things.**]

In identification, which usually refers to a relatively mature mental process of differentiation by which an individual integrates another into a cohesive self-identity, change occurs in a fairly global manner. In transmuting internalization (Kohut's term), by comparison, bits and pieces of the object or selfobject are internalized. Introduction of the latter term reflects Kohut's concern that, if the therapist actively assumes a role of idolatry, he thereby encourages only gross (nonselective) identification. This can obstruct a gradual integration and transformation of the patient's own psychological structures, and also hinder the progressive building up of new ones. In transmuting internalization, however, aspects of the idealized other are slowly, selectively, and partially internalized, then reassembled in the psyche of the patient. This means a piecemeal assimilation of an ongoing identificatory process—"microinternalization." Instead of being an irrational, wholesale idealization or repudiation of another, it includes recognition of realistic imperfections of the object or selfobject, as new aspects of the clinician are continually internalized and integrated into the emerging self.

Transmuting internalization is the outcome of two related and repetitive consecutive processes: first, feeling understood, and then, learning to understand. The infinitely repetitive process of microinternalization requires therapist and patient to go over the same topics again and again, with increasing refinement. The insight here is part of the internalization process, at times as a technique, at times as a result, and at times as a building block for the therapist–patient relationship.

Alas, some therapists—not to mention patients—have little tolerance for such a painstaking and protracted process. They consider repetitions as meaningless chatter, a waste of time for both, although occasionally there are those profound moments. Not every minute of the session can have the same degree of profundity, but even when what the patient says *seems* "meaning-less," it is never without meaning. Thomas Moore (1994a) tells an anecdote of those in therapy often asking him, "Aren't you tired of hearing the same things over and over again?" "No," he replies, "I am quite happy to hear the same thing." He believes in an alchemical circulation, that the life of the soul depends on a continual going over and over of the material of life. I personally never hear the same thing. Each time it's different, though seemingly the same. "New veins can be found in old mines," said Ferenczi (1928). The more traumatic the environmental events and the more conflicted the intrapsychic struggle, the greater the need to retell one's story, differently each time. As the poet Tennyson's "ancient mariner," long lost at sea, repeatedly pro-claimed to anyone who would listen: "Until my torrid tale is told, I shall not cease to speak." But the tale can never be told. [**No one tells or hears the same tale twice.**]

THE THERAPIST CANNOT HELP BUT ERR

> *Carolyn:* My boyfriend B is in one aspect no different from my parents. He screams at the top of his voice, "What's wrong with you? Calm down. Relax." I'm an anxious person. If I react to something with a little more than average emotion, they all behave as if I'm crazy. They don't know why I react that way, nor do they try to find out.
>
> *Me:* Unknown, and unfound!
> [**The Healer is definitely human and errs.**]
> [In the past I might have explored her emotional response to their behavior:
> "And how has that made you feel?"
> Or sympathize:
> "What an awful feeling that must be."
> Or empathize:

"How horrible!"

Or go after the content:

"Do you think your selection of a man is overdetermined?"

Or be more specific:

"Do you think your selection of a man is determined by a parental pattern of disapproval?"

Or seek some transferential process:

"Do you wonder whether I consider you crazy the same way that they do?"]

Carolyn: I'm not sure what that means, exactly. I must be doing something wrong that prompts such reaction from the people that I'm the closest to.

Me: They know you and found you out?

[This was a serious mistake, most likely prompted by her negation of my previous statement, thus a narcissistic injury to my interpretive powers.]

Carolyn: That they decided I'm this crazy person, period? I guess so did you, when first you said unknown and unfound, and now you're saying you're known and found. So I deserve what I get then. I feel horrible. I can't even count on your being on my side. Everyone seems to be conspiring to show me how bad I am. My parents, my friends male and female, my therapists, they all take me down. Why do you think I came to you, really?

Me: To find your unfailing other.

Carolyn: Damn right. I'm not interested in any "designer therapy." I've seen enough therapists not to fall into the same just-say-amen approach to every utterance of the therapist, you know. Remove the letters T, h, and e from the therapist and what do you get?

Me: I'm sorry, what I meant was . . .

Carolyn: (interrupts) I don't care what you meant. I know what you said. You should mean only what you say. Don't try to wiggle out of this. I know you're very good at it. But as they say, virtuosity at times obscures one's virtue. That's not what I actually wanted to say. This actually turns out to be a compliment.

Me: I hope you said what you meant.

Carolyn: In reality you guys were mostly well-meaning people. It's just your professional "entity hunting" that gets in your way or you get anxious.

Me: And make anxious misconstructions.

Carolyn: Yeah! I think so. You know your mind is not free from itself. Enough. I give you victory in your retreat.

Me: Victory?

Carolyn: Well, yes. To keep my faith in therapy, and furthermore . . .

Schafer (1980) said, "The analysand can do no wrong because he can do no right" (p. 64). It seems to be the reverse for therapists. They are highly loyal to their mistakes and not very motivated to report them. [**That is, unless failures go to their heads.**]

After all these years of clinical work, there have been only a few occasions that I did not regret either having said something in a session, or not having said something and thereby missing an opportunity. As soon as a patient walks in, I feel a kind of anxious anticipation, not knowing what will present itself thereafter. This attitude of expectancy is natural, even good, as the clinician comes prepared for a mutual adventure, similar to chess master Savielly G. Tartakower's remark on the game's opening position: "Mistakes are all there to be made." [**The incorrectness of the bullfight is what makes it appealing.**]

Common mistakes can occur across a very broad spectrum — from devastating to the patient to embarrassing to the therapist. For example, the therapist can create a chaotic situation by not getting patients' negative feelings out of their hiding places, by too early interpretation, by interpreting the meaning of what the patient says before addressing his or her resistance, or by interpreting the resistance before it is fully developed. Less chaotic, but more embarrassing, mistakes are related to not gathering all of the relevant information before offering recommendations. A recently divorced friend of mine told me that a consultant therapist had spent the entire first session on his immediate reasons for treatment. After an initial consultation that was largely devoted to descriptive details of the patient's clinical symptoms of anxiety and depression, including periods of inactivity and boredom, the therapist recommended that he take up some hobbies—"like playing a musical instrument." The only problem with this otherwise reasonable advice was that my friend was already a professional pianist!

Friedman (1988) takes a quite original posture on the subject. For him, to talk about mistakes in psychotherapy itself is a mistake. To speak about "errors" in psychotherapy, he says, is misleading because due to contradictory duties that are required, the therapist cannot help but err. The therapist is not even squarely in a false position. He has to balance perception with influence, objective dispassion with expressed concern, and he has to shuffle several roles in order to maintain a therapeutic posture while at the same time to be "real," to be both a man of mystery and a seeker of truth.

Friedman feels that the clinician has only two choices: how much trouble to invite and from what direction. If he really cannot avoid mistakes, he should learn precisely what undesired consequences may be caused by his erroneous actions. Basch (1980) says that the erring therapist need not worry. Whenever he went wide of the therapeutic mark, the patient indicated in some way that he had not registered the meaning of what was said—that is, he disavowed the therapist's comment or interpretation and went on to use the therapist in a way that made sense to him. It may be further consolation to therapists to hear Karl Jaspers (1963) say that learning results not merely from experiencing anew, but rather in the experience of error. [**You should always quit while you're behind.**]

SUCCESSFUL FAILURE

Carolyn: I got this sudden idea last night. See what you think.
How to say this? I think I'm quite an introspective
person. My knowledge of literature and philosophy, my
previous therapies and analyses, and now you should
compensate whatever leftover deficits I may have. Didn't
Caesar cover his defects with laurels? I like helping
intelligent people. I make a good living doing psychotherapy, but I don't really enjoy it. I thought maybe I
should become a training analyst.

Me: Suddenness has the structure of a question.
[In the past I might have said something equally bad.]

Carolyn: Well, of course. The question is put to you. I already
have the question in my mind: whether I'll be good at it
or not. Can I go through the ordeal and the politics of
the institute? I don't know. But you seem to disapprove,
to say what you just said. Sudden or not, there is the
question of my going ahead with this idea, investing
time, energy, and money. Why don't you come out
straight and say, "You're too sick to be a training
analyst." This is what you're thinking, aren't you?

Me: You're right. Thank you. You correctly sensed my dissent.
I'm not sure why I felt that way, but it isn't intended to
be an insult.
[The Healer is an authentic, imperfect being.]
[In the past I might have gotten defensively interpretive:
"You're angry at me that I wasn't encouraging you."
Or seek her disidentification with me:
"What do you think of the fact that I'm not a training
analyst?"
Or focus on the "suddenness":
"Sudden?"]

Carolyn: Ok, now that we got that out of our way. Which way
am I right?—that I shouldn't be a training analyst, or

that I got you? Actually it doesn't matter. If I got you in your defensive style of communication, you the master therapist, then I can easily aspire to be a training analyst. I don't know why you dissent, because you believe in the concept of the wounded healer. If my craziness doesn't interfere with being a therapist, it shouldn't interfere with being a training analyst either. Do you think training analysts are healthier people? I heard this real story from an analysand herself. She's being analyzed by a very senior training analyst from the most kosher of all institutes. She's on the couch talking about her recent financial difficulties, she hears sounds of rustling papers for quite a while. Curious, she turns around and sees her training analyst counting his money. Puzzled, she says, "What on earth are you doing?" He replies, "Well, you were talking about money, yessss?" She says, "How does that relate to your playing with your money? What if I were talking about shit?" You see. Anyhow, you may be right or you may also be wrong. But here you are again. What is wrong with you? Why are you out to demoralize me? Don't tell me why I really don't care. Fuck you. Nevertheless I appreciated that you thanked me. My parents never . . .

The issue of mistakes seems of more concern to therapists than to patients. Therapists have to grow to recognize that the world of their profession is not based on eternal verities. They must learn that they are not always right, nor need to be, about their understanding of the patient's world. As Edwards (1982) advises, one should not even aim to always be right. Having a predetermined fixed response or role—imposing a strict standard or rigid rule for a presumably perfect therapeutic word or deed—is neither possible, nor advisable. Thus in the matter of mistakes in psychotherapy, it is not even preferable to be *too* correct. A grain of wrong actually belongs to good taste, says Nietzsche.

The process of psychotherapy involves oscillations in small increments between "getting worse" and "getting better," between failures and mini-successes. No treatment is ever a total failure, as it is joked; it can always be used as a bad example. More seriously, if every gesture were thoroughly rehearsed against making mistakes, it might give an impression of spontaneity, but it would not really be. Furthermore, it would be exhausting and ultimately ineffective.

Ironically, some of the negative repercussions of psychotherapy come from its effectiveness, insofar as collective reviews of research have typically shown greater variability of outcomes in treated than untreated groups. They have even shown that a proportion of treated patients get worse. Strupp and colleagues (1977) were more specific in their findings that personality characteristics of the clinician impacted upon therapy effectiveness. Qualities such as coldness, hostility, seduction, pessimism, and narcissism of the therapist contributed to negative outcomes, as well as having an inappropriate goal or goals for the patient, fostering overdependence, and breaching confidentiality.

Specifics aside, in some fundamental sense the therapy has to fail in order for the patient to succeed. Here is how it goes: Patients first must become more vulnerable within treatment, if they are to become less vulnerable outside. For example, the patient must regress and repeat the traumas of his or her past in order to deal with adult desires and disappointments. Here psychotherapy can come closest to a delayed mourning process, as the yearning patient may grieve over earlier real or fantasied events, unmet wishes, and unresolved conflicts. He or she may relive the memories of those who failed him, for example, an absent or unavailable mother, an abusive father. At bottom, he may grieve the loss of his or her own former self.

So, too, the therapist must, in fact, first *fail* the patient—as did others in his or her life. Only then can both patient and clinician simultaneously examine and understand that process of frustration and failure as it takes place in treatment. Psychotherapy thus necessitates, first, a process of failure on the part of both parties, which acts as a new version of an old scenario, and helps to understand the current one by experiencing it in vivo. [As Camus said, when you understand one thing through and through, you understand everything.]

ONE FEELS BETTER BY FEELING WORSE

> *Carolyn:* (Crying) Life is hard for me. Even simply managing ordinary stuff of daily living is at times overwhelming to me. I got this bill from my gynecologist. The insurance was to pay 80 percent of it. They only paid 20 percent by mistake. I had to make half a dozen calls to have it corrected and still couldn't. I feel totally inadequate. I mean, why do things like that always happen to me, and there's no one to turn to? I don't know what to do.
>
> *Me:* How to contain the unexpected?
>
> [The Healer teaches only eternal verities.]
>
> [In the past I might have inquired whether there were any mistakes on my bills.
>
> Or even become more centrifugal:
>
> "What about the fact that you are paying 100 percent of my bills?"
>
> Or pick the issue of dependency feelings not being met:
>
> "Do you feel that I'm one of those 'no ones' to turn to?"
>
> Or be empathic:
>
> "Too lonely!"]
>
> *Carolyn:* (Stopped crying) That isn't nice. You're supposed to be on my side. It's bad enough that I'm in pain and feeling sorry for myself, but now you are saying that I'm also an immature person. Maybe I am. Well, how does one become a mature person, if not taken care of during

her immature years? I never felt taken care of even as a child, whether you think so or not. Actually I've done a good job in spite of that. I'm allowed occasionally to sulk about my past, am I not? Even if I can't yet contain the unexpected, I'm mature enough not to expect much from anyone (little smile), including you, especially today. As to your bills . . .

Although Freud (1925a) discarded the cathartic cure because it brought no lasting change, it has been popularly endorsed ever since by hypnotherapists, gestaltists, primal scream therapists, and New-Age proponents, and even in cafés and bars. They seem to presume that there is a superior self-knowledge in the emotions. If you could "really feel," they exhort, "then you would really know!" In fact, anything that requires cognition, reflection, or introspection is frowned upon as overintellectualization—part of the patient's *problem*, not part of the cure. One can easily agree with the Cartesian concept of "I think, therefore I am," or perhaps, "I think, therefore I know." If pressed, one could even proffer the philosophy of "I feel, therefore I am." But there is something very queer in the assumption of "I feel, therefore I know," says Ricoeur (1965).

The common belief is that one feels good by just getting things off one's chest. However, it is difficult, if not virtually impossible, to feel good in a sustained, absolute, and enduring way by any method, never mind by catharsis, which is known to last a very short time. At best one can feel better. Affect is like an addiction; somehow one needs frequent, if not steady and escalating, doses of feeling good. And those who feel *too* good, like those on the upswing of an affective disorder, are most certainly on the way to feeling much worse. Therefore, therapy cannot and should not promulgate the promise of making people feel good, especially by offering what they do not have or never had. If anything, patients need time to feel worse, such as revisiting the pain of the past, before they can expect to feel what they did or don't have. As Malan (1979) put it, "the aim of therapy is not to make up to patients what they have missed, but to help them work through the feelings about not having it" (p. 141).

KILLING GENTLY WITH EMPATHY

>   *Carolyn:* I thought about taking a whole bottle of antidepressants last night. I don't know whether they would have killed me or not, but I remembered your telling me why you wouldn't give more than two weeks' supply of it. Anyway, I was afraid of botching it up and surviving with a paralysis or something. Then I thought about calling you, as you instructed me at my dark moments I should do. Well, it was about midnight, too late. Why bother you? So I decided to bother the one who deserved to be bothered. I must have woken B up. He was kind of groggy and there was a female voice in the background, so I hung up . . . That's it. . . . Say something. . . . What is this silence?
>
>   *Me:* Working silence!
>   [In the past I might have gone rigorously after her suicidality:
>   "What pills do you have in the house?
>   What else could you have done to kill yourself?
>   What other thoughts went through your mind to stop yourself?"
>   Or I might have empathized with her pain:
>   "Hearing a female voice in the background? How painful!"
>   Or seek a transferential dimension:
>   "If not by a midnight call, I may deserve to be punished by your suicide?
>   Do you feel I'm botching up your treatment?"]
>
>   *Carolyn:* Okay. It was obvious, he was comfortably sleeping

and had a female companion, not suffering at all with our past. Now it was all mine. He wasn't there even to be receptive to any message. But why do I have to do all the work in all my relations, whether starting or terminating? Well, work hard on your silence because I'm quite desperate! I don't want to live like this. You seem to be totally oblivious to my pain, and not taking my killing myself seriously.

Me: I have learned that human life may easily end at the far side of despair, but it could also start anew there.
[The Healer always seeks positives to balance the negatives.]

Carolyn: It's easy for you to say that. Plus you're misquoting Sartre. That far side of despair is a concept for people who've never been there. That's the reason I think of for your lack of empathy for my despair.

There is only one philosophical problem, says Camus, whether or not one should commit suicide. Patients experience that dilemma more intensely. Suicide is one of the most dramatic and tragic expressions of a person's despair, and every therapist's nightmare. This is because there is really no foolproof way of preventing suicide, not even locking up the person for life. Even then, the truly determined individual would find a way of killing himself, often in the very best controlled situations. On the other hand, a therapist may inadvertently bring about, through some mistake in communication or behavior, the very act he is trying to prevent. The most common of these errors can be the least suspect of all: empathy, the all-purpose therapeutic tool. Indeed, the expression of overattunement, which is a form of excessive or erroneous empathy, may in fact precipitate suicide by projection of the therapist's existential ambivalence about living.

The second most common mistake is also related to empathy, this time not having any, at the same time asking—or expecting—the patient to stop having suicidal thoughts. In fact, suicidal ideas are escape valves to be left alone, making life bearable at times of unbearable circumstances. As Nietzsche put it, "The thought of suicide is a great consolation. With the help of it, one has got through many a bad night." The act of talking about something that one is feeling, rather than simply feeling, is the first step toward control.

There is an emotional context and corresponding psychic reality to a person's wish to die, or its common counterparts in living. Since there is no such thing as a zero or null context, as Spence (1982) says, the therapist must understand the meaning of the patient's suicidal ideation only against a set of background realities. Therapies may demand that the therapist be empathic, but they don't instruct him about when and how, and especially when *not* to be. [**One must go to temporarily painful places in order to find permanent joy.**]

THE THERAPIST WOOS THE PATIENT BY FOLLOWING HIS FOOTSTEPS

> *Me:* Welcome back. Did you have a good vacation?
> [In the past I would never initiate the session; I definitely would never use a sentence suggestive of positive expectation; I would have considered the "welcome back" seductive, too enthusiastic, and presumptuous—the patient didn't come back and at least not to me.]
>
> *Carolyn:* Thank you. Yes and no. It was good to be in the sun, to swim, sleep late, just hang around. Of course, the most important thing was that after such a long interval I was ready to face the family. My parents were both delighted to have me. They didn't indulge into "whys" of my absence, not returning calls, etc., as if they understood. I kind of gave a quick explanation that I was going through a stage that needed some isolation includ-

ing from them, that inward travel requires the curtail-
ment of the outward one, you know. My brother couldn't
make it. Anyway, after the initial excitement of reunion,
it was all empty. Furthermore, Mom isn't doing well,
so it was a little gloomy. Anyhow, before I left for vaca-
tion I was talking about making some changes in my
world—a kind of New Year's resolution, looking at the
people in my life and making some sense of all that.

Me: You didn't mention your father!

[The Healer follows the patient's footsteps.]

[In the past I could have done worse.]

Carolyn: Yeah. He was there, too. Still his same old self; drank
most of the time. Would you believe he gave me a big
wet kiss on my neck? Old lech. Anyhow, coming back to
my New Year's resolution. The first change that I want to
make is to stop the treatment.

Me: You didn't mention the therapist!

[In the past I would have explored whys, hows, try to
delay, if not stop, the termination by interpretation of
flight from the treatment, "the wet kisses" of the
therapist, the fear of intimacy, by explanation that such
desires are common, but one needs to stay to overcome
the resistances, etc.]

Carolyn: The therapist? Well let's see. He is a kind of
cognitive security but . . . You seem to focus on me as
if there are no external circumstances. My analyst used
to bring every external subject to our relation, and the
two other therapists were either all too empathic or just
discussed the external events, kind of supervising my
life. You, I don't totally get. You ask a question but not
with the intention of introduction of a subject, as you
don't follow through or you introduce a subject and then
ask no question. Do you worry how much I can dwell in
my mind without cracking up? And however you start,
once I pick up the thread you are nowhere to be found,

and the moment I realize that I've been carrying the whole load I look at you and you say something totally from left field, and I wonder whether you were listening all that time I was talking. Interestingly enough, that's what my mother did, even this last . . .

The therapist may decide to focus treatment either on the patient's inner life (especially fantasies of the past) or on his outer life (especially realities of the present) and cast the treatment into a certain course. Obviously, these don't have to be mutually exclusive. The choice depends on many variables, including both the nature of the early intrapsychic conflicts and the actual current events through which they are played out. The therapist makes this choice through inductive as well as deductive reasoning. The first aim is to find a small number of pervasive issues that appear now in relation to the therapist, but which run through the course of the patient's illness and can be traced back through his or her personal history. Next is to explain how the patient's attempts to resolve these central conflicts have been not only maladaptive (that is, producing symptoms and character pathology), but adaptive (that is, characterizing his or her general style of pleasure, productivity, and personal relationships).

The therapist must recast these overriding issues into the therapeutic mold. If the central conflicts are oedipal in nature (i.e., originating in the triadic developmental stage), the material needs to be recast to reflect the inner life of the patient. Then the patient is helped to take a certain distance from the issue and try to reconcile his wishes, fears, and defenses as they are expressed or repressed within himself. On the other hand, if the central conflicts are preoedipal in nature (i.e., originating in the dyadic developmental stage), then the material should be recast to pertain to the external life of the patient. Here attention is directed to the interpersonal (rather than intrapsychic) role in the origins or perpetuation of the damaged or deficient patient. Terman

(1984/1985) warns us, however, that attributing a self-injurious attitude to the patient's inner life—no matter how true it may be—only re-creates the original injury.

People do not value anything except what they made themselves, says Semrad (1980). That is why Roth (1987) advises allowing therapy to set in motion an organic and self-directing process. Calling psychotherapy "the art of wooing nature," he proposes that it is the patient who inevitably is in charge—despite active "wooing" on the part of the therapist. He suggests that, although the clinician is the one to oversee the treatment, comment on it, and try to influence its momentum, for the most part the patient does what he wants. He offers Kutuzov's story in Tolstoy's *War and Peace* to illustrate his point: The Russian commander-in-chief was asked how he manages so masterfully to maneuver thousands of soldiers in his army. To this he replied, "It is rather simple. I look to see in what direction the army is moving, and then I give the order to go in that direction." As long as the patient has an embryonic sense of self, he'll only need some clearing of the path from the therapist. This is because given the optimal circumstances, the psyche self-regulates. [**One knows by following one's own footsteps.**]

LEARNED UNLEARNING

> *Carolyn:* Last week I went to the cognitive therapy center to check out whether they could do something for my anxiety, or is it my depression? Anyhow, they gave the whole program, the homework, the manuals, published papers on their efficacy, biography of their guru, Dr. Beck.
>
> *Me:* Good.
>
> [**The Healer is always willing to unlearn.**]
>
> [In the past, with transferential listening I might have

explored her frustration and disappointment in me. Now all I want is for her to find solace in any way she can find it.]

Carolyn: But they got this lay religion attitude about them. They keep oversaturating me with their messages of their effectiveness, their belief system, and how wrong-headed you are, I mean psychodynamic people are. I got a little offended, with their attacks on your indulging me in my subjective senses and your, your sort of psychological, ahem-ah . . .

Me: Psychological decadence!

Carolyn: (laughs) Gosh, I was so afraid that you'd be upset with my going to that center. Now, you see, they applied to me a hard-hat psychology, and you, you have this nonquarreling attitude that . . .

The standardized techniques with their operational manuals are getting more and more popular in this age of cost saving. But at what cost? First these simply started as research protocols, but now they have dramatically moved into the mainstream of general clinical operations. How can psychotherapy be practiced by a manual and reduced to explicit formulations? Louis Fierman (1965) expressed great doubts about such reductionism: "We could never describe or formulate one single sentence as the therapeutically desirable response of the therapist to a given behavior of a given patient because no formulation can guarantee that when the therapist makes this response under given circumstances to the given patient, that it would be therapeutically spontaneous and genuine expression of the therapist's mind" (p. 161). Communication between patient and therapist is never linear, as Lacan (1977) emphasizes—it is cumulatively spiral, mediated by both directions. If there are manualizable aspects of the psychotherapy, they cannot be at the level of interpersonal relationships.

The therapist's actual interactions and verbalizations vis-à-vis any patient are really a series of improvisations. It is the quality and spontaneity of these creative interventions that differentiate clinicians from one another. The issue of improvisation reminds me of a call I received from a colleague. He said that he has been treating a middle-aged man who recently complained of mild but recurrent chest pain. Inquiry into his current life circumstances revealed that the patient's business partner was trying to ease him out and take over. To make matters worse, the partner was also having an affair with the patient's wife. Yet the patient could not acknowledge emotional reactions to either home and work situations, or actively deal with the stress that he was under. As might be expected, he was totally unable to make a connection between these distressing events and what was physically happening to him. In fact, he was indignant that his medical doctors could not find anything physiologically wrong.

Under the circumstances, it was not too surprising that the referring therapist found the patient to be uncooperative and unreceptive to treatment. The patient denied to the therapist having any psychological problems, was unable to express or verbalize his feelings, and showed a complete lack of ability and motivation for self-examination. He revealed only an impoverished use of language, could not free associate, had no fantasy life, and insisted that he didn't dream. If he had had any dreams, he could not remember them, even if he tried. In consultation with the psychotherapist, and for a few sessions that followed, the patient had been aloof, detached, testy, irritable, demanding, and contentious.

What was the upshot of these unsatisfactory sessions? The therapist said he would like to refer this patient to *me*! And when I asked, "Why me?" he replied that he could not get Otto Kernberg on the phone!! I made an appointment to see the man. He was worse than I expected; the only thing he was concerned with was whether it would be difficult to find a taxi in my neighborhood.

What could I do with such a person? To my own surprise, I found myself asking whether he could tell me a joke. It is the first time I have ever done this (I guess, out of desperation). In immediate reply, he sternly informed me that he did not know any jokes, in fact that he dislikes jokes and hates joke tellers. Then he remained totally silent. Well, so much for my improvisation! However, he did show up to the following session—with three joke books in full view. He promptly put them on my desk, and superciliously said, "If you are so interested in jokes, here they are; you can read them yourself." When I asked whether he himself had read them, he replied that he "just glanced" at them. After some more proddings about the ones he had read, the patient proceeded to tell me the following joke:

> There was this businessman who one day lost all his money in the stock market. He came home, to where he lived on the 28th floor of an apartment building. He opened the window wide, turned around, and announced to his wife that they had lost every penny they had. The wife suddenly ran across the room and jumped out of the window. Thereupon the man calmly leaned over the ledge, looked down, and said, "Thank you, Paine Webber."

Of course, this opened up the whole area of his passive wishes for his wife's death as well as the suppressed rage he had been trying to contain—and much more. The point here is: How can such an interaction be anticipated and manualized? The learning process has to allow for the as-yet unknown, and even the unknowable. A manual may be useful only insofar as it is just a simple foundation, a primitive beginning (even if it were a wrong start), only to be corrected and revised, evolving step by step as a mutually learning experience. It is never static. ["**We can only learn if we also always unlearn at the same time**," says **Heidegger (1971)**.]

PROMISES GENERATE ANXIETY

Carolyn: The cognitive therapist at the center promised me that within sixteen sessions I'd be cured. Apparently 80 percent of the patients do get excellent results. If I fall into that unlucky 20 percent group, they have this heavy-duty form of the therapy that they are almost sure will help me.

Me: How can one refuse such an offer?

[The Healer's only claim is good faith effort.]

[In the past I might have listened unconsciously with a territorial purpose and in a lapse of taste make some skeptical statements about their restrictive paradigm.]

Carolyn: You're not disappointed in my going for it?

Me: My disappointments have always preceded me.

[The Healer's only claim is good faith.]

[In the past I might have said with a pseudo-graciousness:

"Of course not, I hope it'll work out for you. But I'm always here, if you want to come back, just let me know."]

Carolyn: Stop these fake enigmatic profundities. I'm not that smart. What do you mean?

Me: That I couldn't deliver what I didn't promise.

Be wary of a therapist who promises you a result, any result. Some therapists believe that it is perfectly acceptable, if not actually advisable, to make a reasonable promise to meet a therapeutic goal and to do one's best to deliver it. Such assurances temporarily may reduce anxiety in the patient and the therapist, but ultimately the therapist's obsession about curing the patient's symptoms will generate greater anxiety in both parties. While a positive expectation is a basic element of psychotherapy necessary for therapeutic change to occur, the promise of removal of symptoms—no matter how judiciously done, how circumscribed the presenting problem, or how presumably certain the prospective results—is counterproductive. As Dewald (1964) says, "Since the symptom represents an unconscious attempt at resolution of an intrapsychic conflict through the construction of a compromise formation, any promise or assurance that the symptom will be removed unconsciously represents a challenge to the patient's defenses" (p. 142). Therefore, insisting on ridding the patient of his or her distress, however seemingly benign and superficially helpful, is not a good idea. Instead of eliminating expressions of illness, such attempts at taking them away may in fact make matters worse. By endangering the defenses that are currently in place, the therapist may push the patient to seek symptom substitutes, thus generating even more manifestations of conflicts, and their inevitable accompaniment, of anxiety. [**The less you claim, the less you have to recant.**]

SNAIL'S PACE: TEACHING OLD GENES NEW BEHAVIOR

> *Carolyn:* You see, if I didn't have this anxiety, I could handle everything else fine. When I don't have this jumping-out-of-my-skin feeling, I feel totally normal. Half of a Xanax is better than ten sessions of psychotherapy, including the cognitive one. But they say with a medication you're dealing with the symptom, not the problem, that I should change my way of thinking to prevent the symptom from occurring. With you I'm focusing on everything else except on anxiety, only to realize later that with all that introspection I'm just becoming more introspective, but doing nothing about the anxiety itself, falling into a kind of, a complacency of . . . ah . . .
>
> *Me:* Complacency of introspection!
>
> [**The Healer says, "Let's open the window."**]

[In the past I might have explored the developing negative transference, or warned her about the tolerance building, thus limited value of minor tranquilizers, or preach about the value of tolerable anxiety, that without it one may bask in the bliss of stagnation.]

Carolyn: Even so, will it lead to allaying my anxiety? My analyst used to explain that my anxiety was a manifestation of some infantile conflict and if we worked that through, it would go away. The Kohutian therapist said that my self wasn't well glued, and that under internal or external stresses I may feel like I was getting unglued. The other therapist, the eclectic, sent me to a psychopharmacologist who prescribed the Xanax.

Me: They, me, and you, we are all trying to alter your body–mind response system.

Carolyn: Well, we're not doing a very good job, are we?

Me: Not really.

There are three broad categories in psychopathology: defects, deficits, and conflicts. To illustrate this point, let me give you examples of driving a car: If you have a problem with your eyesight, it is a *defect*; no amount of driving lessons will help— you have to get glasses. However, if you have good eyesight, and you don't know how to drive, it is a *deficit*—it can be corrected by training. On the other hand, if you have good eyesight and are well trained to drive, but you have a fear of driving or are ambivalent, and thus cannot make a decision whether you should drive to visit your mother-in-law or not, then that is a *conflict*— neither eyeglasses nor any amount of driving lessons will help.

Similarly, in the makeup of the mind, there can be defects of thinking that characterize schizophrenia or of affect in manic-depressive psychoses; there can be deficits that result in personality or self disorders; and there can be conflicts that cause neuroses. It is possible, of course, that their manifestations occur separately, simultaneously, or successively, not only combine with but compound each other. For example, as Pine (1990) says, detachment as an early developmental deficit may represent failure of attachment, or as a later developmental conflict may reflect defensive avoidance of interpersonal contact. Eagle (1984) has suggested that the two sources of psychopathology can easily overlap, insofar as developmental deficiencies frequently interfere with the capacity to deal with conflict, while unresolved conflicts in turn often trigger developmental regressions or arrests. Furthermore, one cannot proceed with the next stage of development without proper mourning of the last, says Roth (1987). [**This is postdepression depression.**]

Psychotherapy primarily deals with conflicts and deficits. Patients with neuroanatomical, physiological, or chemical defects can be given psychotherapy for their deficits and/or conflicts, or even for coping with their defects—but not for defects per se. Although psychotherapy for the defects themselves is generally considered inappropriate and ineffective, Eric Kandel's pioneering research has begun to suggest a different conclusion. Genetic work with sea snails, which explores the neurophysiology and biochemistry of psychological phenomena, is clearly demonstrating the integration of psychology and neurobiology on a molecular level. His studies of social and sensory deprivation, of sensitization and habituation "training" processes, and even of the development of anxiety have become phylogenetic models for comparable biological mechanisms in humans. His findings during conditioning, of both structural and functional changes in synaptic transmission (e.g., changes in neurotransmitter release and enzyme levels), are striking, and go a long way toward welding the long-standing mind–body split that has plagued the psychiatric field since its inception. These explorations also reveal that genetically determined pathways can be interrupted, as well as restored, by learning. By demonstrating how psychological disturbances reflect neuronal and synaptic changes, he has further proposed that treatment with psychotherapy can, in fact, act on these biochemical events—that the alteration in synaptic functions produced by external phenomena can allay anxiety or impact upon other neurotic conditions.

FREE-FLOATING PARADIGM

Carolyn: Did you kind of know what my problem was before, if ever, or do I find that out for myself? Like, do you have it in your mind or do you say to yourself, "Ah this is a patient with, for example, anxiety disorder, schizophrenia, or hysteria." Do you know what I mean? Do you have an opinion about me? Am I fitting into some category? You must have seen other patients similar to me.

Me: Opinion "Yes," conviction "No."

[In the past I might have explored our intersubjective field:

"You wonder whether I can help you!"

Or her own intrasubjective field:

"Are you concerned as to how sick you are?"

Or tap her narcissism:

"Whether you are one of the many patients of mine."

Or:

"Whether you have a special condition, if not a special relation, to me."]

Carolyn: So we just wait and see until it becomes clear?

Me: Without the excess of lucidity.

Carolyn: We are trying to be clear, but not lucid? Is therapy like the rest of life, a public performance on the violin, in which you must learn the instrument as you go along? Do you realize the agony associated with that? My analyst wanted me to free associate to seek the original conflict. The Kohutian expected me to micro-internalize to him to remedy my deficit, the eclectic was an all-purpose explorer. What do you want, what are you searching? I mean, what do you want me to do?

Me: (Sigh)

Carolyn: Okay, what is it that we may want to find? Whose fault is it for what I am, or what I'm suffering from? I haven't been able to figure that out.

Me: Maybe the fault lies in the question.

[For the Healer, searching is not the only way of finding.]

Carolyn: The fault lies in the question? So, how do you ask the question without fault? Or are you suggesting that the questioning itself is the problem? I'm more confused now than before. Was it Tarachow who said, "Two people are separated more at the end of a conversation than they were at the beginning"? Now I know what he means. Can you really find a peaceful existence without searching for it? Can you understand what makes you tick without asking questions? Is the truth so incoherent? I think you and my father could get along fabulously. In Florida he was suggesting that all our self-knowledge is wrapped in romantic camouflages, and that . . .

Each school obliges the therapist to listen to the patient within its particular paradigm. For example, in the Freudian conflict framework the technique of free-floating attention is designed to form a connection to the patient while giving free play to ideas aroused in oneself. If the therapist focuses on one area attentively, he may miss important material. As Freud (1912b) said,

As soon as anyone deliberately concentrates his attention to a certain degree, he begins to select from the material before him; one point will be fixed in his mind with particular clearness and some other will be correspondingly disregarded, and in making this selection he will be following his expectations or inclinations. This however is precisely what must not be done. In making the selection, if he follows his expectations he is in danger of never finding anything but what he already knows; and if he follows his inclinations he will certainly falsify what he may perceive. [p. 112]

However, Freud's free-floating attention may not be enough. A bifocal attention—use of simultaneous and/or alternating of conflict versus deficit models of listening—may be more productive. As Kohut (1971) said:

> As we listen to our patients' free association, we will hold both viewpoints in suspension—the classical one that alerts us to the presence of evidence for the transference reactivation of structural conflict, the self-psychological one that alerts us to the presence of evidence for the transference reactivation of thwarted developmental needs—in order to determine which one of them will lead us to the more psychologically valid understanding of the patient. [p. 155]

Now this only represents two theoretical positions. Imagine if you have to keep multiple theoretical perspectives in mind while you're listening to a patient, which may be especially difficult for beginning therapists. In her last lectures, Karen Horney was optimistic when she compared the therapeutic situation to that of learning to drive a car: Initially, she observed, there seems to be an overwhelming number of details that demand attention, but as the different tasks are gradually mastered, the process eventually becomes automatic. Similarly, as our understanding of the patient increases, our observations of the psychotherapeutic process fall into line, and the easier it becomes to pay attention. However much this is intended to comfort, it can't totally succeed as we also consider the prevalence of car accidents.

Attention is a special form of *presence*. It is neither overpresence nor underpresence. Therapeutic attention is generally content free, so as not to lead the patient. The therapist's way of being present is determined partly by his personality and his own neuroses. Obsessive therapists tend to have too active or inactive attention. They try too hard to be spontaneous and get lost in minutiae. Hysterical therapists display perfunctory attention. The therapists with paranoid traits (not all that uncommon) are rigidly attentive, hyperintentional, and constantly search for confirmation of their interpretations.

Bugental (1987) suggests that the client's concern (consisting of pain, hope, and commitment) is complemented by the therapist's concern (consisting of need, vision, and sensitivity). Just as the fully concerned client is most apt to be fully present, so the fully concerned clinician is most apt to be both recipient and provider of presence. The therapist's presence is a planned one, in Pine's term, a "prepared explorer," one who tries not to get completely lost in the immediacy of the moment.

Freud (1912b) described psychoanalytic listening as consisting simply in not directing one's notice to anything in particular, and in maintaining the same evenly suspended attention in the face of all that one hears. [**One's hearing improves with interest.**] In psychotherapy, the therapist's unconscious is the receiver of the patient's unconscious material, and evenly suspended attention is a mental state to allow such reception, an inter-unconscious tuning in. Freud's recommendation is geared toward preventing the therapist's intrusions into the patient's material due to his or her selective attention—such as trying to relate to the patient's verbalizations with "experience-distant theoretical preconceptions" (Chessick's term). Similarly, Pine (1990) writes that uncommitted listening to the patient occurs in the context of broader theoretical commitment, but the challenge of therapeutic listening remains that of suspense between theory of mind and ignorance.

"When ordinary man attains knowledge, he is a perfect sage; when a sage attains understanding, he is an ordinary man," says Camus. For the "sage," eternal verities may seem as small as the world, but they are as large as one's aloneness. They are not decodable by his normative competence. For the "ordinary man," all perfections are inauthentic. He never provides easy and quick answers, but has only difficult questions. The only truth, for him, is the appropriation of transmaterial.

5

Cutting the Gordian Knot Is Not the Equivalent of Untying It

PACE OF NEUROTICS: EACH PERSON HAS A UNIQUE INTERSUBJECTIVE TIMETABLE OF CHANGE

A would-be seeker asked a Sufi: "How long will it take to arrive at the point of true understanding?" The Sufi answered: "As soon as you get to the stage where you do not ask how long it will take."

—Idries Shah

Carolyn: Given all your "unlimited impossibilities," if we continue to meet twice a week, how long do you think I would need to come?

Me: It depends on the nature of that "need" and how well we could work together towards attaining it.
[For the Healer time and space contain only questions.]
[In the past I might have wondered whether she is dissatisfied with the pace of treatment or whether any material from the previous sessions might have evoked

some negative sentiment, or I might have given some approximate time estimate and qualified it.]

Carolyn: I guess my need is eventually to be happy. But the word *we* bothers me a little. I hope a greater load of the work will come from you, because I don't even know how to work on becoming happy. So it's mostly on your shoulders. You're the expert.

Me: You can only be happy if you don't make the happiness the purpose of your life. As to my carrying the task, even if that were feasible it would only deprive you of your will.

Carolyn: My will? Like fully actualizing myself? No, no, a proximity is sufficient, please, I don't mind—deprive me, deprive me.

Is there any way to predict the length of treatment? Is it as long as one's insurance company pays, as the contemporary cynics suggest, or is it dependent on some measure of psychopathology, such as the partial resolution of conflicts, improvement of symptoms, or modification of character traits, as the absolutists advocate? In response to the patient's question, "How long will treatment take?" Freud proposed a trial treatment. He likened the therapist's response to the answer given by the philosopher to the wayfarer in Aesop's fable. When the wayfarer asked how long a journey lay ahead, the philosopher simply answered, "Walk!" Only afterward was this apparently unhelpful reply explained, giving the grounds that he needed to know the length of the wayfarer's stride before he could tell how long his journey would take. However, Freud soon recognized that the comparison is not a good one because of the inherent nature of the pace of the neurotic.

In general, one reduces one's pace the longer one walks. So, the lengthier the treatment, the slower the progress. The neurotic also tends to alter his pace, if not the actual direction of his path, first progressing (by remembering and revealing repressed material), then regressing (by resisting interpretation or other efforts by the therapist). This means moving forward followed by moving back, not in a straight and even trajectory, but with irregular strides. Freud thus concluded that the duration of treatment is almost unanswerable.

Neurotics also have an inconsistent step, because they are characteristically conflicted about where they are going. Despite desires and fantasies to be somewhere else, they are inhibited by anxieties and fears. Therefore, their movement is uneven and the direction can change, even reverse itself. It is easy to stray off course, considering the complex uncharted territory that needs to be traversed. In fact, the sicker the patient, the more frequently he or she may make a wrong turn, especially having begun on a wayward path early in life. Many neurotics wittingly or unwittingly retrace their steps on their own, even if their choices are incorrect or dangerous. Under the guidance of the "well-traveled therapist," the patient is supposed to go back, to return to a more familiar place before he can face the future. As Leighton and his associates (1968) have put it, "The ceremonial [of psychotherapy] itself, or some parts of it, constitutes a symbolic reenactment of something which went wrong in the past and which is now being set right. . . . therapeutic activity is concerned with making this [reenactment] come out on the side of the patient. . . . The patient does it over again . . . without the mistake" (p. 1178). Nonetheless, no matter how motivated the patient is (and how sure-footed the therapist/guide is, for that matter), the time required for such an arduous hike is not really predictable. Although to others it may look like strolling aimlessly, the therapist takes his time to consider all the necessary factors before he makes his own first stride. [**A Japanese gardener was scolded for not doing any work. After being hired for days, he just continued sitting and looking at the garden. When questioned, he responded that the first task of creating a good garden is to take in the landscape.**]

ABORTIVE VARIATIONS: SHORTENING THE GESTATION PERIOD CHANGES THE DELIVERY

Carolyn: This onion-peeling metaphor would be laughed at in the kitchen. You take a sharp knife, put the onion on a wood board, bang. Fast, efficient, and no tears. Furthermore, I already cut the onion with the previous therapists. Here are its roots: I am in love with my father and I keep longing for a paternal man as a lover who must reject me for my own good. If not, I'll reject them to protect my psyche from the substitute incest. So here we are. Then what?

Me: Is that your own conviction or an objective appraisal by someone else?

[In the past I might have gone after the mockery or explained the reason behind the slow process of self-discovery.]

Carolyn: Any such professional jargon should be identified as a misdemeanor. Yeah, that's what the therapists told me. And you know I saw more than a few. It doesn't totally ring true. But these people are all trained therapists. They must know what they're talking about. How long should I be seeking for and where do I go to find it, whatever that "it" is?

Me: Well, that "it" is neither found nor perhaps lost.

Carolyn: Fine, may I have "it" now? You didn't answer the question of "How long do I have to suffer?" They say anyone who has passed through an ordeal patronizes those who have not had to undergo it. I think it's the other way around. Hasn't science progressed enough to have quick access to the unconscious and quickly resolve the issues?

Me: It is on the *longissima via* that we reach the inaccessible.

[**The Healer doesn't promote fast growth, as it would have weak roots and be easily torn up.**]

In her book *Postcards from the Edge*, Carrie Fisher's heroine, the coke-carrying member of the sensation generation, says that instant gratification takes too long. Similarly, even short-term therapies are considered too long by the same people. The brief therapies of Luborsky, Mann, Bellak, Sifneos, Davanloo, and the like, are the microwave equivalent of a slow-baking, unlyrical compression of long-term therapy, a variation on an intentionally terminable theme. [**Are brief techniques this generation's lite therapy?**] The basic principle of all brief dynamic therapies remains the same: Take patients who have reached a certain stage of development (commonly, a triadic conflict level), and instead of slowly peeling layers, cut into the heart of their intrapsychic content, defenses, or budding transferences; then provide explanations, clarifications, and generic-genetic interpretations addressing the current life of the patient. [**Are we now subject to the tyranny of technique?**] Thus Kramer's (1989) question of whether cutting the Gordian Knot is really the equivalent of untying it—whether there is some extra benefit for the patient in dealing with complexity—is answered with Stern's (1985) recognition that clinical issues are issues for the life span, not phases of life. Nearly four decades earlier, Reich (1949) came to a similar conclusion: "The laborious unraveling of the knot is still the shortest way to real success" (p. 37).

Such short-term psychodynamic psychotherapies are practiced in vitro, rather than in vivo, as is the case in long-term psychotherapy. Well, if lengthy treatment allows one to reiterate conflictual events of early childhood, how can the patient possibly repeat his or her life very quickly? Therefore, isn't "brief therapy" ipso facto abortive? In contrast to a plateau of emotional intensity and cumulative insight that comes from the time-independent sessions, the quickened pace of short-term work may generate more intense (yet more superficial) encounters, and on occasion, be accompanied by sudden insights that can dissipate as rapidly as they arise.

I heard this little joke the other day about brief therapist Habib Davanloo. He started with twelve-session treatment, increased it over the years to fifteen, twenty-five, and now forty sessions. If he tries harder, he'll discover psychoanalysis! Also, there is now a maintenance cognitive therapy. It's supposed to terminate in fifteen sessions. So, are we one day going to see a paper titled "Cognitive Therapy—Terminable or Interminable?" Some recommend a repeat of the whole fifteen sessions, as needed. But, as Roth (1987) says, "Psychotherapy is like marriage, it is something you hope you have to do only once" (pp. 104–105).

THE ORIGINAL CONFLICT RESOLUTION: LONG SOUGHT AFTER, BUT NEVER SIGHTED

> *Carolyn:* I've been reading some of the case studies in the analytical journals and books. Patients present themselves with all kinds of complicated problems. Analysts help them find their original conflict and work it through, patients are then discharged from treatment and live only in common misery thereafter. How come that didn't happen to me? I went back as far as remembering myself in the crib. I'm still the same neurotic self. Me and Woody Allen. What's even more disconcerting is that I seem to remember differently each time I go over the details of my past, as if I have multiple selves. Could I be a multiple personality?
>
> *Me:* You are entitled to only one and the same self.
> [The Healer's ignorance verges on the holy.]
> [In the past I might have questioned her reading analytical material with a subliminally discouraging tone, differentiated the simple from the simplification, inquired more about the "multiple personality" matter.]

Carolyn: Oh, what about the question of resolving my original conflict and walking away from my only and the same neurotic self? Forget the original, how about so many present conflicts I have with men, women, bosses, friends, neighbors, and conflicts as to what to do with my life, my hair?

Me: Surplus conflicts are like pond flies: they skip and skim upon the surface.

Carolyn: OK, let's hurry to get to the bottom of the pond, damn it! Just don't drown me in your orgiastic appetite for metaphors.

Tuttman (1982) suggests that regression can be a curative factor; sometimes a patient will have to return to old memories and feelings in order to move forward. Yet, sometimes we are less damaged by the actual trauma of our childhood than by the traumatic way that we remember that childhood. Classical psychoanalysis is such a traumatic path of remembering, as it keeps repeating the past trauma in the present. The business of the past, says Edwards (1982), only needs finishing. But how can psychoanalysis finish off by reliving the past?—especially if you consider the mind rewriting one's childhood experiences again and again. Bachelard (1971) says:

> When, all alone and dreaming on rather at length, we go far from the present to relive the times of the first life, several childhood faces come to meet us. We were several in the trial life (*la vie essayée*), in our primitive life. . . . Our whole childhood remains to be reimagined. . . . A potential childhood is within us; when we go looking for it in our reveries, we relive it even more in its possibilities than in its reality. . . . What a lot of beings we have begun! Reverie toward our past then, reverie looking for childhood seems to bring back to life lives which have never taken place, lives which have been imagined. [p. 126]

Therefore, using the concept of "resolution of the original conflict" as an outcome criterion, has probably derailed most therapeutic endeavors. Not only does more digging not recover more material but, in fact, as the monk Matthieu Ricard said, "Plunging down into the psychoanalytic unconscious is a bit like finding some sleeping snakes, waking them up, getting rid of the most dangerous, and then staying in the company of the rest" (Revel and Ricard 1998, p. 262). Furthermore, "To relive a few events of long ago is only a limited remedy which no doubt allows some blockages to be whittled away but doesn't eradicate their primary cause. It's no use to keep on stirring up the mud from the bottom of a lake if you want to purify the water" (p. 260). Recently a colleague of mine, who is one of those devoted advocates of interminable analysis, said that he was beginning to believe that the search for one's oedipal past is the modern-day psychiatric equivalent of the unicorn, long sought after but never actually sighted. And the quest goes on. As Reik (1956, p. 49) concluded: "Men will nevertheless continue to pray: 'Lord, give us this day our daily illusion.'"

GENTLY MAKE HASTE

Chessick says that if you plot a graph of activity of treatment, the result shows peaks and valleys and long plateaus. And that slowness is welcomed by most. Investigations of intellectual versus emotional understanding of oneself have shown that there is no good alternative to the slow incubation of insight. [**Few get tired of self-understanding.**] The therapeutic effects of heightened arousal alone, or of "eureka" phenomena, do not last. The repeated interventions over a substantial period of time are required for therapeutic change to be well assimilated into one's life. Despite occasional conclusions to the contrary, clinical research suggests that for lasting results, the therapy must last. [**Nonetheless, some therapists make nothing happen too slowly.**]

EVERY RELATION IS TIME LIMITED

I offer short-term therapy for encapsulated and present-oriented conflicts, such as depressions related to recent loss of a job, health problems, divorce or loss of a loved one, and the like. It's not that I believe that such situational conflicts don't have earlier roots, especially in those patients who have overdetermined reactions. But as Carl Rogers once said, in half an hour, you can accomplish only thirty minutes' work.

For better or worse, time-limited therapy is not on the same spectrum as long-term therapy, although it is easy to assume that there is a linear or quantitative relationship between the two. Rather, the goals as well as the very nature of their therapeutic processes and interactions are different. For one thing, short-term therapies tend to provide the patient with cognitive, or even emotional knowledge, but *not* with transformative insight that requires much deeper delving. Taken to an extreme position, the difference is like between reading a map and walking the terrain. Freud (1910b) stated it even more harshly: "If knowledge about the unconscious were as important for the patient as people inexperienced in psychoanalysis imagine, listening to lectures or reading books would be enough to cure him. Such measures, however, have as much influence on the symptoms of nervous illness as a distribution of menu-cards in a time of famine has upon hunger" (p. 225).

Moreover, the very concept of a shortened version of long-term therapy may be misleading in terms of the respective roles of technique versus relationship. In actual practice, the more one focuses on techniques per se, the shorter the treatment becomes. On the other hand, the more one focuses on the therapist–patient relationship, the longer the treatment can get. Furthermore, every person has a certain innate timetable. This can have direct implications for whether short- or long-term therapy would work. Chessick warned that if the psychotherapist is not aware of each individual patient's unique timetable in the proceedings toward maturity, he may find himself abandoning patients, pressing too hard, and becoming discouraged. To compound the matter, *each therapist and patient pair has its own intersubjective timetable for resonant healing.*

GROUNDING IN ABANDONMENT

> *Carolyn:* I didn't think your taking three weeks off would be traumatic at all. In fact, the first week I was glad that I had this extra time for myself to do things that I usually neglect. The second week I began to miss you. I was sad. I wondered whether you were thinking of me at all, or whether this was for you a totally separate matter and you were simply having a great vacation. The third week I was angry. Three weeks, my God, what kind of practice do you have that your patients could do without you, and if so, why would they need you? Then just two days before your return, I had realized that my anger was partly, if not mainly, directed at my last therapist, who terminated my treatment with the rationale that he felt he couldn't help me anymore. I was totally surprised and traumatized. I thought I was very much engaged with him, and he with me. He meant so much to me. I realized that since I began treatment with you I've been waiting for you to do the same.
>
> *Me:* The time-released trauma.
>
> **[The Healer always tries to emphasize the commonality of human experiences.]**
>
> [In the past I might have reassured her, subtly defended and put down the other therapist (I am not one of those cry-by-night therapists!), searched for early separation-related experiences, apologetically reminded her that I had warned her about my vacation pattern at the

beginning, and finally, empathized with her anger and taken some narcissistic pleasure about being so needed.]

Carolyn: Why do you think he terminated the treatment? His explanation didn't make any sense. Have you ever heard of a therapist stopping the treatment of a reasonably introspective, working, reliable, and paying patient who never bothers the therapist on nights or weekends? I was maybe twice a little too angry at him when he kept changing my session time, and he in return slapped me with a diagnosis of narcissism, stating that my frustrated infantile dependency was turning into rageful episodes and that in between I was totally "affect lamed." At another time, I asked why he became silent to my tongue-in-cheek statement that he should have a sign at the door, like the one Dante put over the Gates of Hell, "Abandon hope all ye who enter here." He replied, "You are demanding an insatiably compassionate talkative womb," or something like that. He wasn't that literate. But I didn't quit. I thought it was pedantic, that's all. Are you guys so fragile? I mean I was devastated. This is the man who claimed to be my selfobject? Obviously, self or not, I was an object to him, an undesirable one. I seriously thought about killing myself. To be rejected or hated by your own therapist? Son of a bitch. So I decided, instead of killing myself, I'll kill him. Once I heard a patient burned herself with gasoline in a car parked in front of her analyst. I thought I'd go pour gasoline outside of his door and ignite it, and watch him exit, see what he had to say, he was very big on exit lines. Or pour gasoline on me and walk into his office and hold him tightly so he couldn't run away. He was very big on "emotional holding" also.

Me: Tyranny of dependence.

[**The Healer differentiates the behavior from the Self.**]

Carolyn: Watch out, you're treading on thin ice. So what if I were dependent? Otherwise why be in treatment? I mean, doesn't that come with the territory? Didn't you say that the dependency was the precursor of attachment, which itself is the undifferentiated ground of being human?

Termination of therapy can be reminiscent of a funeral—after a natural death—with corresponding grief reactions of sadness and anger. This phase of treatment reactivates latent negative transference, even after a successful outcome. Termination by the therapist understandably creates greater trauma to the patient and, to some extent, to the therapist himself. What's more, the therapist's premature termination of treatment will not be experienced as a death, but as a murder.

A great deal has been written on the prevention of patient dropout, but not much about the prevention of *therapist* dropout. We know, most commonly, that patients drop out if their transferences are left unattended or if the patient doesn't feel empathized with or even simply understood.

Therapist dropouts are more insidious, and most of them are countertransferential, a consequence of the therapist's reluctance to know or to learn something about himself. It often plays out either with deficit patients, with whom the therapist feels drained and helpless, or with negatively engaging patients, with whom the therapist feels chronically rejected and diminished. A much less understood phenomenon is the therapist being pulled into a "dyssynchronous role-responsiveness situation" (Sandler's 1976 term), a set pattern that may or may not be congruent with the therapist's own predisposition.

Ultimately, the therapist's dropout is related to the patient's nonresponsiveness to attempts to form an empathic bond, whether passive or active, with passive empathy "a waiting, sentient attitude that echoes the patient's statements, and supports and reflects his emotions" (Havens 1986, p. 17). However, here empathy is only a context, an observation platform. If nothing else happens, the inevitability of stalemate ultimately negates the self of the therapist. In active empathy, there is a potentially much more serious trauma for the therapist as he swings into the patient's emotional life. If the therapist is rejected, such a patient's repudiation of an empathic connection can shake the therapist's very own grounding. No insight, self-reflection, or special maneuver is of much help here. I believe that for the therapist (not to mention the patient) there is an inevitable sense of abandonment in failing to establish a mutual bond. The therapist drops out—if he himself is still in need of another to ground himself. Such self-grounding is not grounding in separation; it is a totally lonely existence.

The Tibetan Tarthang Tulku (1984) warns us that to the extent that we divide our world into self and other, and establish ourselves as agents acting upon and responding to situations, we commit ourselves to a view grounded in separations. While being self-grounded in separation means a capacity to struggle for an differentiated and independent self, being grounded in inseparability, or fusion, obliterates us, and makes us too vulnerable to others. [Very few survive the tyranny of the other.]

IF THE OTHER IS NOT SEPARATE, IT CANNOT BE LOST
(Arnold Modell)

> *Carolyn:* This is like mutual meditation. I vacate my mind. I focus only on my breath, I inhale and exhale if my mind goes to thinking. I bring it back to my chest and my abdomen. As the air comes in and out of me, I become part of the atmosphere, penetrable, and dissolved in nature. It isn't that I inhale the air you're exhaling or vice versa in this room. Oh well, maybe that too, but mostly it's as if my mind is being molded in clay and I'm passing it to you and you take it, you reshape it and give it back

to me. I guess my last therapist didn't have the same reciprocal experience. We seemed to be mostly in denied frontal opposition to each other. He simply did not need me or want me.

Me: Even in the frontal oppositional relationship there is some oblique interdependence.

Carolyn: If there was, he definitely showed no sign of it. Are you sure, is this another explanatory prop of yours? I mean, do you have any dependence on me, oblique or otherwise?

Me: Doesn't even frontal opposition require the existence of the other?

[The Healer is always self-reflective.]

[I was wondering why I was competing with her previous therapist, who was not even in the ring, who left willingly a long time ago. So am I using him as a prop, not for an explanation but for a paranoid alliance?]

At one time or another, the therapist unconsciously allies with the patient to an extreme extent, even colluding with him or her against others. **[This may be considered as the virtues of his fault.]** The desire to establish such a tenacious tie may be traced not necessarily to the patient's need or wish, but to the *therapist's* yearning for fusion (which is the main unconscious reason of interminable therapies). Each one of us, to a greater or lesser degree, wants to re-create a state of symbiotic bliss, an expression of the earliest desire to merge with mother. Freud referred to it as an "indissoluble bond," which was attributed to infantile helplessness. Thus it represents in the practitioner a difficulty in maintaining his or her own separateness, the unresolved resultant of trying to come to terms with one's aloneness in the face of basic attachment needs.

Every person has the temptation as well as fear of breaking down ego boundaries, the urge to regress in the character of their object relations, the desire to dissolve into another. In fact, Walant's (1995) study of the alienated self suggests that our society's long-standing denial and devaluation of merger phenomenon throughout the life cycle has actually increased the likelihood of personality and addictive disorders, precisely because autonomy and independence have been overly encouraged at the expense of enduring attachment needs. In infancy, this early primitive need requires direct, sensory physical contact, whereas in childhood progressing on to adulthood, the need seems gratified by verbal and social as well as physical contact. With the further development of the psychic capacity for ideational and symbolic gratification, this universal fantasy of fusion generalizes from persons as objects to substitute symbols and abstractions. The individual then behaves as if fused or dominated by such concepts as cosmic forces, unconscious forces, moral absolutes, God, Duty, Truth, or Country. These become substituted in fantasy for the other that was in infancy the mother. If this primary need for social contact is frustrated, the individual is left with heightened subjective awareness of his own existence, individuality, aloneness, separateness, and autonomy, all of which arouse primary existential anxiety. The person longs not only to be united with the original mother, but also to form an indissoluble bond with the external world as a whole.

What drives the patient into the office of the therapist is the wish to step out of this isolation, although he may not know this. In fact, both therapist and patient suffer from the same universal symptom of aloneness and need for attachment, an expression of the unconscious wish for a subterranean connection, to return to the original undifferentiated state. It represents a fundamental need for contact with another person or persons, and its psychic derivative may be conceptualized as a universal wish or fantasy of oneness, an "illusion of fusion" (Fierman's term).

The practice of psychotherapy is a lonely business. The therapist, despite outward appearances of being engaged with others, must acquire a tolerance for loneliness. This is one of the professions whose confidential nature requires that the person not share his daily activities with anyone, including with the members of his family. The capacity to be alone is not only one of the most important signs of maturity, but also an absolute necessity for the psychotherapist. Although the practitioner is naturally not immune from human frailties, he cannot expect to use his patients as objects for his own behalf, to satisfy some unsated needs for connectedness.

———————◆·◆·◆———————

Change occurs by understanding the way of sameness. It is an arrival at a state of felicity, wherein time and space, self and others are undifferentiated, in order not be preoccupied by them.

6

"In the Ordeal of the Self, There Is No Salvation by Immunity" (R. M. Unger)

THERAPISTS ARE NOT IMMUNE FROM THE INFLICTIONS OF THEIR PATIENTS

> I have lived on the lip of insanity, wanting to know reasons, knocking on a door. It opens. I've been knocking from the inside.
>
> —Rumi

Carolyn: As this young woman, a new patient of mine was talking, I was saying to myself what a fraud I am. She was telling me about a party that she went to. As she walked in, she felt dizzy. She was so anxious that she couldn't even focus her eyes, even though she rehearsed her entrance the whole week before. Finally, she saw an old friend and latched onto her. After a glass of wine, she felt relaxed and talked with a few guys, but none of them either asked for her telephone number or expressed any interest. So she left alone and on the way back bought a box of Entenmann's, went home and ate the whole thing. She thinks she's "ugly, fat, and not that smart." Now who does she sound like to you? My God, if I have the same problems as my patient, how on earth can I sit there and behave as if I can help her? I think I made a mistake. Never mind being a training analyst. I shouldn't be practicing even in the red-light district of psychotherapy. One cannot just go to classes, get some supervision, collect a few credentials, and declare one-self a therapist.

Me: The world is your classroom.

[**The Healer believes that everyone has the capacity to reach a state of felicity.**]

[In the past I might have explored her wondering whether I was equally disturbed, and which way.]

Carolyn: So, I should just plunge into living? I've got to build up my self-esteem, I need some success experi-ences . . . of any kind. Incidentally, I was intrigued with what you said, something like "Self-esteem is unearned." It's so true, I watch this . . .

A visitor to a monastery, awed by the devotion of its monks, asked the director of the monastery what reason people give when they come here. "Everyone who comes here," replies the director, "does so for the wrong reasons." Obviously he was implying the right outcome. The same goes for psychotherapists. Some may come to the field to help others, some to be scientists, some looking for a day hospital for themselves, and they may be all the wrong reasons, righting themselves along the way. This is because, if the embryonic features of the emotional problems with which the patient is struggling are present in therapist himself, he will be unequivocally on their side and establish "reciprocal understand-ing" (Storr's term), which means that the more he learns about himself, the more will he be able to understand his patients. The more he learns about his patients, the more will he be able to understand himself.

Burning at the stake used to be a popular method for deciding whether or not someone was a witch. Perhaps what the practice lacked in fairness, it made up for in finality. Similarly, Ancient Hindus tied a bag of cayenne pepper around the head of an accused witch, and suffocation was the only proof of innocence. By a comparable, but not as definitive a method, one can decide whether someone is neurotic.

Maslow's (1970) definition, which views neuroses as a failure of human growth, implies a universal continuum. It encompasses all the standard psychiatric categories as well as all the stuntings, cripplings, and inhibitions, and a host of other diminutions not traditionally thought of as mental illness. After all, every one of us has inevitable developmental deficits and conflicts in our formative years and ongoing environmental stresses in our everyday lives thereafter. One's psychological trauma is a chronic process, and rarely a discrete event. We all share the same universal pathology of yearning for infinity and search for oneness, an ontological hunger. On some fundamental level, we all want to fuse with an all-powerful other, never quite ridding ourselves of a seemingly insatiable desire to merge with mother—Jung's mythological substratum to human experience.

In addition, there is the common garden variety of strivings, wishes, and fears of dependence versus independence, aggression versus passivity, shame and guilt, self-esteem and self-doubt. It is not only our patients who are perpetually trying to survive the indignities of life, while at the same time attempting to maximize their potential with regard to love, sex, and work, or who suffer from reminiscences. We all do. But some of us distance ourselves from them by articulating them clearly. Dr. Coyne Campbell (1941) observed that the patients who were brought to him because they had been judged to be seriously maladjusted, or even insane, showed one chief symptom: they were unable to tell him clearly what was the matter. That may differentiate people in gross psychopathology. But when it comes to the existential matter of selfhood, the dynamic process of adaptation and actualization, of being and becoming, we all live in the same psychic bubble that cannot be articulated. At certain times in our natural lives, we all suffer at least from some modicum of anxiety and depression, the two most common products of inherent human struggle, or to use Frank's (1974) generic term, *demoralization*. As painful as that may be, it makes our job easier. "I am a human being; nothing human is alien to me," says Alexander Moszkowski (1971) in *Conversations with Einstein*.

THE ESSENTIALS OF MIND ARE THE SAME

You'll feel less alone, simply by recognizing that we all have the same emotional stratum.

—Anonymous

One of T. A. Dorpan's comic strips reads: "Half of the world are squirrels and the other half are nuts." This is only half true, although at least half of the world seem to be therapists, formally or informally. In some fundamental way, therapists and patients all share a common well, a source of instincts, perceptions, intelligence, creativity, the basic affects of love and hate, fear and desire, and the like. Part of our unconscious is a collective one. And there are no psychological supermodels. Jung (1936a) distinguished a personal unconscious from a collective unconscious, the former embracing all the acquisitions of personal existence—the forgotten, the repressed, and the subliminally received, thought, and felt. Simultaneously, the latter originated in an inherited brain structure, referring to all those psychic contents that are peculiar not to one individual, but to a broader human universe, that is, to a society, a people, or to mankind in general. In other words, the collective psyche comprises the psychic functions that are deep-rooted hereditary elements; they are transpersonal portions of the individual psyche, phylogenetically developed and inherited. By contrast, the personal unconsciousness plus the consciousness constitute the ontogenetically acquired, developed segment of the psyche; it is that portion that gives us our individual differences. These essentials of a particular human being, our "ontological structures" (Heidegger's term), allow only minor variations on the theme.

To comprehend a patient, the therapist must go on a dual search, seeking to find out both what is *unique* (selective) as well as what is *universal* (shared). The former view looks for what makes the patient singularly special, at his or her worst and best; it searches for those individual qualities that define and distinguish the person from others. At the same time, the latter view takes a quantum leap in the other direction to find what he or she has in common with other people, not necessarily from a psychopathological perspective, but on the larger level of what fundamentally binds or connects the patient to all humanity with similar struggles.

THE THERAPIST AS A SURROGATE NEUROTIC

Carolyn: I dread seeing this patient. He's a chronically depressed, bitter guy and inadequate, who blames everyone for his problems except himself. If he loses his erection during sex, it's because his wife "moves"; if he's late to work, it's because of the "dysfunctional subway system"; if he isn't getting better, it's because I'm "incompetent." I hate him because I can't find him. When I ask him whether he takes any responsibility for all of the things happening to him, he replies, "Of course. Don't I come to my sessions regularly and talk?" Then I began to wonder, maybe he's right. No, he isn't. Then I present the case to "Oldie," this old-bag supervisor of mine who fakes listening. She doesn't remember the material from the previous sessions, then keeps repeating "Empathy, empathy" as if it's a mantra. Meanwhile, the administrator of the clinic keeps double-scheduling patients like the airlines. But they all show up and there isn't another therapist, a later-flight equivalent, here, only the same therapist working even later hours. Last evening I came home from work around 9 P.M., the electricity was out, everything in the refrigerator was spoiled. I called Con Ed. They claim I haven't paid their bills for three consecutive months. So I had to go there this afternoon in person, pay all back payments in cash. That's why I was late coming here. It's a long trip from the village to uptown, you know. There are usually no cabs, buses are unreliable, and the subways smell.

Me: To find someone is to develop him.

[The Healer is foremost an educator.]

[Later I'll get to the negative sentiment about coming uptown, coming to see me, the worth or lack of it, and draw her attention to the parallel between her and her patient's complaints.]

Carolyn: So find me and develop me. I'm at the end of my rope. I'm sorry but you said the unbearable must be shared, so there.

It has been said that each time your patient loses a symptom, his therapist acquires it; together they generate dovetailing neuroses. Unfortunately, therapists may tend to acquire symptoms without patients losing theirs. There is a cumulative effect of distressing interpersonal relations in therapy-soaked life. Kernberg (1965) has said that this especially happens when the psychotherapist is in the presence of severe regression in the patient, which can manifest as primitive rage and vengeful attack. He goes on to suggest that the patient's aggressive behavior tends to provoke from the therapist counteraggressive feelings and attitudes, as if the patient were pushing the aggressive part of his self onto the therapist, and as if the countertransference represented the emergence of this part of the patient from within the therapist.

Most likely, this mutually responsive phenomenon is pervasive to the therapeutic field and indigenous to it—an occupational hazard. For example, in his study of empathic communication between therapist and patient, Havens (1986) has referred to the "contagion of every affect." "If you gaze for long into an abyss, the abyss also gazes into you," says Nietzsche. Others, such as Ivey (1995), have clinically observed the dangers of attunement when working with alienated and affectless patients, such as the reciprocal feelings of boredom, detachment, loneliness, impotence, and even dread. Perhaps some therapists are more sensitive than others, and what is worse, the most empathic clinicians may well be the most susceptible ones. As a defensive maneuver, to leave the chair half empty doesn't help.

Independent of the therapist's and patient's preexisting conditions, there exists a mutually being stirred, a kind of Jungian "unconscious infection" between patient and therapist. Havens also pointed out the other side of the empathic coin when he warned that while sharing the patient's inner life, there is always the possibility that what seems like the therapist's receipt of another's mental experience is really the therapist's transmission of his own. Psychology has no self-help manual for such afflictions. [Not only do we make patients neurotic about their neuroses, we could also make them neurotic about our own neuroses.]

TOO PROSAIC A DARKNESS

Carolyn: I think that rich people have no shame. I'm treating a daughter of a very wealthy family. She lives in the West Village, trying to "find" herself by rejecting her parents' lifestyle. So she doesn't accept any help from them in terms of paying my fee, although she effectively negotiated with me a reduced one, which she is always a few months behind in paying, meanwhile coming to sessions in a chauffeur-driven car. The other day she said nonchalantly, "Isn't it interesting that we have the same taste? We have the original." I looked at her puzzled: She was referring to my one-hundred-thirty dollar print of Franz Kline. But that's all we have in common, if it is. She is gorgeous, she changes boyfriends as frequently as her hair color, she's rich and well connected, she got accepted by every law school that she applied to. I think her parents had something to do with it, though. I watch her in awe as she talks about the utter meaninglessness of her life. What fucking meaning could she be talking about?

Me: The world isn't as real as we think it is.

[The Healer offers a perspective that may promote tolerance, not envy.]

[Later I'll deal with her envy, her latent homosexuality, her deprived self now and in childhood.]

Carolyn: Fuck that. To me it's quite real. I tried your idea of "holy listening." It just isn't in me. I listen as a human who is self legitimizing and end up anxious and angry. Let me ask you this . . .

In my training, I mostly have treated persons with unfair fortune, whose external world was discernibly more deficient than mine. They have been sicker and poorer, with many more obstacles and fewer opportunities. In short, in virtually every instance of interpersonal environment, psychological endowment, and circumstance, they have been less fortunate than I. What I found was that, with the exception of some social guilt about this discrepancy, I could easily remain empathic and sympathetic to their plight.

However, what I must also admit that I had was an occasional sense of superiority, which I—and especially the patient—certainly could have done without. If this latter feeling had any saving grace, it was the warning it offered me of an impending problem with our therapeutic relationship. I was okay as long as the patient could regard me as a good role model. I believed that I had earned this status through training and effort. At the same time, I was unable to appreciate that I had been excessively empowered by many inherited and accidental vicissitudes of fate.

Despite the above, I seem to have sustained some semblance of therapeutic equilibrium between esteemed therapist and suffering patient. I have retained those professional and personal qualities traditionally deemed essential in all healers, a recognition that the therapeutic agent holds a special position in the community, which is derived from certain powers and knowledge that he has acquired. I've been able to establish Ehrenwald's (1966) "therapeutic presence," defined as the therapist's personal belief and confidence in his or her own ability to be of help. Simultaneously, I've been the legitimate recipient of the "therapist's myth," the expectation of help on the part of the patient based on his or her trust in my capacities to do so.

But now, decades later in private practice, some patients are more or less my peers, if not superior in every discernible dimension. What's more, we probably have similar troubles. Many of the individuals I am trying to help are clearly more fortunate than I in a variety of ways. They are multitalented, good-looking, rich, successful, independent, and worldly, as well as surrounded by a wide circle of family, friends, and admirers. Bestowed with every asset and advantage, whatever their troubles, they also appear to have the best resources to surmount them. [**Can this be a mirror countertransference?**]

As a consequence, the therapeutic balance has changed, at the expense of therapeutic potency, my personal narcissism notwithstanding. As sociologist Talcott Parsons's (1951) early study of variables of the doctor–patient relationship necessary for successful treatment showed, the therapist will not be able to exercise therapeutic leverage if we regard him in too prosaic a light. But, in fact, the therapist is always in a "win" situation. [**If** you are more endowed than your patients, then you are simply lucky; if you are less endowed, then you are truly fortunate— bestowed with an unparalleled opportunity for growth.]

————————◆•◆•◆————————

There are no patients, there are no psychotherapists. There are only the uninitiated. There is no behavior that makes no sense, or that makes sense. There is only the inevitable. There are no neurotics, and there are no normals. There are only degrees of equanimity in view of the human dilemma. We are all seeking.

7

Man Transcends the Norm, Going Beyond What Can Be Measured— Therefore, He Has No Norm

"THE MOST COMMON OF ALL DISEASES IS DIAGNOSIS" (Karl Kraus)

To accept oneself as ill means something like a *capitis diminutio*—a lowering of the flag!

—Karl Jaspers

Carolyn: As if dealing with patients isn't enough, you get administrators who demand that you give the patients reimbursable diagnoses. You mentioned "exit diagnoses"; well, that young rich girl's exit diagnosis is "bitch." Now that is not reimbursable. You also cannot give diagnoses that presently or in the future may interfere with the patient's work life. So every patient gets the diagnosis of adjustment disorder. I guess it's the adjustment to managed care. That means we're not to terminate patients who keep adjusting and also are paying. I'm sorry about the "bitch" diagnosis. Actually I would be hard

put to make her diagnosis. I can only throw in borderline disorder and narcissistic personality to sound intellectual. But what does all that really mean? You think
everyone in treatment, as she is, has a Telos. Well, you're
wrong.

Me: No size fits all.

[For the Healer there is no normative certainty.]

[In the past I would have pursued her "you are wrong";
how else am I wrong; or the bills that she hasn't paid; or
was she trying to find out whether I would terminate a
nonpaying patient, or what do I think of her diagnoses?]

Carolyn: No, it doesn't. How do other therapists, and you, of
course, live in such an ambiguous profession? There is
no certainty of anything. This isn't in any way a science,
nor is it remotely medical care, you know.

Me: Is it at least aesthetic appreciation of life stories?

[The Healer offers an appreciative perspective.]

Carolyn: Not to me. I would rather go to movies for that. If it's
carried to the point of . . .

The diagnosis of experience diminishes the meaning of both
terms. There is the universal tendency of mind to order experience into form. The *Diagnostic and Statistical Manual of Mental
Disorders* (1994), with its now famous (or is it infamous) acronym
DSM, is an externally regulated, standard language of general
psychiatric knowledge for researchers, diagnosticians, insurers,
and clinicians alike. It has become a dogmatically applied numeri-
cal system, a form of nosological tyranny imposed upon the field,
attempting to diagnose all ordinary and extraordinary psychological experiences. James Hillman (1996) goes even further:

The whole of that thick, heavy, and lightweight book [DSM]
provides accounts of the various ways the daimons affect
human fate and how sadly and strangely they often appear in
our civilization. This book prefers to connect pathology with

exceptionality, exchanging the term "abnormal" for "extraordinary" and letting the extraordinary be the vision against which our ordinary lives are examined. Rather than case history, a psychologist would read human history; rather than biology, biography; rather than applying the epistemology of Western understanding to the alien, the tribal, and nontechnological cultures, we would let their anthropology (their stories of human nature) be applied to ours. [p. 31]

Hillman wishes to reverse our thinking in psychology as it is taught and practiced, ambitiously seeking to redeem this field from some of its sins.

The *DSM* has four sins to be redeemed. [**Poetically inflated?**] They appear in the form of four axes. Recently, a fifth one, a global assessment of functioning on a scale of 1 to 100, has been added to the other four axes of the *DSM* (i.e., Axis I, clinical disorders and other conditions; Axis II, personality disorders and mental retardation; Axis III, general medical conditions; Axis IV, psychosocial and environmental problems). Even these five axes not only cannot differentiate the psychological troubles of the individual in all his uniqueness, but if anything they diminish him.

The overall diagnosis with its five axes overlooks a host of other relevant variables, especially positive resources and assets, from intelligence, abilities, and talents, to family role models and social networks, that should be taken into account in any comprehensive clinical appraisal. Even the sixth axis (proposed by Karasu and Skodol 1980), which was designed to reflect past and present conflicts, defenses, coping styles, and ego functions, is limiting. So you may wonder how many such "axes" can you grind? As many as you have to, because psychotherapy is a finely ground process.

Even at its finest, collecting biographical information about the patient is a form of objectification of the person's subjectivity. It is a type of intrusion into one's emotional life without regard to the consequences and ramifications of such psycho-peeping. Like biography, making diagnoses is a prying, peeping, and even predatory process; like biographers, psychological diagnosticians are "psycho-plagiarists" (novelist Vladimir Nabokov's term).

Despite wishful thinking by *DSM* proponents, psychotherapy as a treatment modality is not designed to cure *DSM*'s illnesses, or any other categories for that matter. Rather, it is at best geared toward potentially remedying the deficits and resolving the conflicts of the individual. The patient's expressions of distress, whether they take the form of depression or anxiety, somatization or dissociation, still will always differ from patient to patient, person to person. One of the qualifications of the therapist is the lack of interest in quantification. Thus the good psychotherapist undoes the diagnoses. Friedman (1988) says that "Half of the task of training" is to "understand strangely." The "other half" is to "perceive normally" (p. 545).

Shapiro (1965) says that the neurotic person does not simply suffer neuroses, as essentially one suffers from tuberculosis or a cold, but actively participates in it. Thus the creation of categories rarely serve the patient, and what is more, could counterserve to stigmatize. In fact, such labels often end up being used for procedural, bureaucratic, or even punitive purposes by the practitioner. Basch (1987) has pointed out that, in regard to borderlines, diagnosis is often a sign of the therapist's negative feelings toward a patient who will not play the game by the rules and leaves the therapist at a loss.

Worse is that the whole field, complains Leston Havens, is in the untenable position of attempting to define sickness before it has defined health. Such a stance fails to recognize that psychotherapy as a major modality of treatment accomplishes its art by not being illness-specific, but person-specific. The individual is *not* a diagnosis, and any such equation or categorization is a form of misguided reductionism. Even the characteristic imprint that the patient leaves behind, which Havens calls "fossil diagnoses," is phenomenologically more relevant than any formal classification. The former is a sudden, sometimes powerful experience of "here is a new person," an experience that normally causes an element of surprise. This means not only once or twice, but progressively seeing the patient in a fresh way.

In the final analysis, evaluating and understanding patients in psychotherapy requires finding new approaches or pathways that are not easily subject to the regulated tyranny of diagnostic formulae. O'Hanlon (1993) captures this notion with his "possibility therapy," which is the antithesis of an attitude of foreclosure that circumscribes who the patient is or what his or her future will be. In White's (1993) words, it is a stance of "indeterminacy within determinacy," for which the only capacity that a therapist needs is a curiosity, a capacity that evokes a certain relentlessness to break up our familiarities.

THE DIAGNOSIS IS A CONCLUDING FORM OF OBJECTIFICATION

> If you ever recognize the patient, you have already lost him.
>
> —Anonymous

Carolyn: This supervision scheme is a farce. "Oldie" isn't helpful at all; nevertheless she demands that I follow her advice. If I follow her advice, I'll have no patients. I don't know how she got to be so important. Anyway, I'm sure of neither my diagnoses nor what I should be doing with my patients. My diagnoses change with my relations with my patients and I improvise the technique as I go on. Didn't you once say that what's meant in the psalm, "Sing Unto the Lord a New Song," is improvisation? I think you were not exactly reaching. Some days the bitch is like me, a garden-variety neurotic. Other days she seems psychotic, as if belonging to a different species. Insurance companies may not recognize this methodology, but I believe every therapist feels the same way. They're just too complacent to say so.

Me: Your negation of the system brings you coherence.

[The Healer is one who seeks positive influence, even within negative events.]

[In the past I would have first gone after my "reaching," thus how did I get to be important; then explore her identification with me and her attempts to resist it, especially by her projection.]

Carolyn: My friends say I matured a lot. I used to always say to myself in a difficult situation, how would Dr. K. handle this? Now I don't even go through such a step. I just handle it the way that you might have. You know, I used to take notes on your statements as soon as I would leave the session and . . .

Freud, as a diagnostic system for psychoanalysis, separated those who could from those who couldn't form a transference neurosis, deeming the latter untreatable. He tried to distinguish between the content and the structure of pathology. He conceptualized psychoanalysis as a cure for neuroses; later on, his followers elaborated on it for the more severe and intractable psychoses and character disorders. Most recently, psychotherapeutic modalities and techniques are being specially designed and researched for the treatment of certain designated disorders and a host of different diagnostic categories. The obsessional development of nosological systems to describe psychological disturbance has reached new heights (and new lows, for that matter), with operational manuals and their varied revisions. Apart from the matter of disagreement and controversy over the inclusion and validation of specific conditions is a more fundamental concern— the impact on the individual of the diagnostic process. Whatever rubrics are applied, the critic Anatole Broyard, for one, spoke of the disapproving quality in the language of diagnoses. Bugental (1987) said that it is countertherapeutic to let any of the nonindependent dimensions come into the foreground of the therapist's consciousness during interviews, as such objectification will be incorporated into his subconscious.

The opposite extreme of the objectification of the individual by diagnosis and by treatment rests in the existential schools—an uncommunicative form of subjectification. Within their theoretical framework, they see all men defined and unified by what is intrinsically human. They are not separated, or stigmatized, by extrinsically imposed societal standards of sickness or health. According to Hanly (1985), however, simply engaging in an exercise to change oneself serves as a denial of real responsibility, freedom, and choice. In the aphorisms from his bedside teachings and writings, the great physician Sir William Osler (1961) provided a middle ground that did not totally discount diagnosis. In aphorism 181, he advised his students to care more particularly for the individual patient than for the special features of the disease.

There seems to be an almost unbelievable enthusiasm generated about labeling others in general. An avid interest in making diagnoses is understandable, a common manifestation of our a priori assumptions about the meanings of experiences in order to protect ourselves from the anxiety of existence. It constitutes a necessary stance of concluding, of maintaining a structured, safe, and predictable view of one's world. It works only for a short time. There is a viable alternative: [**Reach for "a stance of not concluding"** (Margulies 1984), **where you'll find the ultimate serenity and predictability.**]

THE NATURE OF THE THERAPEUTIC RELATIONSHIP AS A DIAGNOSTIC ENTITY

Jaspers's (1963) monumental book on general psychopathology sought a methodology that would differentiate the patient's symptoms not by manifest content, but rather by the way the patient experienced them and by the way the therapist experiences the patient. Insofar as the relationship between therapist and patient constitutes the supraordinate influence that transcends all other variables, it may provide the most reliable information about the patient. In fact, Kohut and Wolf (1982) have made this intriguing observation: "It was not the scrutiny of the symptomatology but the process of treatment that illuminated the nature of disturbance of . . . patients" (p. 44). According to Kernberg, it is the fundamental type of transference that is formed—classical (or advanced) versus narcissistic (or primitive)—that has remained as perhaps the most telling dimension of patient evaluation. These two expressions of patient relatedness are viewed as maturational markers. They not only comprise transferential axes upon which all psychotherapeutic practice is pivoted, but forecast the kind of therapy that ensues. Then psychotherapy can really begin, for in the process of healing the original label is diminished, if not ultimately destroyed. As Reik (1952) earlier observed,

> "Sympathetic understanding" is not . . . as you might expect . . . present from the start of the work. It is one of its optimal results. It comes toward the end of treatment or emerges when the [therapy] has progressed considerably not in a quick diagnostic testing. One may compare its development with the reading of a really great novel. You do not love its figures immediately or it would not be a great work of art. It takes time and some psychological work on your part to penetrate to the essence of the personalities you are reading about, to learn what makes them tick and what the motives are that determine their actions and feelings. . . . The more [the therapist] discovers of those emotional undercurrents, the deeper he goes into the domain of unconscious processes, the more his patient becomes "sympathetic" to him. . . . At the end he cannot but help to see in [the patient] a human being like himself, struggling with the same conflicts that are common to us all. . . . At the end

the [therapist] realizes that there no longer exists a gulf
between him and his patient. [pp. 129–130]

There, you no longer talk about therapeutic relations, but "the
therapeutic union," even to the point that the therapist's heart rate
has been found to follow a pattern similar to that of the patient.

In our becoming, we may constitute ourselves as an object in
the eyes of the other, and later on either through imagery—
fragile—or real identification with the one who saw us as an
object. In therapy, it is symbolic identification, that is, the patient's
changing his introjects and internalizing the therapist, in one form
or another, that is considered the most potent, nonspecific change
agent in psychotherapy. In his dictionary for psychotherapists,
Chessick (1993) points out, "There are three terms that have been
mixed up repeatedly and that represent subclasses of the clinical
mechanisms of internalization: identification, introjection, and
incorporation" (p. 165). Before him, Campbell (1989) reflected on
a comparable confusion: "Some writers use incorporation synony-
mously with identification and introjection. Others equate incorporation with introjection and define both by which the
mechanism of identification takes place. Others differentiate
between them on the basis of the phase or level of psychic
organization and development at which the assimilation of the
object takes place" (p. 364). Along maturational lines from
primitive to mature, incorporation (an internal process of oral
ingestion, engulfment, and often destruction, of the object) and
introjection (a process wherein the object or partial object remains
somewhat more separate within the self and carries on a relationship with that foreign body) are both archaic versions of identification (wherein the self is unconsciously modified to resemble
the object as an inner presence). Projective identification is
another common form of relation between therapist and patient
that is diagnostic.

The noun *projection* was originally posed as one of several
defense mechanisms by which the person dealt with primitive

impulses by perceiving them as coming from outside oneself. It harkens back to Freud's (1911) case of paranoia, in which the patient endowed another with his own internal persecutory feelings. George Klein introduced the dual terminology of *projective identification* to accommodate the double aspects of this phenomenon as both intrapsychic fantasy and interpersonal relationship. For him, it consisted of aggressive penetration into the object as well as reinternalization of that object. And Ogden (1979) has gone even further to accommodate diverse schools of thought in his portrayal of the fourfold meanings and functions of this term:

> It is a psychological process . . . that is simultaneously a type of defense, a mode of communication, a primitive form of object relationship, and a pathway for psychological change. As a defense, [it] serves to create a sense of psychological distance from unwanted (often frightening) aspects of the self; as a mode of communication, [it] is a process by which feelings congruent with one's own are induced in another person, thereby creating a sense of being understood by or of being "at one with" the other person. As a type of object relationship, [it] constitutes a way of being with and relating to a partially separate object; and finally, as a pathway for psychological change, [it] is a process by which feelings like those that one is struggling with are psychologically processed by another person and made available for reinternalization in an altered form. [p. 362]

The relationship between therapist and patient has been described from many different perspectives, which inevitably overlap to create a compounded process. Most commonly, it has been known that the change by internalization of the therapist—therapeutic union—requires a long-term relationship with the patient. The ultimate union is a spiritual one, which transcends all other relationships, and once it is established everything would fall in its place. It has no therapy-related restraints, especially because there is no time element in the spiritual union, only the element of distance. [**When there is no space between you and the thunder, you'll be hit with the lightning, according to a Japanese saying.**]

TO CONNECT ONE'S PSYCHIC LIFE TO AN END ITSELF WOULD LEAVE THE PERSON STANDING IN THE VOID

> *Carolyn:* My eclectic therapist sent me a patient. I was very pleased, until I saw the patient: a 68-year-old woman with every possible medical illness imaginable, on dozens of medications, can only pay what Medicare would allow, talked a whole hour about nothing except that she doesn't sleep well. I could have gotten out of my chair, gone for a walk and come back, and most likely it would have made no difference. She's been in treatment on and off by numerous therapists, mostly trainees. She couldn't remember the names of any. The last trainee was supervised by my therapist. That's how I got dumped on. So "What did you learn from all these therapists," I asked her. "Not much," she replied. "Then, why do you go to see them, like now?" She said the treatment may help her not to get worse. What would that "worse" be? I asked. She never thought about it. No one ever asked that question. But if I wanted, she could tell me about her family. I said, maybe later. "For now, would you not want to know the worst case scenario, if you never saw any therapist?" She replied, "How can I be in treatment without seeing a therapist?" I don't believe that any self-knowledge would help me to deal with this patient. What does introspection have to do with all this, my career, my personal life?
>
> *Me:* The introspection is only an interim medium.
>
> [**For the Healer no mental activity is an end product.**]

[In the past I would have explored her feeling toward her previous therapist and specifically "dumping this patient on her"; that is, did the therapist think that she could identify with this patient; how come I do not refer patients to her, and her putting down the therapy (introspection as a code for me).]

Carolyn: Yeah, yeah, yeah, from the cult to self-therapy to spiritual quest. I wouldn't mind telling you this. I hate such patients. I didn't quit my sophisticated career with the intention of a life with morons. I thought the field of psychotherapy and analysis meant the ultimate refinement of the mind. Now I can hardly stay awake. Where are those interesting patients that I read about in the books and articles? I thought I'd be treating and be treated by people like myself, not some old, burned-out schizoids.

Me: You only want to associate with stars. In the circle of your intentions, those stars serve to perpetuate the enchantment of self with self.

[For the Healer the anger and frustration are just by-products of unconvinced self-love.]

Carolyn: No, even you are not in my league. You couldn't continue that with the next verses of Wordsworth if your life depended on it. Psychotherapists are formulaic and their patients deserve it. Furthermore . . .

Therapists are always looking for "good" patients. For some, a good patient is someone like themselves. Then there are those who seek the worn-out criteria of "YAVIS" cases (i.e., young, attractive, verbal, intelligent, and successful): ["**There is less here than meets the eye,**" as Tallulah Bankhead said of a Maeterlinck play.] YAVIS cases may or may not be such good patients, but they are sought after by therapists because these patients do proceed naturally, gathering momentum. I know for certain that you cannot refer a DOPUR patient (i.e., dumb, old, poor, ugly, on relief) so easily. Beyond this, the selection criteria for patients is pretty much similar for nearly all therapies, including a good measure of motivation, an interpersonal capacity to relate to others, a certain stability and responsibility in one's personal life, and some semblance of self-cohesion. Dynamically oriented psychotherapy may also add a few extra qualifications, such as ability for monitored regression and capacity for insight.

Of course, with all these desired qualities, you may wonder why such a person would require treatment. In reality, it is a gross misconception that only sick and disturbed individuals need therapy. In fact, as in "the rich get richer" metaphor, the healthier the patient, the more he or she can get from psychotherapy. Then, taken further, the best patient would be the one who doesn't need it at all!

I would say that if a person can talk about him- or herself, he is halfway to being a good patient. According to Lacan (1977), the subject begins analysis by talking about himself without talking to you, or by talking to you without talking about himself. When he can talk to you about himself, the analysis will be over. Lacan always preferred to be witty at the expense of being right. In fact, that is exactly the point where the psychotherapy can begin—the real moment of the patient talking to the therapist about himself, person to person, and about himself. Some can never get that far, like those medically ill with psychosomatic symptoms. They are the patients with "alexithymic" characteristics (Sifneos 1973), who use their symptoms in defense against experiencing affect and to ward off insight. For starters, they are not aware of being under stress and look upon emotional problems as malingering, and regard revealing their dependency as shameful. What's more, they are prone to operational thinking that is extremely detached and pragmatic; are unable to find appropriate words to verbalize everyday events in their life, especially feelings; and have an impoverished capacity for fantasy.

The difficulty is not that the patients will not speak about themselves to the therapist, but that even good patients will not give up easily what they are telling you about—their neuroses. It is common clinical knowledge that, although the patient wishes relief from his neurotic suffering and disability, he does not want to give up the neuroses itself since it represents his attempt to solve a psychological conflict, and as such represents the best level of adaptation he has been able to achieve on his own.

Man's wish to know and to be known is exaggerated. Thus patients frame their problems in such a way that it is unknowable, thus insoluble. This is because, in spite of the stated wish to change, they would like things to remain the same, or at least not to be responsible for the change. To really change, the patient must be fully responsible for it, while recognizing that treatment itself—*not* the therapist—is inducing the change.

The person will be on his way to patienthood when he begins to acknowledge the need for his or her symptoms—as a precursor to *not needing* them. The patienthood role means having four nonspecific elements: (1) the individual's awareness of his or her pain, that is, the capacity to experientially acknowledge that one is suffering; (2) the inability to cope with that distress, that is, realizing that adapting to the situation is beyond one's control; (3) the wish to change the situation, that is, desiring relief and being willing to do something about it; and (4) the belief in the ability of another to help, that is, recognizing that one cannot go it alone and has to put trust in someone else's expertise. [**This is still a too pathomorphic look at a person.**]

How many people do you know who have all those special qualities that fit the standard description of the most promising patient? I don't know many *therapists* who could fit that depiction of an ideal candidate for therapy. Although we, the therapists, may not find the perfect patient, we can easily make a patient out of anyone (no matter how perfect his life may be)! You know the story: A patient says, "I'm the happiest person in the world, Doctor—I have a wonderful wife, the kids are fine, I'm wealthy, I'm healthy, and I enjoy my work." The therapist responds, "How long has this been going on?" [What our profession lacks in common sense, it makes up for in sense of humor.]

In the totality of both subjective experiences and objective reality, not every part of the person is accounted for and gathered in. And "the more the individual asserts the (objective) reality of his (subjective) experience, the more likely he is to be regarded as mad" (Wright 1991, p. 73). Yet man transcends the norm, going beyond what can be measured—therefore has no norm.

8

The Ultimate Engagement Is Through Our Common Destiny: I—You—It

THE THERAPIST BECOMES THE "THERAPIST" ONLY IN THE RELATIONSHIP TO HIS PATIENTS; ALL RELATIONS ARE NOT METAPHORICAL

Carolyn: "The bitch" canceled the last session two hours before her appointment and didn't show up for the next one, without leaving any message. Very unusual. I got worried, whether she was sick or something else. You know, this is New York. So I called her. She was home with a flu, very apologetic for not having called me. I asked whether she had someone cooking her chicken soup, you know things like that. She was so happy to hear from me. "Doctor," she says—she calls me doctor, sorry—"I have learned so much from you in such a short time and I feel so totally understood for the first time in my life." I told her that she desired to be understood. "I know, I know," she said. She was thinking of coming three times a week and paying my going rate. Would I have the time for her? Gee whiz. She really became a good patient, I must say. The past doesn't necessarily live in the future, I'm sorry. She's a very forward looking woman, like me. Her present dilemma may belong to the past, but the moment it is spoken, as my yoga teacher says, it is no longer now, therefore does not exist. I want her to focus on the future.

Me: Like writing the script and acting the scene at the same time.

[**For the Healer, people must follow their bliss.**]

[Later I'll explore her ambivalence toward her patient, that is, bitch vs. good patient, her discomfort of being a therapist ("she calls me doctor, I'm sorry"), her low self-esteem ("gee whiz"), superordinating her yoga teacher to me, whether my time focus was misdirected, etc.]

Carolyn: Actually I'm just acting, and hoping that there will be some . . .

An unusual attachment occurs between therapist and patient, according to Orlinsky and Howard (1987), through a common endeavor, mutually fostering a sense of role identity. This constitutes a therapeutic union that consists of three essential and distinct parts: first, "reciprocal role investment," which reflects the degree to which each participant is personally committed to his or her role, rather than simply going through the motions; second, "empathic resonance," which refers to the ability of the participants to communicate and be on the same wavelength, rather than talking at or past each other; and third, "mutual affirmation," which refers to a sense of caring for one another's basic well-being.

The therapeutic union is further strengthened by "interactional rituals" (Goffman 1967). These are countless patterns and natural sequences of behavior that have positive social value. For example, "Just as the member of any group is expected to have self-respect, so also he is expected to sustain a standard of considerateness; he is expected to go to certain lengths to save the feelings and the face of others present, and he is expected to do this willingly and spontaneously because of emotional identification with the others and with their feelings" (p. 10). Thus, both members cooperate in performing their respective roles, within the tripartite ingredients of the therapeutic bond. The only prediction worthy of considering then becomes how well the therapist not only fulfills his respective roles at any one point of treatment, but also adjusts to inevitable fluctuations in the patient's roles.

All schools of therapy consider the relationship between therapist and patient as a crucial variable in the therapeutic process. Even the learning theorists and behavioral schools have begun to recognize the role of the relationship, or at least to acknowledge the need for "relationship skills" on the part of the therapist. For a long while, behaviorists had insisted on giving credence to their techniques alone, whether deconditioning, relaxation, reciprocal inhibition, or cognitive structuring. Ultimately they realized, however, that unless one paid attention to the nature of the transference (and resistance) and maintained good interpersonal rapport, the patient did not follow behavioral instructions. Therapists could no longer simply be conceived as a "social reinforcement machine." The bottom line was their recognition of the complexity of ambivalence—that most patients did not want to change in spite of their overt wishes to do so, and that human change does not occur in a vacuum.

In contrast to a regressive transference relationship, which has been likened to that of parent to child, the type of relationship that the behaviorists formed most closely approximated that of teacher to student. The educative relationship usually is more time-limited than the parental one; it may begin with adulation of the teacher leading to disappointment, if not to resentment, and ultimately it ends up with rebellion against the educator and education. Well, as they say, every teacher becomes a bore eventually. Perhaps that is why behavior therapies are short-term therapies.

Even the sex therapists have moved away from strict technical training exclusively in the classic manner of Masters and
Johnson. The sex therapist Helen Kaplan told me a fitting joke: A
couple comes to see a sex therapist. The wife complains of her
husband's lack of sexual desire. The therapist takes one look at the
husband, who appears 100 pounds overweight, and decides that if
the husband could get into better physical shape, the problem may
go away. So, he recommends that the husband should run ten
miles a day and then call him in ten days. The couple leave, and
exactly ten days later the therapist receives the awaited call, in
which the breathless husband says, "Doc, I have done exactly
what you recommended. I have been running ten miles every day,
for the last ten days." Impressed with the patient's compliance, the
therapist anxiously asks, "Well, then, is your wife any happier?"
To this the husband responded, "Doc, I have no idea—I'm exactly
100 miles away from home!"

Incidentally, quite incorrectly, Freud was assigned the image
of a cold and distant therapist. He was anything but that. He once
said he was no Freudian. He certainly knew the profound powers
of the transferential relationship, as well as the importance of its
personal and humane aspects: he would send postcards to his
patients, give them food, and have contact with them outside of
the confines of treatment. In fact, in the famous case of Rat Man,
for example, it was the patient who protested that Freud's
"Cordially yours" correspondence was too intimate. [**The use of
relationship as a technique is in bad faith.**]

INTERNAL DIALOGUE BEGINS TO GERMINATE
IN AN INTERSUBJECTIVE FIELD

You may say anything you really, truly feel. Anything at
all, no matter what it is.

—George Bernard Shaw

Carolyn: Well, the honeymoon is over. Actually I'm surprised that it lasted this long. The bitch stopped talking. She comes to sessions, but it's like pulling teeth to get her to say something. She stares at my breasts, and that really makes me uncomfortable. What's worse, I get wet, you know, down there. I think I blush—not right now, with her. The worst is I occasionally glance at her crotch. Am I a lesbian? You think she figured that out and that's why she isn't talking. With the Oldie's suggestion, I raised the issue of homosexual attraction with her, her fear and wish and wanting to flee from the treatment. I think the Oldie herself is attracted to me. Anyhow, the patient totally denied it and even laughed. She confessed that she kissed and fondled other girls during her high-school years and liked it, but she preferred boys. You know, I also had two such relationships with other women. So the bitch and I are again in your "intersubjective synchrony," except that boys don't prefer me at all. I can't even find them.

Me: Fish are in the water.

   [The Healer is always hopeful.]

   [Later I'll get to her sexual attraction to her patient, her doubt about her sexuality, my not empathizing with her frustration at not having a man in her life.]

Carolyn: What does that mean? Does it mean that guys are in the bars and I should frequent bars, like looking for Mr. Goodbar? Do you want me to get killed? Who is the fish?

   (She stayed silent for a very long time.)

Me: I, you, she, man, and it.

Carolyn: Laughs. "It"? . . . The anger, the sex, the love, the fear, the wish, the therapist, and the silence, and we are all in the water? Excuse me, who's supposed to free associate here—the patient or the therapist? You use language as if it has no more than instrumental and referential function. Some of us, you know, have a life to live. Let's have a "closed association." How do I find what I'm looking for and where do I throw a wider net to catch one of them for good?

Me: What you have not found yet may be related to not knowing what you're looking for.

[For the Healer, determination is undermined by the very purpose it was to serve.]

Carolyn: I do. Man. Now as I say it, it sounds utterly ridiculous. This interchange couldn't lead to ever deepening dialogue. I reduce myself to just being a woman in need of a man. My God.

I usually instruct my patient to tell me whatever comes to his mind without censoring; I emphasize free association—a means to access latent resources—and encourage the patient to talk as if talking to oneself. **[Isn't this also a travesty of communication?]** This kind of internal dialogue, which occurs without an audience, tends to be more "sincere" according to Reik (1952), than behaving as if one is speaking to an audience. However, such initial instructions on how to elicit uninhibited speech on the part of the patient are strictly procedural and activate the most powerful resistance and transference. Even if useful, at least initially, psychotherapy inevitably must become increasingly revelatory (with more and more resistance to these repressed revelations), and one can't simply keep repeating the same instructions.

Some patients are easy, says Yalom (1989): "They appear in my office poised to change, and the psychotherapy runs itself. Sometimes so little effort is required of me, that I invent work, posing a question or offering an interpretation simply to reassure myself, and the patient, that I am a necessary character in this transaction" (p. 167). Of course, most others are not so easy. Many technical strategies have been designed for difficult patients, and the therapist becomes a very necessary character in these transactions. I personally follow Carl Rogers's enduring idea of making the situation so safe that things that cannot be said will be said, and things that cannot otherwise be experienced will be experienced.

Basically I remain quietly present. It is not that I make no sounds, but I am silent in content, a kind of dynamic inactivity. I do not introduce topics as a way of encouraging the patient to talk. If you ask whether patients fare better by such a do-nothing approach, I would offer you Jay Haley's (1981) tongue-in-cheek response—that assuming 50 percent of the patients in psychotherapy clinics get better spontaneously, a therapist who did nothing would have a 50 percent chance of success! And the therapist who happened to be present in this spontaneous improvement would get the credit. Nevertheless, P. B. Medawar (1967) insisted that even poking would be better than just looking. At least that would lead to anecdotalism in the study of human behavior. In any event, both the psyche and the body are self-regulating systems, and some psyches are better in self regulating than others. "The same mind that created the problem can solve it. The Gordian knot inties itself," says Peter Kramer (1989, p. 12). The patient's need to be honest with himself is one of the self-regulation factors. Therefore, success resides more in the patient than in the therapist. The concept of interpsychic regulation implies that an important aspect of expertise lies in the therapist's capacity to select those patients with whom he can work most effectively.

Haley is too seasoned a clinician to take his advice that the therapist does nothing literally, so I assume he means that simply the presence of the therapist is underestimated, and doing or saying are overestimated. When the therapist cannot establish an intersubjective monologue, he'll feel he has to add something else: External dialogue. This manner of thinking is a forerunner of the more recent intersubjective view, which "seeks to illuminate phenomena that emerge within a specific psychological field constituted by the intersection of two subjectivities" (Atwood and Stolorow 1984, p. 41). Yet even intersubjective discourse requires both a sender and a receiver, as well as a message mediated by a code in a reciprocal interpretation or "reading": it is transsubjective. [The person's relations to everything is ultimately mediated by, and derived from, its merging with the transmaterial.]

ONE HITS THE MOVING TARGET BY NOT AIMING AT THE CENTER

Intimacy is the epiphany of the hard work at living by both parties. It grows with crises and adversities. In psychotherapy, most of this hard work must be carried out by the therapist, especially during the crises of the relationship with the patient.

Glover (1955) divided the crises in therapeutic encounter into two categories: The first treatment crisis is characterized by the patient provoking an argument because of the nonjudgmental attitude of the therapist, which generates guilt, just as some lovers cannot tolerate the pleasure of being loved and thus provoke fights. The second crisis is characterized by the patient wanting to flee because the therapist gets incorporated into the patient's fantasies. On the latter occasion, the therapist can be perceived as a punitive judge, strict task master, or high-and-mighty parent. And in either state of crisis, if the therapist becomes defensive, the patient would feel misunderstood and become even more vituperative or prone to act out. Of course, the therapist in return should be warned against himself being on the defensive (or on the offensive, for that matter) or worse, also acting out.

It isn't that the treatment relationship always stays stable, or that the mutual discourse between therapist and patient should be obliged to remain harmonious at all times. This would be unrealistic, and probably countertherapeutic as well. Chessick (1989) has depicted intrapsychic realignment by noting that if you plot a graph of any activity, the result shows peaks and valleys as well as long plateaus. Comparably, adaptation (or maladaptation) to therapeutic crises, chronic or otherwise, with highs and lows and reciprocal readjustments, are part-and-parcel of the essentials of treatment.

In actuality, the psychotherapy process is a state of permanent mild crisis, and the therapist must constantly remain on alert. These chronic crises are primarily related to the subtleties of the therapeutic relationship. First and foremost is the establishment and maintenance of trust, which will be tested in every stage of psychotherapy. The patient always needs validation, though the request manifests in constantly changing defensive patterns. The therapist does not meet the patient's shifting demands by deliberately aiming at the center of the patient's pathology.

EMPATHY STEMS FROM THE EMBODIMENT OF THE WHOLE AS SELF

> *Carolyn:* Sunday night I went to a Kabbalah reading. There was this extraordinary rabbi, a kind of Jewish mystic, who talked about the Sephirot, the Ten Commandments' equivalent of emotions. There in the background of niggunim—do you know what I am talking about? Wordless melodies—you're supposed to find your self. Because you are not who you are. Your external intentions are bad infinity.
>
> *Me:* And your kavannah?
>
> *Carolyn:* My goodness! My internal intention was to thank you. Yes, in order to see the fish, one must get close to the water. I got close to the muddy waters of Kabbalah Sunday night, but fishes! My, my, my, I've exchanged cards with two guys and smiles with a few others. Even if nothing comes out of all this, I was happy that I did something different, that I could do something different, and maybe in that expanded arena that I would become more aware myself, which is now what I want. But what I am and the rest may follow or may not.

Me: Even the absence of what you want belongs to you.
[**For the Healer the mastery in one's house is compensation for its emptiness.**]
Carolyn: Are you an ex-Kabbalah groupie? Well, these Jewish guys . . .

Therapists tend to suffer not only from transexperiential alienation, but also from its self-experiential form. "The final mystery is one's Self. When one has weighed the Sun in the balance, and measured the steps of the Moon and mapped out the seven heavens star by star, there still remains oneself," said Oscar Wilde in *De Profundis.* Therefore, the therapist first must attempt to find himself. Then if a patient is more similar to the therapist, consciously and unconsciously, the therapist has a better access to the patient's mind. My patients are not so homogeneous, and our similarities are not particularly pronounced. Nevertheless, there is a baseline of information and intuitive knowledge immediately available to me with a patient with certain characteristics such as age, sex, education, and more so with psychopathology. No matter how attenuated the information is, if it is available, I am more likely to be empathically predisposed to that person. Kohut (1971) agrees: "The reliability of our empathy, a major instrument of analytic observation, declines the more dissimilar the observed is to observer" (p. 37).

Empathy is the therapist's allowing himself to be used as part of the patient's self. It is an affect with that precognitive nature. Empathy is defined as a mode of observation that attempts to capture the subject's inner life. It requires the observer to draw out of him- or herself a state of experience that approximates that of the other. Such assessments allow the therapist to find the answer to fundamental questions, such as What is the patient experiencing? and Where are these reactions coming from? Under these therapeutic circumstances, what the therapist empathically finds out may be true transexperientially, but first he or she must be able to answer even more basic questions, such as What am *I* experiencing, and where are *these* feelings coming from? "Embry-onic features of the same emotional problems with which the patient is struggling are present in the therapist," says Storr (1979, p. 169), if he could tune in himself.

In short, first one has to empathize with oneself. R. D. Laing (1967) said, "Each person, not being himself either to himself or the other, just as the other is not himself to himself or to us, . . . in being another for another neither recognizes himself in other, nor the other in himself" (p. 74). The self-unaware therapist cannot empathize with himself; therefore he cannot empathize with others, which in turn generates a pathologizing interactional pattern and alienation in himself and others.

The patient's affects are the best transmitters of data. The search for correctness may not help in finding the other, but empathy does. Yet empathy is not intuition. In fact, it is the oppo-site. As Kohut (1977) cautions, "Whereas empathy is the . . . analyst's greatest friend, intuition may at times be one of his greatest enemies—from which it follows that, while the analyst must of course not relinquish his spontaneity, he should learn to mistrust explanations that suddenly surge up in him with unques-tioned certainty" (p. 168). Similarly, Levenson (1976) says,

> The therapist would not have to be correct in his formulations as much as he would have to be in harmony or in resonance with what is occurring in the patient. A new mutual under-standing might result; not one person understanding the other's truth. It may sound outrageous to suggest that it would be possible to do good therapy without ever really under-standing what is going on as long as the therapist is involved in the expansion of awareness and is using his own partici-pation to further elaborate and actualize the patient's world. [p. 8]

This is especially true if the awareness is expanded to the whole: the embodiment of everything as self, not just a species-wide bond.

"Withinness" (Dorsey 1976, p. 70)—being both subject and object of one's experience—proceeds from intersubjective monologues and culminates with transmaterial silence: "The Amongst Itness." "It" points the way to the unforeseen, and, ultimately, to unity.

9

One's Neurosis Is the Best Place to Seek Enlightenment

No play, no analysis.

—D. W. Winnicott

"EVERY THERAPIST PLAYS WITH THE PATIENT"
(Kenneth Wright)

Carolyn: I had lunch with an old classmate of mine, and we shared a bottle of wine. So I came to the office a little high. You know, I can't drink much. I was horny, so I sat in the spot the bitch sits in and masturbated. I'm embarrassed that I'm not embarrassed to tell you this. I'm definitely attracted to her, but also hate her. She has this sense of entitlement, smugness that things will come to her. Anyway, her session was six o'clock, and by then I was totally sobered up. But I still wanted to be a little nutty. So I took my bra off and wore a white silk shirt. She came to the session full of sugar and spice, telling me about an older guy that she met and how he was so loving and affectionate and how safe she felt with him, meanwhile frequently glancing at my chest. I felt my nipples hardening. Then I said to myself: What the fuck am I doing? This is an immature woman, an erotic illiterate. She is looking for nurturance but willing to be sexual to get it. Of course, I would never act on it, but even having these thoughts and feelings are so screwed up.

Me: Psychomorality?

[**For the Healer the mind is pure and innocent, even in its lack of purity and innocence.**]

[No subtle ethical scolding or pursuing her lesbian tendency, no indulging of her doubts about whether she is suitable for this profession.]

Carolyn: Everything in my psyche is OK as long as it's contained there and not inflicted on others. I haven't been able to reassure myself about the latter. Anyone who has a contact with me will be subjected to my psyche. Maybe because I'm still a beginner . . .

Me: And one always remains one.

Carolyn: And if you're loving, diligent, and always learning, you may feel whatever you want? Is that it? If so, I can't be a therapist. I don't want just to feel, I want to have it, concretely: to squeeze her head between my breasts almost to choke her, and have you watch it, so that you may stop this stifling game, your soliloquizing, and your nonideological muffling. Maybe it is the man thing. My father used to preach to us about the inexhaustible curriculum of self-improvement from which one never graduates. Well, I don't even want to be a student, never mind the graduation, if it means nonbeing. He was . . .

Considering that psychotherapy involves the repeat of past feelings, repressed desires, and unfulfilled wishes, not to mention the range of experience and personal history that it represents on the part of two parties, it stands to reason that the patient's (as well as the therapist's) transference is neither all-positive nor all-negative. It is ambivalent by nature, so that one receives and unconsciously displaces a mixture of both elements, perhaps one or the other playing a more dominant role at a particular point in time or in relation to specific events. Therefore, the term *transference* itself is misleading as a singular noun, because it erroneously connotes some one-dimensional, monolithic, and homogeneous entity. Rather, transference phenomena are plural, multiple, and diversified, and make themselves felt through excesses. Indeed, early on Freud warned psychoanalysts of extensive and often excessive manifold forms, which can vary between the extremes of a passionate, completely sensual love and the unbridled expression of an embittered defiance and hatred. Karl Menninger (1958) describes such transference neuroses as artificial induction of a therapeutic illness.

Furthermore, transferences are phase specific. Kohut has focused on the preoedipal phase-specific relationship between therapist and patient (i.e., selfobject transferences) to depict types of primitive relating that harken back to very early infancy, and the affect of these infantile experiences is absorbed in character defenses, and thus is intractable. Their pathological anchoring could overtax therapists' empathy. For example, in a mirroring transference, the patient would see in the therapist's eyes the gleam that an infant could see in his or her mother's eyes and interpret that "delight" as one's own lovability—"I am perfect," "I am beautiful," "I am smart." In an idealizing transference, the patient would see the therapist as a calming, safety-generating person, just as the infant seeing the mother serves as an internal soothing function—"I am strong," and "I am invulnerable." In a twinship/alterego transference, the patient would see in the therapist a certain degree of likeness to himself, making the connection between the two—"You are part of me." The sequence from the mirroring to twinship type of transference reflects a maturational process; nevertheless, the greater the reliance on an archaic selfobject relation, the more serious is the pathology. The object transference is still further along in the developmental process, less primitive and narcissistic—marking one's arrival at the oedipal phase. But that arrival is never free from its precursors.

Greenson (1967) said that all transference phenomena are ambivalent because the nature of the object relationship that is transferred is more or less infantile, and all infantile relations are ambivalent. Even in our most mature selves, we still carry the remnants of earlier object relationship and narcissistic transferences and they crowd out most other issues. The selfobject transference reflects the reactivation in the relationship with the other of an archaic level of experience at the stage of *non*differentiation. It is what gives to this relationship its symbiotic, fusional quality. It may have once been absolutely blissful, but primitive yearning for merger can also become accompanied by fear of fusion.

More mature interactions may reflect a greater separation between self and object. It can also encompass love of an idealized other in all its varied, substitutive, and excessive or diluted forms of attachment and affection—trust, admiration, sympathy, respect, concern, and sincere interest. Yet under certain regressive circumstances, including the often frustrating and intensified context of therapy, therapists are also susceptible to experiencing and transferring very intense mixed emotions, desires, wishes, fantasies, and fears to their patients. [**One's transference may be one's neuroses, but also one's neuroses may be the best place to seek enlightenment.**]

THERAPEUTIC MISPRISION

> *Me:* I wonder whether "the bitch" becomes steady content
>   here as your way of avoiding some other subjects?
> *Carolyn:* An interpretation? Well, you see she embodies all

my life issues. If I can figure out my relation with her, I think I would figure out lots of others. Didn't you once say, "When you understand one thing through and through, you understand everything"? Make up your mind. I have many more issues, I'm sure. Which one do you want to discuss?

Me: Heterosexual panic!

[**The Healer tells it as he feels it, right or wrong.**]

[**Not** "What comes to your mind?" or "What are those 'many issues'?"; **not** "You seem to be irritated by my question"; **not** whether you could not feel safe with such a self-contradicting therapist.]

Carolyn: Not really, you see when I watch your crotch, I don't want to have sex with you either. Your penis is your breast, it even gives out some milky stuff, ha, ha, ha. It isn't real milk. Man's penis is a failed breast. You know that all you guys have breast envy. Gosh, I was in such a good mood when I came in, you spoiled it. . . . The reason I said last time I should be in treatment with a female therapist was because of the same synchronicity that you're writing about. You have no idea, at times, what I'm talking about. When I described the sensation of having the bitch's head in my bosom you looked bewildered. The more I talk about her, the more confused you seem to be getting. I'm not resisting talking about myself by talking about my patients. And if I *am* resisting talking about myself, it's not because of the heterosexual panic, you pedantic reductionist. I fucked more men than the number of papers you published!

Me: Did I tap an inner inquietude?

Carolyn: Look, I don't turn the other cheek; the last such person died on the cross. Life is a tale told by an idiot, full of sound and fury, and psychotherapy makes the biggest noise.

Me: You clipped off the "signifying nothing."

Carolyn: Ah, okay. Now I'll come down. You don't have to reach for me. There will be no resistance from me, provided that you drop that interpretive ladder.

Me: And lie down where all ladders start.

John M. Dorsey (1976), who was Freud's patient, tells a story that the professor told him about his dog Jofi (a chow). It is about the therapeutic misprision. Apparently when resistance of the patient mounted, this usually quietly sitting dog would get up and leave the room. Also, she would signal the end of the hour by getting up and yawning. In contrast to Jofi's misprision, Freud stayed put and attentive, as he was keenly aware of the importance of unconscious resistances. Consciousness is inherently reflexive and critical, but also flexible and changes its position. The unconscious is less so and the source of most resistances in treatment. The resistance is a natural force, says Freud, related perhaps to the inertia discovered by Newton to reside in all matter, a reluctance to change position. Therefore, it has to be part and parcel of every treatment wherein change is the goal. As the neurosis of the person is contained in this resistance, the therapist always works either in the middle of the explicit resistance, or at the edge of latent ones. They are never static.

Dealing with a patient's latent resistances depends on the particular pathology and the person in question, along with other situational considerations, especially relational variables. Obviously, there are some standard techniques, and even specific directives in psychotherapy, including those for reducing resistances. But even Freud, who was as determined in his technique as anyone ever was and who established many principles (e.g., suspended attention, neutrality, abstinence) realized that he was well advised to call his own proposed rules "recommendations." He disclaimed their unconditional acceptance and opposed any mechanization of technique, yet he knew that the therapist must face the patient's resistance or lose him. Chessick (1980) went further in noting the therapist's responsibility in therapeutic confrontation:

> The mark of the professional psychotherapist, in contrast to the novice, is the capacity to recognize silent defenses and resistances at work in the therapy and the willingness to have it out with the patient in regard to these vital defensive systems, even at the risk of incurring great anger on the part of the patient and spoiling the pleasant atmosphere in which the patient, on the surface, seems to be intellectually cooperative. [p. 182]

To "have it out" (therapeutic scolding) successfully through an interpretive stand, however, requires that the therapist understand that interhuman aggressivity is essentially intrasubjective and used by the person for self-integration, however temporarily. And as neither fights nor "flights avail against danger from within," as Freud put it, therefore the therapist doesn't really have the patient on his side. But the therapist must remain steady in his empathy, try to feel the patient's own experiences, and articulate them with the patient's expression. That closeness must be reflected in the most subtle minutiae of their relationship, if the therapist intends to interpret the resistances. The therapist must even use the same words as the patient, and those words have to mean the same thing. In an advanced developmental level, the patient and the therapist, according to Balint (1968), "speak the same language." True, the patient may reject the interpretation of resistances, may be annoyed, frightened, or hurt by it, "but there is no question that it *was* an interpretation" (p. 14). The therapist would be able to chip away at the resistances of the postoedipal patients by emotionally neutral interpretations. But in primitive stages of developmental maturation, patients' resistances cannot be tackled with interpretations, partly because the words would not have the same meaning, and the message would never be received. With these patients, the good therapist has it out, not by chipping away resistances by neutral interpretations, but through dissolving them by empathy, that is, by forming an emotional foundation upon which such interpretations are sustained. Of course, all effective interpretations are formed upon an affective foundation. The affective bond at an archaic preverbal level provides an emotional stratum upon which all understandings grow, in which all messages are received and imprinted. If the stratum is not yet consolidated, messages will not be received. [Japanese Proverb: Just because the message may not be received, doesn't mean it is not worth sending.]

ONE COULD WOBBLE AGAINST THE BACKGROUND OF STILLNESS

Carolyn: You know more than anyone else that I came to this profession not just looking for a day hospital for myself, and to market my pathology. I read your writings, you know. You are at times very wrong. My "self" isn't going to "crystallize" by being a perennial patient. I told you what happened with the previous therapists. I agree with you that my main goal is myself, and the profession is only one of the dimensions of it. My life can't be reduced to what I do, but I have no life outside of what I do. The best thing you can do for me is actually to introduce me to a good man. I translated one of your highfalutin' sayings to a real-life lesson: "One needs to attain enlightenment before one attains it." I say one should attain a guy before one attains him. The way that a child could make a woman a mother, a guy could anchor a woman and make her whole. Actually I'm not sure, now that I said it. Meanwhile even though all my friends would kill me for saying something like this, they all want a guy, especially if he's handsome and has money and no children from a previous marriage.

Me: An anchor is useful when one stops sailing.
[**The Healer is not for a passive contemplative life, but for an active and rigorous one.**]
[The focus wouldn't be on her reading of my work and her feelings about it, or her retaliative reducing me to a matchmaker and my abstract uselessness.]

Carolyn: Screw it, I want to stop sailing, stay in a safe harbor. I want an anchor. What have I gotten for all these years of sailing? I'm chronically nauseated and wobbling. I want an anchor, yes definitely, just throw me one. (Silent for a few minutes.) I'm sorry, actually you already threw one anchor to me, yourself, but you see it isn't enough, not that you say it is. You see, not only are we not in the same boat, but I don't even have a lifesaver jacket. . . . It . . .

Occasionally conflicts seem to resolve with the therapist's interpretation and with the patient's corresponding insight, but most often not. Very few people have just classic triadic conflicts, which involve unresolved sexual and competitive desires or wishes. Even they carry some dyadic conflicts about the earlier issues of attachment and individuation, which do not change as a consequence of becoming conscious of them. Quite frequently I hear patients volunteering such ostensible insight and not simply cognitive insights or intellectualization. Rather, they are emotionally felt insights, but nevertheless lead to repetitive dead ends in treatment. These dyadic conflicts serve a preemptive purpose with their persistent existence—the formation of the nuclear self. It is also possible that triadic conflicts may not be resolvable with interpretations, either. Psychoanalysis is essentially a psychology of conflicts, not necessarily a remedy for their cure.

Those who are stuck in the dyadic (i.e., preoedipal) stages of development may not yet have formed their basic self, which is Balint's (1968) "basic fault." These people are constantly confronted with their limitations. Their selves have to be reassembled.

One has to reach the oedipal stage of development to build the tripartite psychic structure (i.e., id, ego, superego), to be able to make use of interpretations, and potentially to resolve conflicts without endangering one's very core selfhood. Persons with dyadic conflicts have not yet stabilized their nuclear self. Insofar as their tripartite psychic structure is not maturationally able to contain the intrapsychic conflict as an independent mental representation, such conflict is not accessible and thus not resolvable by insight. These persons cannot take distance from themselves without risking fragmentation, because the self is still in the process of becoming.

In fact, all conflicts first serve toward the formation of the self. Dyadic conflicts, which are simply deficiencies in the structuralization of the representational world, may deceptively present themselves as resolvable conflicts, imitating a neurotic scenario. Yet these earlier conflicts are actually part of prior developmental activity—the formation of object constancy and self-identity. What appears on the surface to be genital activity is actually in the service of pregenital aims—self-structuring. These patients manifest dyadic conflicts that are the genuine imitations of the triadic conflicts. They are not something to be interpreted away. Instead, these turbulent and often rageful struggles between love and hate, and unmet wishes for intimacy versus fears of engulfment, are still in the service not only of gratification (or vindication), but of *validation*. To solidify weak boundaries between self and others as well as to stabilize the self, they are part of the "glue" that is required for internal cohesion and indispensable for man's strivings for survival. In Kohut's (1977) words, "And no satisfactory definition of the concept of a cure . . . can be given if we fail to determine the patient's greatest terror—whether castration anxiety or disintegration anxiety—and his most compelling objective—whether conflict solution or the establishment of self-cohesion, . . . [unless] he can establish the conditions that will guarantee his psychological survival" (pp. 280–281).

COOPERATIVE RESISTANCE: ONE GROWS DEPENDENT ON ONE'S OPPONENT

Carolyn: I really think that I should be in treatment with a female therapist. I don't think you really understand what it's like to be a woman. Don't interpret this again as "heterosexual panic" because it's not. I don't even have a homosexual panic. Panic is not the problem. My anxiety is related to my not feeling self-confident. It's like jelly inside of me, not bones. And I don't like your one-liners in answer to my problems. What does it mean, that I'll either find or lose myself forever? I don't even know why I should be reading Auden. Don't give me homework. I can hardly handle the material from the institute. Furthermore, high doesn't rest on low. Low rests on low, and high is totally elsewhere. I am low, not even resting on anything, and you are high and resting on your laurels. I went over the things that you said to me in the course of treatment. Are you a therapist, or a philosopher, or a minister? For example, once you said, "Obedience is a part of attention." Well, you're not going to get that kind of attention from me. I want you to teach me life without expecting that I will learn it.

Me: To let you wish to learn how to learn?

[**The Healer is loyal to superordinate paradigms without negating the ordinates.**]

[**Not** interpreting again her wanting to leave me; defensively exploring how I do not understand her, her putting me down with my "one-liners"; our desynchronous place as she experiences it.]

Carolyn: No, I don't want to learn, nor do I want to wish to learn how to learn. All I want is to be taught. Can't you tell the difference? You keep pushing me, pulling me . . .

All patients desire to preserve their status quo, in spite of expressed claims of wanting to change. Whether one describes patients' resistances in terms of frustration of drive gratification, maladaptation to reality, irrational cognition, repetition of old internalized relations, or as related to fears of self-cohesion, they are powerful enough to bring the therapist's attempts to a dead end. This is because the potential change always arouses anxiety, even though discontinuity rather than continuity best characterizes lives over time. Any change inevitably threatens the patient's stability, no matter how precocious and nonadaptive that stability may seem to outsiders. As Strean (1985) has put it:

> Therapists observe a universal paradox in psychotherapy—all clients unconsciously want to preserve the status quo no matter how dysfunctional it is. . . . Those who accept resistance as part of the therapeutic process are accustomed to hearing the impotent man extol the virtues of celibacy, the unhappily married couple insist that fighting and hating are inevitable features of married life, and the alcoholic or drug addict proclaim that dysfunctional ways of coping are superior. [p. ix]

Conceiving of opposite discrete entities simultaneously is demanded from the therapist. He must particularly be a student of this homospatial Janusian process in dealing with negatively engaging patients, insofar as their negativity is a form of cooperation. The patient's negativity is primarily related to developmental conflicts, especially to the individuation phase. And they'll not deal with these issues, never mind resolve them, as they are commonly associated with their fears of further selfobject failure.

Compliance in the separation phase of development is a duplicitous act stemming from excessive dependency. Otherwise, in all self-asserting relations, the resistance in treatment is expected to develop as an organic phenomenon. It has nothing to do with the therapist's or patient's "failure." In fact, the emergence of negative reactions (every patient has some latent negative trans-ference) may be an early sign of the beginning of a therapeutic process.

For a long time I dreaded (well, at least didn't look forward to) opposition on the part of the patient and tended to blame myself. I am not sure whether any therapist really appreciates its appearance, even though Freud alerted us to the fact that resistance is part and parcel of treatment, that the overcoming of resistances is the part of our work that requires the most time and is the greatest trouble. It is worthwhile, however, for it brings about an advantageous alteration of the ego, which will be maintained independently of the outcome of the transference and will hold good in life.

Yes, defiance is necessary for the progress of treatment, and resistance may accomplish it to the extent that the therapist stands for parental authority and the patient behaves as an embattled child. Insofar as the libido serves the process of attachment, aggression serves to ward off individuation. In spite of knowing all that, I couldn't help seeing resistance as a technical *problem* until I got away from the negative terminology, itself—the concept of resistance—as Schafer (1976) advises, and began to view it as an affirmative phenomenon, defined by what it accomplishes. Mess-er's (1988) defamiliarizing argument, that the patient's resistance is not only or not primarily opposition, but paradoxically a kind of *cooperation* with the therapist, makes the point. But just how much of this kind of cooperation can one take? Apparently a lot.

In fact, according to Jaspers, one grows dependent on one's opponent. Of course, each therapist contributes, in his own idiosyncratic fashion, to precipitating negative reactions on the part of patient. Even simple efforts of the therapist can be construed in an unpleasant light, naturally causing resistance, of which the most effective ones are offered by the therapist. The resistances manifest as various rationalized forms designed to preserve the status quo, in spite of the patient's expressed desire to change, and they have to be understood within the context of his psychopathology. For example, superego resistance is geared to maintaining a guilty status, whereas id resistance seeks childhood gratification from the therapist, and ego resistance attempts to contain impending danger. They may also take the shape of resistance to transference, or as intensification of it, or they may take a primordial form of striving to merge with the therapist. The resistances can be obvious, like prolonged silences, or circumstantial; or they can be repetitious, but relatively unobtrusive, as in slips and inattention. In short, no therapeutic relationship is immune from encountering resistances. And no matter how or when these defensive responses are formed, they should be regarded as necessary, even *desirable* elements in the natural progress of treatment, rather than as obstacles to be overcome. [**Man moves forward stumbling.**]

UNGRATIFYING BATTLEGROUND

> *Carolyn:* Are you bored or something? You seem to be wanting a little fight in every session, either by seemingly saying "Remember your past, who were you then?" or "Forget your past, who are you now?" Or you say, "Forget your unconscious wishes, tell me your conscious ones," or you scold me for not accessing my unconscious wishes. Well, if I were aware of them, then they wouldn't be unconscious, would they? How, then, can I be holding back something if I have no awareness of what that is? You don't listen to your own advice. The other day, you said, "In order to fill a pot, you must have a pot. You don't have a pot." I don't have myself. So how can I really talk about my relations with others, my father, you? To fit all these into my nonexistent pot is something you should intuitively recognize as impossible. They just spill all over the place, never to be contained. That's why I come to one session and talk

about my father a whole hour, but never mention him in the next. It isn't avoidance—it's gone until the next gathering. You overestimate my psychological health and mirror back my self as twice my size. I know you mean well, but you're a distorting mirror. You expect leaps in being from me.

Me: Hmm.

[I just didn't know what to say.]

Carolyn: That shut you up, didn't it? We are not all condemned to be adult, as you think. I plead guilty to being immature and wanting to remain so.

Me: The therapy wasn't supposed to convict you.

Carolyn: Well, the Gospel does, so why not you? Religion and therapy are all male concoctions, you know. If it were left to women, we would have an entirely different order.

Me: The Gospel does so, so the sinner will come forward and be forgiven. Psychotherapy advises that instead of cursing the darkness, light a candle.

[For the Healer litany is inner pollution.]

Carolyn: See, you're saying that I should stop getting angry at you and my parents, basically. Okay, do I find the candle myself, or does it come with $300 a session? If I eventually find and light my candle, am I just to be content by that or is a mighty flame followeth by a tiny spark? I see from your eyes you missed that . . .

Me: Well, you're supposed to learn from your past, not to live in it, especially if it was a sort of inferno.

Carolyn: You old duck! You're okay, if you could only stop peddling so hard.

In the therapeutic playground, it takes two to play or fight. Langs (1981) believes that resistance on the part of the patient is nearly always interactive, and the most effective resistance is the one that is sanctioned by the therapist. The resistance is a phenomenon to which the therapist co-contributes, that unconscious communication between therapist and client inevitably represents the presence of an element of countertransference in every intervention. He refers to it as "communicative resistance." One of the common contributions of the therapist to the development of resistance is premature id interpretation. That is why Wilhelm Reich has recommended that the therapist approach the resistance from the defense, the ego side, which obviates the danger that the patient learns something too early.

Another such contribution of the therapist is advice giving. Langs (1973) believes that advice-giving is almost always a manifestation of the therapist's countertransference, thus untherapeutic. He thus advocates that "the therapist . . . not tell a patient to modify his life situation or realities, thereby depriving him of his autonomy, ingenuity, self-criticism, and capacity for change. He need not promote passivity and helplessness, inadequate functioning, and a poor and disturbed self-image—all of which the patient, unfortunately, will later exploit, and which will haunt the therapist" (pp. 549–550). In fact, the reluctance to give advice itself is therapeutic, says Storr (1979), in that it carries the implication that, once his problems are more clearly understood, the patient will be as capable as anyone else of making his own decisions.

On the other hand, a neutral interpretive attitude can easily generate different undesirable side effects in the patient. Tarachow (1963) justly wrote: "To begin with, every interpretation is a deprivation. This is more so in certain types of patients than others. Nevertheless, every interpretation is designed to rob the patient of something—his fantasies, his defenses, his gratification" (p. 13). The more complete the interpretation, the more aggressive the deprivation. These disturb the patient's neurotic equilibrium, especially if directed toward the interpretation of the id, as they are less congruent with the patient's experience than ego interpretations. Of course, "uninterpreted transference is a form of living within the pattern or symbol, a means of perpetuating a relationship with the original object that has been lost" (Wright 1991, p. 277).

Even knowing that the interpretation is ipso facto frustrating for the patient, it is often the therapist's own inordinate need for professional satisfaction that compounds the ungratified battleground between patient and therapist. This commonly manifests as excessive zeal on the part of the latter to get his or her messages across, often getting more and more frustrated, as they seem not to be received. He becomes despairing about the usefulness of such endeavors and finally may give up. Paradoxically, the problem is in the zeal itself. Excessive zeal generates despair on both patient and the therapist. Didn't the French statesman Talleyrand say, "Above all, not too much zeal"? (especially the zeal in correctness of the interpretation). It is like in orgasm—the harder you try, the less you'll succeed. An "If it works, it works; if not, not" attitude is what makes it work. And we all know that every interpretation is incorrect at a certain level; it is a reductionistic act and can never be carried out in the spirit of "nothing but." The best historical case of excessive, zeal-related outcome is Breuer's treatment of Anna O. Trying to treat her hysterical paralyses, he would put his head on her forehead, at times all night. But she developed pseudocyesis.

ATTILA, THE HEN: NON-PEACEFUL UNION OF THE FAINT-HEARTED THERAPIST

> *Carolyn:* First of all, my father was a tall, handsome, and elegant man. You didn't have to be his daughter to fall in love. He was as unpretentious as a secure man gets. So you two have very little in common. Your badgering me about "me loving you" as a repetition of my early conflict is simply absurd. My analyst made the same mistake. I appreciate you, I mean, but I don't love you. If I'm finding males my age immature, it's not because

I'm looking for my father as a lover. The younger ones are damn immature. Why the mature ones don't pay attention to me is a puzzle. I thought older guys liked "young chicks," ah—younger. This married guy that I went out with the other day was quite happy to get a blow job in the car, but had no intention of taking me out to dinner or seeing me again. You're only partly wrong. "Peacock feathers aren't made from eating thorns." And what is this speaking from the lower bridge? They eat other things too. So stop feeding me thorns: "The only way to have a lover is to be one!"? Okay, but I don't know exactly how. Isn't that obvious? Even my unhappiness is insubstantial. And you contribute to my lack of substance by implying that my imperfections are what would make me lovable. So I keep perfecting my imperfections, and nothing happens. I think you're not in touch with the real world. I need a therapist who will guide me, as I'm incapable of pursuing my "self" alone. The last four weeks we've been discussing this subject. I do need a female therapist.

Me: Four times round is enough for one dance?

[The Healer always seeks unity, even in contrariness.]
[Not to discuss the logistics of termination or to transfer her to a female therapist, nor to pursue the comparative put-down of me with her father, or the thorns that I'm feeding her with (remember the "milky secretion of penis" statement).]

Carolyn: But you've been an aesthetically unrestrained partner in this painful dance. Why? Are you a masochist or something? You have this rhetorical presence. You seem to be more interested in how you say something than in what you say. I used to have such soft sessions with the Kohutian at the beginning. Being with him was like being with my Yoga teacher, even quieter, believe it or not. The sessions used to begin with a mutual recognition of each other with some contentless talk, and then the tempo would pick up a little. We would deal with issues of the week where he would resonate almost imperceptibly with my joy and agony. Toward the end would come rallentando, the tempo would gradually slacken and wind down. . . . With you, if it is love, it's like divine madness, which I embody but you instill. I can't even . . .

Like the silent and peaceful union of positive transference (if aim inhibited), the negative transference also seeks union. Following Fairbairn, even aggression may not be discharge seeking, but object seeking. Not only love, but also fight and hate, require engagement. In one of Noel Coward's plays, a character asks about a couple: "Do they fight?" The answer comes back: "No, they are not that close." The negative transference is a bad sign, only if the therapist does not notice it. Yet this overlooking seems to be quite general, according to Reich (1949), suggesting that "No doubt, this is due to our narcissism which makes us willing to listen to complimentary things, but we are blind to negative attitudes unless they are expressed in more or less gross forms" (pp. 23–24). Of course, "a totally frustrated transference is no transference," Friedman (1988, p. 27) tells us.

Most therapists simply prefer a positive and peaceful bond with their patients, even though such transference could be a defensive idealization. But the therapist doesn't much worry about losing these patients. On the other hand, hostility and anger that emerge before a viable working alliance is established tempt the patient to act out and break off the treatment. Thus, early negative transference must be pursued vigorously, in order to forestall such a development.

There is general consensus among seasoned clinicians that negative transference is the most frequent cause of stalemate. It is not easy to confront the patient with having intense hateful feelings, albeit displaced. In fact, Glover attributed most therapeutic stagnations to the "faint-heartedness" of the therapist in daring to make the necessary transference interpretations. Even Freud wanted to dodge the confrontational anxiety by suggesting that a battlefield need not necessarily coincide with one of the enemy's key fortresses, that is, in front of its gate. Gill (1979) admitted that negativity generates sufficient anxiety in the therapist as well as the patient so that both are motivated to avoid these "potentially disturbing interactions" (p. 266), and Greenacre (1954) warned that "insofar as negative attitudes toward the analyst are not analyzed or even expressed, the need of the patient to be reassured of the love and protection of the therapist becomes enormously increased and demanding" (p. 682). Negatively engaging patients provoke anxiety, and the anxiety generators are not liked. Even therapists are not immune from disliking and its consequence—primitive guilt.

In a more optimistic vein, Greenacre further suggested that the emergence of the negative transference can be an important sign of progress. I guess that depends on the starting point. We know that some patients' malformed or deficient self is organized around primitive rage; without it, they would fall apart. In this sense, the expression of negative transference serves to better buttress a fragile self and to sustain, however aggressively, a more cohesive one. Moreover, in their interactions with others, these fragmented individuals, with rampant and unresolved rage, need to have a libidinal object to attack. Therefore, the only way that such persons can relate is with manifold forms of hostility, anger, mistrust, rebelliousness, assault, and reprisal.

In any event, the critical issue is to recognize—and appreciate from the patient's perspective—the hateful feelings and aggressivity (overt or covert, flagrant or subtle, direct or disguised) that may come the therapist's way. In this context, *any* degree of negative transference is still better than no transference. These patients are especially sensitive to the intrusiveness of the therapist, as they are trying to protect their boundaries. Transferential distancing generates greater intrusion, and its interpretation regulates the psychic tension between the therapist and the patient.

Sometimes in treatment, if the patient feels that the therapist does not intrinsically comprehend his experience, he will surely be disappointed and perhaps angry, frustrated, and resentful. As a result, he may well become at least passive-aggressive, if not verbally hostile, argumentative, and combative. This common occurrence is usually a relatively benign form of aggression directed against an object. (Is the therapist ever simply an object?) In more primitive scenarios, however, Kohut writes about a very malignant aggression as a breakdown product of the *selfobject* relationship. If the patient is virtually merged with the therapist as an archaic extension of himself—the clinician as a narcissistic selfobject—then with the failing of the psychotherapist, the fundamental sense of self is disturbed, stability is disrupted, and the patient may become totally unglued. This fear of fragmentation is what generates profound rage—an active, intense, and uncontrolled anger frequently directed at another.

What, then, is the poor therapist supposed to do when confronted with his limitations? How does one make one's impotence one's ally, à la Whitaker? If he is not empathic, he'll fail inevitably, and if he is empathic, he'll fail sooner or later. I appreciate the charitability of Kohut when he says empathic failures are therapeutic too!—provided, of course, that you recover from them. Nonetheless, it is hard to be an empathic figure for the patient while the patient makes no attempt whatsoever to improve the relationship. Instead, such patients spend all their time simply discharging their aggression onto the therapist. As Kernberg (1975) has portrayed it, "The experience of giving something good and receiving something bad in return, and the impossibility of correcting such experience through the usual means of dealing with reality, is a dramatic part of the [therapist's] work" (p. 61). It is believed that being the recipient of torture is one of the shaman's means of receiving status.

Well, isn't that what the therapist is for—to provide a safe and resilient container of the patient's affect, including his aggressivity? The patient's unleashing of hostility and rage, initially may serve—*to vindicate the unloved self.* [**This comes from the beleaguered literature of the self.**] Such aggression, however, has a preemptive reason for being: to establish and secure a relationship with the therapist (albeit a negative one). As Tarachow (1963) has pointed out, ultimately "the prospects of cure depend on the capacity for love and not on the capacity for aggression" (p. 103). The patient's expression of aggression is never to be construed as an end in itself, but as a step toward the capacity to express positive feelings as well. Just offer him greater investment in treatment.

TOO LOUD TO HEAR: AGGRESSION IS AN ATTEMPT TO DEFINE THE SELF, NOT TO RELATE

Some grumbling people intensely and chronically complain about their spouses or bosses, with whom they appear to be forever fighting. [**Are they injustice collectors?**] They bewail and bemoan their fretful fate, yet these same individuals would never leave the objects of their battles. Nor, for that matter, would they stop squawking and groaning, raging and fuming. I tend to point out this discrepancy to such individuals, only to face deaf ears and annoyance each time. As an alternative, I explore their unrevealed motivations for their "fight, but no flight" relationships. I recognize that they are deriving gratification from their discontented ties to others, unconsciously wanting these battles to continue. As Strean (1985) suggests, "A marital complaint is an unconscious wish" (p. 174), and the same may be said about therapeutic complaints.

Any attempts at trying to find a solution to end the unrest itself interferes with the maintenance of a necessary struggle of these patients. Such patients need to perpetuate conflict with their partners, because the latter objects are merely filling in for parental figures, with whom the original conflict perpetuated in the service of becoming. Behind every chronic aggression and complaint, every negativity, there is an unconscious wish to be validated, loved, and accepted. We tend to appreciate only the final and positively transformed version of the person. [**People see the finished photograph without realizing fully that its origin was negative.**]

SANITY À DEUX

> *Carolyn:* When I asked you, the other day, why don't you practice the way that you write, you got up, looked for a book on your shelves, and xeroxed a page for me. If I wondered whether you were unusual before, now I'm totally convinced. You're not who you are, if you ever were. And I don't know how I feel about it. I told two of my colleagues about it and showed them the poem that you gave me. Both said it must be a symptom of your countertransference, or you're simply getting organic.
>
> *Me:* Things that I have not seen, I now see.
> [**The Healer is always learning and evolving, without denying his past knowledge.**]
> [**Not** how do you feel to be in treatment with someone who your colleagues think cannot contain his counter-transference or is organic?, or what about the poem itself? or cite the last names of ten vice presidents of the United States.]
>
> *Carolyn:* I hope I will too, one day, but I must say that . . .

In describing the uncommon psychiatric techniques of Milton Erickson, Haley (1973) recalls the Ericksonian way of thinking—that if you oppose a patient's delusion, it will be like "trying to block a river; it will just go over and around you. Yet if [the person] *accepts* the force of the river and diverts it in a new direction, the force of the river will cut a new channel. For example, if a person seeks help for headaches that have no physical cause, Erickson will 'accept' the headache as he might hypnotic resistance. He will focus upon the need for a headache . . . to the point where the headache disappears" (pp. 24–25). Erickson would even accept the patient's delusions to divert the flow. The following is a creative example of how to grow within this context:

> When Erickson was on the staff of Worcester State Hospital, there was a young patient who called himself Jesus. He paraded around as the Messiah, wore a sheet draped around him, and attempted to impose Christianity on people. Erickson approached him on the hospital grounds and said, "I understand you have had experience as a carpenter?" The patient could only reply that he had. Erickson then involved the young man in a special project of building a bookcase and shifted him to productive labor. Such a transference sublimation, however, is only successful if the therapist remains involved. [**The solution resides in becoming part of the problem.**]

IN PRAISE OF SYMPTOMS

> *Carolyn:* The Oldie is definitely after my body. She invited me to dinner at her apartment. We'll have a candlelight dinner, she says, and that she makes a mean entrecote. Is this a double entendre or what? This also explains why she was so aggressive and hostile initially with me. She was trying to take down my defenses, and it worked. I got very submissive, at least in her presence. She's definitely an alpha female. And me? I'm sort of what the other sees. You realize I can't refuse the invitation, after all she's my supervisor, but I know for sure that she's going to move on to me. What? . . . What is that look?

Definitely not. I have no interest at all. I would rather sleep with a, with a . . . anything, though I should acknowledge that she must have once been a beautiful woman in her youth. She has this angular face, waspy cheekbones, straight white hair intertwined with blond-ish coloring. Stop that! I'm not as desperate as you think. Well, maybe I am desperate. I mean, what do you want? Should I just kill myself? My God. Can't you hear yourself: "She who tiptoes cannot stand, she who strides cannot walk!" Now you've got me totally paralyzed. Now I know why you must dislike me. You must see in me the totality of your failures.

Me: Also my successes.

[**The Healer is fair and generous.**]

[**Not yet** challenging her projection, **not** engaging again her sexual or otherwise attraction to an older woman/ mother she never had, waiting for her to get there—or her perception that I dislike her.]

Carolyn: Good for you! But do you appreciate that all these issues are generating more anxiety in me than I can tolerate? What if she is really sexually interested in me? You seem to be too casual about it. It isn't the gayness, though God knows that bothers me. She's terrifying to me. Look, I'm not paranoid. Even if you are paranoid, that doesn't mean that people aren't after you, as they say. You should really get rid of me. Look, I'm this anxious, paranoid, borderline woman. The Kohutian was smart for what he did. Who needs a crazy person like me?

A single symptom is like a stone causing ripples in the pond of the personality, of which the cause may have long since sunk beneath the surface, but leaves traces that spread out indefinitely. Therefore, the therapist must view the symptoms of the patient with developmental resonance. He must walk a tightrope between the patient's self-accusation and the accusation of others, or between depression/anxiety and delusions, between becoming the *target* of the patient's paranoia, and converting his projective mechanism to introspection. The exposure of oneself to oneself generates guilt, shame, and self-doubt. Therapists are familiar with the danger of the former, and they also worry too much about the latter. Of course, there is a possibility of generating self-accusations from this process if one is too successful, and ending up with a severely depressed patient. As Melanie Klein (1975) says, however, that is fine; in fact, such depression might be a sign of growth and maturation. In this regard, she says that there are two dispositions: paranoid/schizoid and depressive. In the former, the self is treated as an object, and symbols are things in themselves. This is a stage to pass through and an infant mode of experience. The depressive disposition is an adult mode of experience, and the self is treated as a subject. The goal of treatment is to move the patient from the paranoid/schizoid mode of experience to that of a depressive anxious one.

Biological underpinnings notwithstanding, delusions are misjudgments primarily based on projection. They are firmly maintained false beliefs that are contradicted by social reality. And it is not only the psychotics that have delusions. The distortions of reality by relatively healthy neurotics are, in fact, more recalcitrant and more common. To confront or interpret the content of such patients' delusions isn't that easy. As Shengold (1995) has pointed out, delusions and quasi-delusions are difficult to analyze because they are often not conscious. Rather, they tend to exist as unconscious, or at least as not responsibly acknowledged assumptions and associated affect (involving both promise and dread), which are disconnected from responsible consciousness. Moreover, one's delusions result in resistance to change in life, and comparably give rise to stubborn resistances by the patient in therapy. Yet, as Shengold further reminds us, delusions "are a universal and perhaps necessary burden. And healers of the psyche must be able to empathize with this in order to help their patients to be able in turn to empathize with themselves and to become responsible for, to *own*, this burden of delusion" (pp. 48–49). [**The mind best organizes itself not around its visible disorder, but around its invisible order, relying not on what is there, but on what is not there.**]

LOVE AT LAST SIGHT

Some people's first impression on others, including on the therapist, is negative. This is best portrayed in the comedienne Phyllis Diller's joke. She says, "I walked into a psychiatrist's office. The Doc took one look at me and said, 'Get under the couch.'" Of course, some people may look enchanting in a fleeting glimpse, with all the tender evanescence of love at first sight. But everybody in the long, last sight looks likable. This is the "love at last sight" that Walter Benjamin (1998) talked about. "Coming to know another person very intimately and active dislike are generally incompatible," says Anthony Storr (1979), "and the only patients I have continued to find unlikable are those I have not had time or opportunity to get to know well" (p. 60).

As a psychotherapist, should one like one's patient in order to be effective? I assume that it would help. But if the therapist dislikes the patient and can't quite dispel that feeling, he should try not to summarily dismiss him on that basis. In effect, the therapist may leave alone what he likes, but attempt to under-stand—and work with—what he doesn't. This means that he may need time to see whether he can at least sustain some commitment to the person qua person. As Theodore Dorpat (1977) says, "Feelings come and go; commitment endures" (p. 60).

The basic similarity or complementarity, including the communicative matching, between the two therapeutic members, may be significant, if they are to form a working partnership; this is what Berzins (1977) was talking about when he referred to "symmetrical matching variables" between therapist and patient that contribute to their compatibility. [**The therapist and the patient are each other's fate.**]

Some therapists have placed the greatest priority on the generic selection of appropriate candidates, including their ability to relate well to others, show flexibility, and have good motivation. Others rely on their own specific experiences. Previous experiences of therapeutic success with certain patients can play an important role because they reinforce a sense of mastery with particular persons or types. One of the important aspects of the therapist's expertise may well be the *implicit* selection of patients that one could work with most effectively. Very few therapists can and do work with the belligerent individuals who seem to detest everyone including the therapist. They are full of archaic aggression and destructive rage. Their hatred does not subside when their needs are met or their frustration has been allayed. Rather, for such people, "rage seeks revenge" (Baker and Baker 1987, p. 6). They must continue to destroy others whom they see as the source of their privation. When such persons are in therapy, the malignant process does not easily abate. Under these circumstances, therapy can become a way of life that is vengeful instead of reparative. To them, it is not necessarily for *validation*, but for *vindication*. Dealing with these aversive patients is, of course, an inevitable aspect of the field.

I have always maintained, nonetheless, that if you convey loving feelings toward the person, it can temper a hateful disposition, believing, like James Strachey (1934), that the not-hated patient will hate less. The thesis here is that the patient will gradually become aware of the contrast between the nature of his bad feelings, and those of the therapist who does not behave like the patient's internalized bad archaic objects. Eventually these patients will distinguish between past malevolent fantasy figures versus current benign real ones.

I thus search into the depths of myself to discover whether I am also a culprit, unwittingly contributing to a particular patient's rage at others by my disguised distaste for him or her. Did I identify with the aggressor or have an unconscious urge to retaliate? There is no question that hostile, resentful, and rageful persons do not make the most lovable patients. Alternatively, it is easy to care for pleasant, compliant, joyful, friendly patients. It is the former kind—the angry, the deprived, the depressed, the rebellious—who are really in need of care. As Eagle (1984) observed, "It is precisely the person deprived of love who is most conflicted about giving and receiving love" (p. 130). Yalom (1980) compassionately says, "The therapist cares *because* of these traits, since they reflect how much the individual needs to be cared for" (p. 408).

In fact, patients need empathy the most when they are least likely to receive it. And it is especially difficult to give love when you know you will receive the opposite. This is where the therapist who has a calling differs from another good therapist who has chosen a profession. When Kohut was asked by a young aspiring student, "Do you think I could be a therapist?" he responded, "I don't know—do you like people?" Especially the unlikable people, he could have added. [**Love is the only constituting medium.**]

————◆·◆·◆————

The mind is prestructured to love and to believe. Even its seeming hate is a desperate way of seeking love, and its rejection is a pleading way of yearning to believe.

10

Only Redemptive Relations Are Transformative

I am part of all that I have met.

—Alfred Lord Tennyson (*Ulysses*)

DIALECTICAL FAITH: IF YOU BELIEVE IN YOUR THERAPIST, YOU BELIEVE IN NOTHING ELSE

Carolyn: I don't think I'm getting any better and I don't know whether you could help. I don't mean just "you" as a person, but the psychotherapy. You are my fourth therapist, and I must say more or less you all do the same thing. In your case, much more less. You all clarify some issues, make some connection between my present behavior and my past unresolved conflicts, identify some patterns, you know that kind of stuff. I don't want to be ungrateful. You all have been supportive during my ordeals, but up to a certain point you are not my friend, and at the end of the session you are no longer involved with me; instead you are "Now, to the next patient." It's something, but as you said in connection with some men, "Something isn't always better than nothing." My therapy became a ritual that defines our relationship. I come up here, talk for fifty minutes, you intervene occasionally, then you say our time is up. It's only that *my* time is up, actually. And my complaint is not a form of manipulation, as you seem to believe.

Me: Then, this common frame of therapy needs to be expanded, altered, or dropped altogether.

[**For the Healer, there is no blame.**]

[**Not** explicitly seeking more of the negative transferential material; **not** explaining why we cannot be friends—you may lose a therapist; **not** focusing on her frustration of not having me as a friend, and anger at me for depriving her of that wish.]

Carolyn: This whole field of psychology—the discovery of self-knowledge, understanding the labyrinths of one's mind, defenses, sublimations—is only of interest to adolescents.

Me: Psychology means soul knowledge.

Carolyn: So what. I want to live a full life, a felt life, not an analyzed one. I don't want any of your frames. Do you . . .

The therapist doesn't give the patient what he wants, says Wright (1991), especially his "speechless want" (Merleau-Ponty's term). Rather, he helps him to know what it is that he wants, which is mostly the validation of the life as lived. In response to one of his patient's requests, Louis Fierman (1965) says, "It would be silly if I tried to make your life more interesting. The only thing I can try is to make you more interested in life" (p. 88). According to Schafer (1983), we provide a loving and lovable superego. Jerome Frank (1987) says we help patients to transform the meanings of their experiences, so that they feel better. Bugental (1987) says we help them to hurt better, that is, they will feel better by feeling worse. We provide a psychological cocoon, according to a self psychologist. As Tarachow (1963) observed, the primary temptation is to play mother, of course. Freud declared that the analysis transforms the neurotic suffering into ordinary misery. [**What does the therapist want?**]

Interestingly enough, Freud's wife (who was not an analyst) remarked about her husband that she always sought as much as possible to remove from his path the misery of everyday life. And consider how Menninger (1958) imagined psychotherapy might look to a man on Mars with a very powerful microscope: "Out of a mass of milling, struggling individuals, two of them—here and there—are engaged in a regularly discontinuous series of vis-à-vis meetings. They come together, both remaining relatively motionless; they apparently engage each other in a communication; they exchange something. A balance of some invisible kind is established, and the two separate" (p. 17). What is this invisible balance? It is the experience of being emotionally held to be unambivalently understood. Do we become someone who our patients can anchor on? Are we teachers, parent substitutes, or platonic friends? Are we simply offering hope by capitalizing on the silent language of psychotherapy, as Ernest Beier (1966) suggests, based on the half awareness that their life could be more gratifying than it is? The latter may well be true for the so-called worried well, who mostly need to talk to someone. Karl Menninger pointed out that people have been talking to each other for thousands of years, but the question he pondered was, How did it become worth $60 an hour? Of course, $60 was then. But people have not been listening to each other much anymore, if they ever were.

When the psychoanalyst Hans Sachs was asked, "Isn't what you analysts do exactly what a good friend does?"—rent a friend—he responded, "Ah, perhaps so, but where could you find such a friend?" The psychotherapy encounter may resemble other interpersonal relationships, but is truly different from all of them. More specifically, in psychotherapy the therapist and patient develop a communicative intimacy that does not exist elsewhere.

The therapist doesn't duplicate those relationships of everyday living. Jung called it a personal relationship within the impersonal framework. The role of the therapist is not to become a parent, teacher, friend, or lover, or to actually replace one, although he or she may symbolically become one or more of these. Rather, the therapist supplies another type of relatedness, which has no single prototype in real life. Therefore, the patient's relationship to the therapist is not in reality—although it often may be in fantasy—competitive with parenthood, friendship, or marriage per se; it has its own intimate dimensions. Every human being seems to have an infantile yearning for nurture, succor, and support, in short, to receive from others some semblance of affirmation, comfort, and consolation that constitutes early maternal supplies—a kind of associative narcissism that does not require reciprocation. Although the clinician, unlike the mother, is warned against giving "real" provisions to patients, he inevitably becomes a symbolic figure, and provides "symbolic realization" (Sechehaye 1951), which transcends material gifts. "It is not the apples themselves which count but the fact that it is the mother or her substitute who furnishes them" (p. 140). Wright (1991) says that the symbol does not refer directly to an object in the physical world, but to the concept of that object that is always transitional, "thrown together" for that specific phase of the development. He goes on to say that the transitional object is both a memorial to the lost unity with the object and an attempt to reinstate it in *effigia*.

In our best, we bring to our patients a special type of meaningful relationship that is a healing medium in and of itself. **[The healer is the healing medium.]**

WHEN THE THERAPIST BECOMES THERAPIST, THE PATIENT ARRIVES

Carolyn: I should have known better and never called you back, at the beginning. I told a colleague of mine about that consultation, and he laughed and said you must have one of those fringe psycho-theological listening perspectives. But you weren't a religious type. Before I came here the first time for a consultation, you told me that this was a consultation only, not to expect to be your patient, as you didn't have time for a new client. I think that was bullshit, you were checking me out—whether I'm too crazy or not, whether I'm suitable for psychotherapy. Then you gave me four months of waiting time just to save face. And what kind of consultation was that? You asked no question except the initial one, which I thought was bizarre. You said, "How have you failed yourself?" And after I poured out my heart to you, complaining about three therapists, of which one was totally silent—I assume to intensify the transference—and the other was dropping interpretations left and right, the third first took me in close and threw me out. You ended the consultation by quoting someone that "intense light and intense darkness are equally blinding." And you said, "Call me in four months." You didn't even question the validity of my exaggeration about these therapists. I left thinking that you didn't even have a psychological listening matrix, never mind the psychospiritual one, which I'm not sure what it is.

Me: A moving matrix?

[**The Healer always seeks agreement.**]

[**Not** indulging in her questioning my honesty and my bizarreness, or in her ongoing ambivalence.]

Carolyn: I couldn't tell, I still can't tell. I don't go for that new spiritual hocus-pocus anyway.

Me: Hoc est enim corpus meum?

Carolyn: What?

Me: The old one. "This is my body." The sacrament of the Eucharist, it's the doctrine of transubstantiation.

Carolyn: Well, I don't go for that either. You haven't any . . .

As Ernst Kris (1956) says, psychotherapy begins the moment the patient is given the therapist's name. Patients generally get attached to the person that they go to for consultation and begin to invest themselves emotionally, even though these sessions are presented "merely" as *pretreatment* meetings for assessment only. In addition, there is always the likelihood of the patient's feeling rejected at being referred to someone else by the consultant, even though he or she had been told from the beginning that this might be the case. (Likewise, certainly no therapist welcomes the client's dissatisfied announcement that he would like—or has already made an appointment for—a second opinion.) Given the absence of a perfect solution, I would say that one should always evaluate the patient with a psychotherapeutic stance, even though such an approach at the consultative stage may end up compromising the efficient gathering of data.

The consultation's starting point is the symptoms. It is more diagnostically oriented, as it seeks objective history and information about the life and problems of the patient. As the late Michael Franz Basch (1980) has pointed out, the technique of the initial interview is often based on the model of the medical anamnesis. Here the clinician, like the general practitioner, tries to get as complete a history as possible from the patient on the first visit. The patient's presenting complaints, the description of symptomatology, and its impact on his or her life is carefully explored, with the expectation that a useful pattern will emerge in order to make a suitable treatment referral or tentative treatment plan.

However, if the therapist is too structured and directive in his attempts to gather detailed information about the origins and manifestations of psychopathology, it may interfere with a more spontaneous unfolding of patient information. Unsolicited revelations may better inform the therapist of what is on the patient's mind. It would also serve as a gauge for how free the patient will be to reveal himself when given an unpressured opportunity to do so. Either way, the therapist qua consultant has a circumscribed, time-limited, and goal-oriented task that, by its very nature, can preclude emphasis on the therapist and patient's mutual relations.

By contrast, the therapy's starting point is more interpersonal and relationship-oriented. It must seek to establish and sustain an emotional bond that will facilitate the patient's motivation to remain in treatment. Beyond this, the type of relationship formed between therapist and patient, whether it is composed of a primitive selfobject transference or a nontransferential here-and-now encounter, provides a basic context from which specific strategies can emanate. For example, a genetic interpretation or direct confrontation that is feasible within the frustrated transference of a developmentally advanced individual may not be advisable for an already-regressed patient who needs a more realistic relationship, one that supplies greater support and succor. For such patients, it is not the nature of the interpretation but its empathic modulation that counts. Empathically modulated food giving, says Kohut, not the food itself, is important.

In actual practice, however, both aspects of the clinician as objective versus empathic, and as a real versus fantasied figure, are largely intertwined. Thus, the therapist's technique inevitably becomes inseparable from his or her relationship to the patient because, as in chess, in psychotherapy the therapist and patient influence one another continuously. The clinician's contribution to the treatment process is a dual one: it is both specific (i.e., technical) and nonspecific (i.e., interpersonal). As Gurman and Razin (1977) have put it, "It does not seem any wiser to proceed as though applying 'the right technique' is all we need to do any more than it does to pretend that there are not techniques to apply, but only 'a good relationship' to be offered" (p. xi). The technique is impossible without the relationship, and the relationship by itself would never be sufficient. Interestingly enough, though, the more constant the relationship, the more the technique fades into the background, and what remains is the mutual recognition of their common destiny, no matter how unrealistically formulated. [**Spiritual union is knowingly accepting the other's counterfeit coin.**]

FELT CONTRACT: THE MARKSMAN AIMS AT HIMSELF

> *Carolyn:* I should have asked you, at the beginning, very specifically, "Can you help me, and if so, how?" So it's my fault. In no other business do you enter into a transaction without some explicit understanding. Can you imagine leaving your broken watch with a watchmaker without asking whether he can fix it or not? Am I crazy, or is this whole world of psychotherapy like the emperor without clothes? You ought to be defining what you can deliver, and what you cannot, right?
>
> *Me:* You cannot get "ought" from an is!
> [**For the Healer there are no oughts.**]
> [**Not** how furious she is with me for not being able to deliver whatever she expected to be delivered, or how she feels finding me naked.]
>
> *Carolyn:* Would you please domesticate that statement. Did you learn that from Clinton? You know you used to be a good therapist, I'm told; now you're only a guru. But let me tell you, I'm not a groupie, I wouldn't stand for such . . .

Should a therapist have a carefully articulated verbal contract with the patient—and I don't mean simply the discussion of payment and schedule of sessions, but also the proposed goals, the treatment plan, and the very nature of the work? Redlich and Mollica (1976) suggested that a "fiduciary" approach, in which the patient places total trust in the professional's ability and willingness to make crucial decisions in another's behalf, is gradually being replaced by a more mutual "contractual" agreement. Similarly, Goldberg's (1977) exposition on the need for an equitable "therapeutic partnership" between client and clinician points out that such a collaboration is founded not only on the nature of their power distribution (that is, how *equal* it is), but on the degree to which it is made *explicit*.

I don't usually volunteer a detailed, overtly articulated contractual arrangement, and I never would think of offering a written agreement, as if I were a lawyer instead of a psychotherapist. However, I believe that the patient deserves to be informed, and certainly if the patient asks about relevant matters, I try to respond with contained lucidity. I'll establish some basic guidelines and answer any questions. I'll open up the subject for discussion and explore the patient's concerns and doubts, and especially his potential negative disposition. Although I certainly don't ever expect absolute closure on these matters, it will suffice in setting the stage and forging our relationship in relative synchrony in regard to what to expect from the treatment. As Guntrip (1971) says, the maximum benefit requires congruence between expectation and what actually occurs in treatment.

Even though an excess of openness on the part of the therapist may backfire through overexposure, and the therapist's transparency may be countertherapeutic, I agree with Orlinsky and Howard (1987), who state, "When properly implemented, the contract is essentially absorbed into the substance of therapeutic interventions and therapeutic bond, and simply fades into the background" (p. 15). Then the therapist's relationship to the patient becomes more felt than contracted as it is with one's self.

TRANSFERENTIAL FITNESS

Carolyn: I am not an object. How dare you use the term "object relation"? Even you are not an object. We are two objects relating to each other? One of the objects talks for two hours a week, and at the end of the month gives an object to the other object who pockets it and calls it a month. (Silent.) And you men are all alike. You just don't relate as emotional beings. My father was also like that. Concrete, get things done, move on. If I were to tell him details of something emotionally disturbing that occurred that day, he'd say, "All right, get to the point." "Dad," I would say, "I want to talk to you." "Didn't you right now?" he would reply. "No, I got lots of things to talk about." Instead of listening, he would grab me and kiss me on my neck. Dirty lech. Ah, what's the use? I see your eyes shifting, as if saying, "Get to the point." Well, the point is I need a woman therapist who can resonate my "subjective sense of self." Now how do you like this summary?

Me: I like it.

[**For the Healer honesty and self-confidence are related.**]

[**Not** "I wrote that article ten years ago, and I regret that I did." **Not** "It's a shorthand, a professional lingo, it's a bad idea." **Not** "Yet I wonder how much your anger at me is related to your father treating you like an object."]

Carolyn: You liked it? Yeah? Ha. Good. You know I wasn't implying that you're a dirty lech, too. You're quite OK there, kind of asexual, in fact. If you weren't married, I might have suspected you're gay. Not that that matters. You do have certain feminine traits, maybe it's your anima. Now that I think about it, down deep you're more like my mother than my father, kind of passive but more soothing than . . .

Skinner once told a story of two behaviorists who were making love. Afterward, one asked the other: "It was good for you, but how was it for me?" The threat in all relationships is being reduced to an object. Jean-Paul Sartre (1957) has said that at a certain point, the Other may look at him and make him an object of the Other's universe, suggestive of Martin Buber's (1937) objectifying type of connection, the "I–It" relationship. Such objectifying relation negates the other person, and obviously that is the worst sin a therapist can commit.

Freud even charmingly mind-twisted his strongest in-house opponent, Jung, into full compliance with this transferential listening perspective. Jung (1936b) recounts that encounter of his with Freud: "The enormous importance that Freud attached to the transference phenomenon became clear to me at our first personal meeting in 1907. After a conversation lasting many hours there came a pause. Suddenly he asked me out of the blue, 'And what do you think about the transference?' I replied with the deepest conviction that it was the alpha and omega of the analytical method, whereupon he said, 'Then you have grasped the main thing'" (p. 500). Even Freud's interest in attachment was in the service of promoting transference. "It remains the first aim of the treatment to attach [the patient] to it and to the person of the doctor," he said. Furthermore, "To ensure this, nothing need be done but to give [the patient] time. If one exhibits a serious interest in [the patient], carefully clears away the resistances that crop up at the beginning and avoids making certain mistakes, [the patient] will of himself form such an attachment and link the doctor up with one of the images of the people by whom he was accustomed to be treated with affection" (1913, p. 139).

In analytical perspective these two tasks, the transference and the attachment, are two indivisible parts of a whole. The therapist accomplishes this by fitting into what Freud calls the "transferential template" of the patient. The transference is a form of recognition, the reality that we give to our perceptions of the early phases of life—it is the most powerful form of attachment. The therapist induces attachment by listening to the patient's transference in light of a developmental perspective. At the same time, he neither reveals it, as it will bring sessions to an impasse, nor just renounces it, which will bring the sessions to a dead point, unless the therapist offers himself as a real relationship. While straddling between transference and attachment-inducing techniques, the therapist must also balance multiple other conflicting agenda. As Friedman (1988) says,

> The therapist has to have wishes, and he has to have a view that precludes wishes. He has to feel that he is observing history while he is in fact making it. He has to feel that he is watching something happen, although he is actually trying to bring it about. . . . He has to feel that things are determinate when they are up for grabs. He has to feel innocent but responsible. He has to feel that he is objective when he is biased, distant when close, impassive when needy. [p. 531]

[The only worthy offering is the serenity of believing.]

Dewald (1964) distinguishes the therapeutic relationship from other interpersonal relationships as follows:

> Most non-therapeutic relationships occur on a give-and-take basis in which . . . neither [participant] is permitted for long to exploit or claim exclusive attention to his own problems and desires. The psychotherapeutic situation, however, is different in that by mutual agreement . . . the major (if not exclusive) area of interest is the patient and his difficulties and problems. . . . The luxury of having someone listen to all that is said and treat it with regard, respect and interest is in itself a relatively unique phenomenon, and provides a significant gratification to the patient which is rarely offered in other human relationships. [pp. 179–180]

This "communicative intimacy" is a special kind of closeness that can go further than other professional or even personal relationships in its private revelations and breadth of emotions, without crossing the boundaries of verbal dialogue.

The therapeutic environment harkens back to the memory of the mother as a comforting, tension-easing other, an object for emotional and empathic holding as well as object constancy, succor, and support. Adler (1986) has further suggested that therapists, due to their own earlier experiences and personality needs, may be prone toward a parental mode of relating. In discussion of the attributes of the mother-therapist, Searles (1963) described that special recognition as the patient repeatedly staring at his face with absorbed wonderment. This mother–infant matrix is the most tempting form of therapeutic relationship. There "the therapist uses his own self to reflect or to resonate with the patient's self, not to interact with him as an object. In this sense, it is a narcissistic, mutually reflective relationship; it satisfies narcissistic needs, not appetitive or object relation ones" (Wright 1991, p. 312). Yet the best of such repeated filial ties may be more fantasied than real, more an expression of reverie than reality. They are to serve not the reconstruction of an old context, but rather the construction of new context.

Obviously, the parental bond—whether wishful or real, frustrating or gratifying—is not the only type of relationship that is established, either consciously or unconsciously, during treatment. Based on the degree of consolidation (i.e., primitive to advanced) of the patient's psychic apparatus, a narcissistic (pre-oedipal) or erotic (oedipal) transference may form. The psychotherapist, in turn, may modulate his or her activities in order to maintain some respective alliance with the patient. He may even alternate between different types of relatedness, in which archaic versus classical or selfobject versus object relationships can together compose a "figure and ground" configuration. They occur not only with different types of patient or psychopathology, but at different times with the same patient. Transferential templates have rigid as well as flexible dimensions.

Beyond that, there is no standard approach to fall back on. In this regard, Basch (1980) has said that he doesn't think it is necessary to insist that the therapist be neutral or paternal, or loving, or human, or anything else, because all relationships in human life are defined by their mutuality of function, including the therapeutic one. The psychodynamic situation, he contends, is merely a model of competent behavior. Perhaps one ingredient of this competence is flexibility, as recent research has borne out. Schacht's (1991) investigation of the nature of expertise in psychotherapy, for example, affirmed that experienced clinicians are both more disciplined as well as more improvisational in their therapeutic repertoires. They demonstrated greater innovation along with finer attention to the subtle nuances of the individual patient. For Wolf (1994), this has meant that the skilled practitioner must have a high tolerance of uncertainty in conjunction with a willingness to discard what does not work, along with a special openness to look again, to try something different, even if it doesn't precisely fit it with some preordained plan.

In the clinical situation, the nature of the patient–therapist relationship changes not only during the overall course of treatment, but from session to session, or even from moment to moment. This provides the corrective emotional experience that is not sought as such, but is an essential by-product of the therapeutic work. The therapist must be capable and informed enough to shift paradigms to emotionally meet the patient, wherever he or she is. With these shifting paradigms, the therapist synchronizes himself with the patient, not unlike engaging spokes of a cogwheel. The therapeutic technique evolves from such resonant presence, forming a mutual therapeutic context that can emulate all other transformative relationships. [**At its best, this uncommon intuneness is a normative matrix, emulating only itself.**]

REALITY OF REVERIE

> *Carolyn:* I wish I could get into your head for a little while, to
> see what you're really thinking about me, if you're all

there is. What am I to you? A child to help to grow up, a sick person to heal, an interesting research subject, an ordinary human relationship albeit handicapped, a mind to practice your ideas on, or someone through whom you're seeking your own salvation? Occasionally we have this gaze-to-gaze staring when I get a recognition of feeling, or a sound-to-sound overlap, a sense of familiarity, a period of quiet play, low-keyed but alert inactivity where I can go on being. Then you pull back as if you get scared or bored, turn blank and put me "out there" to observe, I become a "thing," a mental process, a collection of instincts, defenses, forces, determinants. Then I get anxious, feeling totally alone and abandoned, about to be fragmented, I beg you with my eyes to come back. You remain observant as if you intended to systematically generate disequilibrium in me, which I readily oblige and begin to talk nonsense. I can no longer hold any content in my mind, some of which I make up on the spot. Then I see you extending a verbal hand, saying something that promotes understanding as well as a feeling of being understood, a cognitive clarity. The more you present patterns of my life, present and past, the more I feel woven together. But this is like strain trauma, this is your "second individuation process." It's too slowly accruing.

Me: Gray in it.

[The Healer provides no shortcuts.]

[**Not** "these are all your childhood projection type of . . . ," **not** whether I am experienced as, or accused of, sadomasochistic behavior, **not** "how painful," how confusing kind of empathy.]

Carolyn: Though some people remain adolescent all their lives. I hope that won't be the case with me. So far I'm not all that convinced. Will I ever reach that exalted state of mind where "winner takes nothing"? You must like Hemingway. But what you don't know, because you're better glued internally, is that for lunatics like me the nothing is more real than nothing. That's Beckett, you name dropper!

Adult fantasies carry remnants of childhood realities, which jointly get projected to contemporary individuals in one's life. In a now-classic passage from his paper on the dynamics of transference, Freud (1912a) said, "This struggle between the doctor and the patient, between intellect and instinctual life, between understanding and seeking to act, is played out almost exclusively in the phenomena of transference" (p. 108). That means the whole thing is a kind of reverie. Strupp and colleagues' (1977) reformulation improved on Freud's paradigm and made the dynamics of the therapist's contribution to treatment more real, but no less calculating: "Psychotherapeutic change does not depend on the elucidation of historical antecedents but on the reliving and modification of historically meaningful patterns that come alive in the patient–therapist relationship in vivo" (p. 17). These are only two samples.

"A given paradigm in any field merely adumbrates new and unforeseen problems which it proves, in time, powerless to resolve and for which a new paradigm is invented," says Felperin (1985, p. 40). In psychotherapy, however, new paradigms get integrated with old ones. So, today's therapist straddles among them: among a transference relationship, a working alliance, a self-object relationship, and a real encounter; between attachment that is based on the distortions of past events, desires, or fantasies, and current real events; between an objective (i.e., dispassionate) attitude and an intersubjective (i.e., empathic) stance. Moreover, the clinician must remain poised between the opposing poles of reverie and reality. The conscious professional detachment and unconscious transferential attachment can complement or even augment one another. The clinician must both frustrate and gratify. Interpretations of transference, after all, tend to generate frustration, while the induction of empathic connection entails some gratification. Friedman (1988) recommends that, both conflict and deficit theorists "must disappoint the patient only enough to allow him to gratify the underlying needs" (p. 61), and it is the alternation of gratification and frustration that generates the building, or rebuilding, of the psychic structure. Psychotherapy attempts to improve the person's self-system and interpersonal patterns of behavior through the vehicle of a specialized interpersonal relationship. It is one that takes advantage of the basic human need for attachment to a benevolent caregiver as well as the capacity for learning in and through a human relationship. Moreover, because the adult patient, unlike the child, has the ability to reflect on his or her experience, this capacity is usually enlisted in the therapeutic learning process. In fact, as Strupp and colleagues (1977) further pointed out, "Some therapists believe that psychotherapy begins precisely at the point where a patient cannot profit from a good human relationship, and the professional is needed specifically by those persons who are chronically unable to seek out and profit from a good human relationship" (p. 9).

One important aspect of the relationship between the therapist and the patient resembles the earliest human dialectic between infant and mother at the most primitive level of the communication. The synchrony of reactive mood and the complementarity of independent space are required for such mutuality of therapist and patient engagement. Daniel Stern (1977) describes such mutuality in his book on the first relationship:

> If the infant shows a shift in direction of affect from positive to negative by suddenly changing from a smile to a sober face or grimace, the mother can once again respect and even reinforce this signal as a communication to ease off. Instead, the intrusive or controlling response would be for the caregiver to escalate dramatically the intensity, complexity, and richness of her behavioral display. If she does that, she will

usually succeed for an instant in refocusing the infant's attention on her. But in the immediately following instant the infant will show even greater signs of distress or unhappiness. [p. 115]

An effective interpretation, especially a transferential one, develops within a relatively stable therapeutic relationship. First, the patient must be anchored in relation with the therapist. Everyone needs a stable resting place before adventuring to explore the past. In an excerpt from the opening statement of Kierkegaard's (1938) 1843 journal, he said that life must be understood backwards but must be lived forwards, and that life could never be understood in time because one cannot locate the necessary resting-place from which to comprehend it backward. The therapist must provide a resting place for the patient to look backward. As Tarachow (1963) says, "We require the patient to abandon his infantile objects, and offer adult objects in exchange. *Without this incentive perhaps no treatment of any kind would be possible*" (p. 21). Without it, the patient feels alone, abandoned, and resistant to giving up his neuroses, however pathological they are. On the other hand, without interpretation the therapist remains an affectionate presence, perpetuating the patient's benign dependency. It may seem very safe and secure, but it does not foster exploration or insight. I think that this is the most common therapeutic error among the most well-meaning therapists. As Tarachow observed, "The principal temptation is to play the role of mother" (p. 14). [**Do we hide behind the mother's skirt?**] In the therapeutic context, even a "good-enough" mother may not be enough. [**The human quest is not for the lost, but for the found.**]

LOVE CONTAINER: PICKS HIS OWN POCKET

Carolyn: The bitch's new name now is Belle. Belle, still five letters. I really like her. Well, she's so damn likable, who wouldn't? So there. This beautiful thing; now now, that's just colloquial. I'm not making her an object. She fixes her dreamy blue eyes on me and says, "I think I love you." What? I thought something like that was coming, over the last few months. But for her to fall in love with me! No one would believe this if they witnessed the scene. What do I have, my God? All my life I've been waiting for someone like her to love me. She could have been a man. She's the most perfect being you could imagine. Pretty, smart, zestful, great sense of humor, sensual. While she was reciting her love for me I couldn't even hear what she was saying. All I was thinking about was to get up from my chair, kneel in front of her, and kiss her feet. I couldn't even move. My body and my mind were frozen. I brought you over my shoulder to give me strength and wisdom, "Have I done something to promote this?" "How do I get out of this?" "I can't handle this." "I shouldn't be a therapist." "Fuck the therapy, just jump her bones, get a job as an English teacher, live happily thereafter." "What if she leaves me?" Then I wonder whether you had had similar feelings about your patients. Noooo-no, not me obviously, I wish I wish. I wondered whether your young wife was once your patient. I thought it may just work with me and Belle. Then I heard you saying, "The therapist is she who survives her countertransferences." Well, it's easier saying than doing or being.

Me: Being right overrides "being."

[**For the Healer inner contentment requires doing no harm.**]

[The executioner of other therapists' loves?]

Carolyn: So, this isn't right? Whether real or not to the point that it overrides my being? Boy, where did you sharpen your guillotine?

Me: Did you know that the guillotine was invented by a piano maker?

Carolyn: I'll check that! So you're a nice kind of killer? Did you know this yourself, that in Nazi camps inmates played music to other inmates on their way to the gas chambers? How about that? At times you're suffocating me with your truths and your . . .

Yalom (1989) called the psychiatrist a "love executioner." We may have pleaded guilty to a lesser charge. Is it ever possible that genuine love could occur between therapist and patient, or is it always transferential and countertransferential, fraught with idealized fantasy and irrational desire—really meant for some past figure in one's life? Is falling in love in our control? I am reminded of Marlene Dietrich's famous refrain when she plaintively sang of her irrepressible, amorous experiences—that she couldn't help "falling in love again" and again. In the therapeutic context, we expect that the therapist can and must help it. In fact, never mind the falling in love, he cannot afford to display any strong emotions in therapy. [**Emotional self-continence?**] Hamlet, wrote Yeats, if worthy of his prominent part in the play, does not break up his lines in order to weep.

Activation of transference would lead to disturbances of the self, in the patient as well as in the therapist, especially when they mutually enter into a neurotic scenario. The proper mediating between the patient's narration and the therapist's interventions, says Spence (1982), is more often the product of the therapist's private store of associations than specific to the material in question. Thus it opens up the possibility of a subtle kind of countertransference. Commonly such countertransferences of the therapist, especially his countertransferential identifications, are contained in his neuroses. Yet, if compounded with the therapist's theoretically based attention, they lend themselves to serious potential mistakes in treatment because they can fuel the patient's transferences. [**Making itself felt through excesses.**] Two different types of countertransferential identification—concordant and complementary—have varying impact; in concordant identification, the therapist identifies with the corresponding part of the patient's psychic apparatus, whereas in complementary identification, the therapist identifies with the transference object of the patient. It is the latter that especially predisposes the clinician not only to intensify the patient's transference [**Is this an iatrogenic disorder?**], but also to act out the corresponding role assignment, as it shifts the drive aims from the self to the object.

There is also the reality of the immediate encounter between therapist and patient. No matter how well informed, mentally healthy, and professional the clinician is, he is still entering into a complex relationship as he undertakes another's treatment. As Yalom (1980) points out, as the therapist enters into the life of the patient, he or she not only is affected, but can be changed by the encounter. I believe that not enough attention is paid to the "love proper" that can develop between them. I'm not talking about the often sensationalized therapist–patient sexual intimacy and exploitation. Rather, I am referring to the kind of love that transpires between two ordinary (maybe extraordinary) people, which can also occur between therapist and patient. Incidentally, don't those intimate relationships in real life have the earlier remnants of transference? A statement by Freud (1912a) cannot be improved upon: "Transference love consists of new editions of old traces, but this is the essential character of every love" (p. 101).

The real danger is the therapist's narcissism taking over the process. Kovel (1991) states "A more radical narcissism arises when the self is both the object and the subject of desire. At this point we do not experience what has happened to desire; we feel, rather, the immediate pressure of desire forcing its way into self-consciousness. The subject-object unity of self cancels out desire experienced through external objects. What results is an experience seemingly closer to the navel of being and yet

profoundly antispiritual: desire in itself" (p. 143). Such a therapist, who is always in need of being loved by everyone, often finds
it difficult to maintain a neutral role. In Fliess's (1942) metaphor
of a teamaster, he says, the "therapist is supposed to savor his
wishes activated by the patient and spit them out like a wine
taster, rather than letting them go to his head like a drunk"
(p. 221).

Both patient and therapist may be in need of, as well as afraid
of, being loved by the other. The less the therapist experiences his
or her real feelings, recognizes, understands, and puts them to
therapeutic use, the more likely he'll allow countertransferential
contamination to occur. It is the therapist who *isn't* afraid of being
loved who, in turn, doesn't allow its being acted out with the
patient. If he can let himself feel, he may also contain it. But the
therapist must be on the lookout that his love is not a pathological
anchoring, and that his own neurosis is contained and not
consumed in his love for his patient. The worst contamination is
the reverse one—the therapist using the same containment in
his personal life, narcissistically alienated. [**The love contained
within the self is hollow. It picks the pocket of the lost.**]

A THEORETICAL LIFE: THE THERAPIST EXISTS
IN THE DISCOURSE OF OTHERS

> *Carolyn:* I thought you were quite unfair in the last session.
> You are uncharacteristically judgmental and prohibitive
> for a "spiritually endowed therapist," if I may add.
> Weren't you supposed to be equidistant from all that
> shit? Furthermore, how do you know for sure that her
> love for me is just transference and not for real? Because
> I'm unattractive? I mean, really, under the therapeutic
> skirt you're insulting me. The proof? I told my Belle that
> her feelings toward me were a common phenomenon
> between the patient and the therapist and is called

transference. She heard about it or read somewhere that you fall in love with your therapist. But she convincingly rejected the idea. She never felt that way toward anyone, male or female, and she had plenty of both. Let me tell you something: Life is not "a field of infinite substitutes," as you preach. That continental philosophy was aborted before it even landed in America. Here, the center arrests the play of substitution. In contrast to Nietzsche's Zarathustra, who comes down from the mountain and finds that he has come too early, you came to America too late. If you believe that only descent impregnates soul, then why take such a secular moralistic posture, on top of interpreting the whole thing as a transferential fake love and countertransferential real aggression?

Me: Binary straitjacket.

[**The Healer holds tight and leaves the other alone.**]

[**Not** yet "father-me" duplicitous superego interpretation, **not** my depriving her from acting out, never mind sanctioning it.]

Carolyn: If you take off your dubious theoretical lenses, you may see that things in life don't always fit into the textbook formulation, and you cannot present yourself as an arbiter of the human dilemma. You insist on the justifiability of your claim to know, even before the occurrence of the event. Does it occur to you at all that your personal and habitual assumptions from which you operate may be just epistemological knots for someone else?

Me: Yes, it does. I'm reminded of the story of three baseball umpires. The first umpire says, "I call 'em as they are." The second umpire says, "I call 'em as I see 'em." And third umpire says, "Until I call 'em, they ain't."

[**The Healer is modestly self-depreciative.**]

Carolyn: So, you're the embodiment of all three male pigs. That's why there are no female umpires. How could you give me this story as justification of your dissonance posture? I'm so agitated, I can't sleep, I can't eat, I'm confused and you're making it worse with your asinine ideas.

Me: First you raise dust and then complain that you cannot see.

[The Healer presents truths within the larger domain of human experiences.]

Carolyn: It's Berkeley again? Don't you have any empathic bones in your body? (Silent.) Speaking of bones, I had a horrible dream last night. Someone was chasing me with a big bone, hitting me on my head, on my shoulder. I would fall and get up, try to run, he would hit me again, and again. . . . it's a royal road to you, right? I don't want to hear that I'm only interested in a selfish road to my subjective experience. I thought I forgot the other details of the dream. Now it is coming back. Do you want to hear them? All right, I think it was . . .

What do you do when a patient declares his undying love for you? **[Don't shadow the patient with transferential interpretations.]** The therapist may be predisposed to the patient's enticement to fulfill his unconscious wish by playing a predetermined role in his life, for example, lover, mother, sadomasochistic partner, prophet, savior. Because of such temptation, Freud has urged the clinician to avoid acting a part, and Ferenczi (1928) encouraged the therapist to be content with practicing a humbler art of benign presence. There is an explicit caution here to the therapist against eliciting the patient's desires or seductions.

Nevertheless, an important distinction has to be made with regard to offering or reinforcing gratification versus preventing severe narcissistic injury to the patient. The therapist has to evaluate whether the patient is relating as an object (i.e., a separate entity) or as a selfobject (i.e., an extension of him- or herself). This is crucial because objects are what we selectively value for who they are, whereas selfobjects are indiscriminately valued for the emotional stability they provide. Due to this critical distinction, it has been emphasized that selfobject needs being met becomes more important than who meets them. The last thing that deficient patients can tolerate is rejection of their love by receiving an interpretation instead. Rather, the therapist has to provide containment and help the patient to gain the sense of security and selfhood needed for depriving interpretations. With this in mind, I make sure not to disturb the patient's sense of self, if that is being held together by my assigned role, even if it is a loved one.

If the patient is capable of real love and treating me as an independent object, which means that he or she has reached a relatively advanced stage of development, I will venture to make an interpretation. I still do it with caution, because no patient is immune from the possibility of narcissistic injury. At times I may remain silent, and sometimes I interpret the displacement of affect and its genetic nature, or the patient's defensive use of avoidance and resistance. At yet other times I induce the intensification of the transference to promote regression, with the hope of exploring original conflicts or the current conflicted relationship. The therapist's excessive technical proficiency, however, may deprive both himself and the patient of human immediacy. Furthermore, by retreating behind technique the clinician imposes himself on the patient within the false boundaries of a tactical and strategic role. Basing her book on Freud's (1937) view of psychoanalysis as an "impossible profession," Janet Malcolm (1981) said that there was only one way for the therapist to respond to the patient who had fallen in love with him—to simply ask to hear more about it. This approach, actually a stand, almost always is the safest, the most sanctioned, regardless of what is elicited or camouflaged by the patient.

HEAR HERE (AND NOW): "I ALWAYS WAKE UP,"
SAYS THE SLEEPY THERAPIST,
"WHEN THE PATIENT SAYS SOMETHING TO ME"

Carolyn: I feel this enormous vacuum in me. I don't enjoy my
work. I'm not all engaged with my friends. Nothing
much gives me pleasure. I'm not really clinically depressed, just lacking in joy: a zest deficiency. Maybe I
was wondering whether this is something new, or have
I always lacked the kind of enjoyment that some people
either have or say they do? I was always a mature kid, a
little too sober, too phobic, and too worried. My parents,
especially my mother, were themselves anxious people.
So many of the playful stuff, such as skiing, bicycling,
canoeing, were all forbidden. The fact that I had to wear
glasses at a very young age also contributed to my
reticence to be free and let go. I was always on guard. It's
no different now. I still do none of those "dangerous"
activities. I don't even dance or sing. So what is there to
be joyful about? I just dutifully carry on my life, in a sort
of dysphoric mood.

Me: You had a glimpse of euphoria last week, which I . . .

Carolyn: (Interrupts) No, that was an illusion of some sort.
Don't worry. I'm pre-wired to adapt to the indignities of
life. It was the unfamiliarity of the experience that threw
me off balance. As you pointed out, pooling of unfamil-
iar experiences with old and familiar ones makes the
former familiar. I did that. The end result was predes-
tined. My personal history could not have produced a
different end product. So, there's no reason to indulge
into self-pity, is there?

Me: Not even entitled to your pain and to tell me?
[**The Healer's aim is always to connect in the present.**]
[**Not** focusing on her exonerating me as charity or as

defense, **not** empathy for the lifelong deprivation of zest.]

Carolyn: Yes, I feel like I'm not entitled to burden you with such silly things. There are people out there with real serious problems who may need your help. But more acutely, I sense that by subjecting you to my unhappiness I may be making you unhappy. You can't stare at an abyss too long, you once said, without the abyss looking back at you. This was when I was a little too preoccupied with my hypochondriacal self and visiting lots of doctors. I also wonder whether I'm staring at my internal vacuum a little too much and that I may end up falling into it. Meanwhile, I'm not sure what I expect from you. If you listen to me silently, as you are right now, it's deafening, and when you say something, even if it's just verbal caressing, it's worse. What upsets me more is when you subtly invite me to go on or inquire as to what else happened and make empathic sounds with exclamations at the end, like "How awful!" "Unbelievable!" They always are either overshooting or undershooting, and I watch you watching my reactions to your statements, and then you keep making successive approximations until you find the precise feeling I might resonate with. It's so exhausting. I end up forgetting what was it that I was here for and zero in to our interactions as if that's supposed to be the most important matter. Incidentally, why did you just say that?

The time focus of the therapeutic observation is not on the patient's present life, or on his past, but on the moment, as Bion (1967a) suggests. The "analytical observation is concerned neither with what has happened nor with what is going to happen but with what 'is' happening" (p. 272). He is obviously emphasizing the need to focus on the patient–therapist relationship as it is transpiring in the here and now, which sometimes gets lost in the classical historically oriented stance. That is why a good therapist would be fully alert to hear any reference the patient may make about their relationship, however oblique. This doesn't mean that the therapist constantly makes self-referential interventions. May and his associates (1958) brought this position to its unsurprising extreme: "Beyond all considerations of unconscious determinism . . . the only thing that will grasp the patient, and in the long run make it possible [for the patient] to change, is to experience fully and deeply that [he/she] is doing precisely this to a real person . . . in this real moment" (p. 261).

I believe it is without the therapist doing something, and definitely not precisely. Therapeutic presence has the same elusiveness as the proverbial virtue of the good hostess: it is unnoticeable when it is there and becomes conspicuous only when it is absent.

EMOTIONAL DIALECTIC: THERAPIST AND PATIENT FIND THEMSELVES IN EACH OTHER

> We played music for you, but you didn't dance. We sang a funeral song, but you didn't show any sadness.
>
> —Matthew 11:17

Carolyn: At times I feel like you don't understand me at all. Maybe you don't treat people as sick as I am. You say things to me as if I'm a normal person and expect accordingly some sane responses. When I take you to some dark alleys, as you know borderlines do, I see that confused look on your face. You obviously have never been there. You may have been the author of your life. I've been living without any script, never mind having written it. So I look at you for a role identity and you look at me and shout, "Now act." I'm trying to figure out how to gain your peaceful deliberative resignation, and you keep suggesting that I should cultivate my capacity to suffer. I can't locate myself inside of time; you insist on "now." I'm trying to put up some temporary theoretical scaffolds to do the fixing of my self as a person and as a therapist, while you see them as polarizing; I want a full life, and you say even T. S. Eliot lived only partly; I tell you my "hows," and you ask why and again why; without being so explicit I search for my truth, you also want relevancy; I seek to answer the new questions, you question the old questions; I pour out my pain, you want to tap cheap emotions; I despair about my not being curable, which is an energizing pessimism for me, while you believe that the trip to Lourdes is never made in vain. You seem to be promoting the art of counterfeiting one's self. I've had it! You are Karasu and you think that I am always at Kairos.

Me: Kairos?

Carolyn: Ha! It's a fate. It means moments at which the person is ripe for profound change.

Me: Rumpelstiltskin.

Carolyn: What?

Me: Another fairy tale, in which the queen broke the wicked dwarf's power over her by guessing his name.

Carolyn: No. I'm not trying to break your power by describing you. It's just my constant fear of my otherness that you may be representing with a tacit knowledge, that I don't know how to get the depth of knowledge and I don't know how to go on with my shallow subjectivity . . .

All patients struggle with the sense of self, independent of their manifest reason for coming to treatment. Those therapists who are unaware of their own similar struggle could derail the therapy for a very long time. Storr (1979) tells of initiating a patient without such grounding: "My work really started with him when I made it clear to him that I recognized his nonexistence. He made the remark that over the years all the good work done with him had been futile because it had been done on the basis that he existed, whereas he had only existed falsely" (p. 137).

Self-knowledge depends on one's original misconstruction, and the knowledge of other depends on one's original loss. So, in therapy, through their reciprocal role investment—while the patient and the therapist confirm each other's role identity through mutual resonance—they seek to reconstruct, if not construct, their original loss. Just as the therapist's empathic understanding helps to "locate the missing self" (Havens 1986) of the patient, so the newly understood patient enhances the sense of self of the clinician. An interactive feedback phenomenon occurs in joint recognition of one another. From this dual process of affective identification, each member of the dyad forms symbolic representations of nascent aspects of the respective recipient's unacknowledged or unaffirmed selfhood. [**The patient finds out what the therapist knows, which is what the patient has always known: That is, no one is himself.**]

These complementary mirroring or identificatory processes simultaneously occur in psychotherapy. Wright (1991) describes a juxtaposing of two selves, or partial selves, that can give the illusion of oneness, at least temporarily, in which the therapist finds that part of himself seems to fit the patient. He depicts it as a matter of "*matching* an inner form of his own experience with something in the patient that resonates with that form" (p. 313). However, therapists should never lose complete sight of the recurring resonances, in which their internal experiences repeatedly reverberate from within and without, continually changing their selves.

We try to locate another on the observation platform of intersubjectivity, says Friedman (1988), "on the intersection of his horizon with ours. If we could not blend our own needs with an author's, we could not read books" (p. 430). We understand ourselves in the other's response. Therefore, part of the training of the psychotherapist must involve the cultivation and expansion of his "interactive repertoire" (Colarusso and Nemiroff 1981, p. 377). Psychotherapy is, and also should be, emotionally demanding of the therapist, says Storr, not only for the benefit of the patient, but for himself. Finding the other can also be both enhancing and healing to the therapist. Orlinsky and Howard (1987) believe that "therapists who approach their sessions in a self-attuned state are better able to be fully involved and empathically resonant with their patients" (p. 6). Yet whether and how the therapist should emotionally engage with the material and which way is more beneficial for the patient remains controversial. Here the field can learn something self-justifying from the world of art, wherein the actual opposition between two emotive theories is best summed up by contrasting a statement from Bach with one from the composer Ferruccio Busoni. The former said, "A musician cannot otherwise move people, but he can be moved himself," and always "conveys his feelings to them, and thus most readily moves them to sympathetic emotion." The latter stated: "Just as an artist, if he is to move his audience, must never be moved himself—lest he lose, at that moment, his mastery over the material—so the auditor who wants to get the full operatic effect must never regard it as real, if his artistic appreciation is not to be degraded to mere human sympathy" (Langer 1979, p. 223).

A complementary process, which is sometimes subtle and even unconscious, may also occur in which involvement in a therapeutic bond leaves the therapist in a state of enhanced self-relatedness. Unlike typical transferences and countertransference, I am referring here, rather, to feelings and affects that are displaced neither from the patient's nor from the therapist's past. This is a new by-product of their real encounter, in which the patient may affirm an inchoate aspect of the therapist. It is this reciprocal "human echo" (Kohut 1977) that enables the clinician to more fully recognize, or actualize, an otherwise latent aspect of self.

In one form of mutual relationship—reciprocal mirroring and self-reflection—the patient recruits the therapist to use his own self to resonate with the patient's self. Depending on the stability of the therapist, what occurs may constitute either a dual narcissistic bond or a healthy narcissism in the form of a mutually reflective relationship. The latter satisfies self-sustaining needs, rather than object relationship or appetitive needs of the former. In Wright's (1991) words:

> The therapeutic relationship is not . . . first and foremost an *object* relationship. The therapist is neither doing to the patient, nor, in the ordinary sense of the word, being done to. . . . He is there to put himself at the disposal of the patient—a parental function perhaps, but it is a knowing and understanding function, not an interrelating one. To make the contrast with an ordinary object relationship, we can say that the therapeutic relation is a self-to-self relationship. [p. 312]

When such deep connection is made separately by both parties involved, then the knowledge of the other becomes mutually effortless. We know best what we experience. In ultimate mutuality, the sender and the receiver virtually disappear.

CLOSE CONTACT WITHOUT GENERATING ANXIETY PROMOTES ATTACHMENT

Carolyn: Even though I see you only twice a week, I have you always in my mind as an anticipatory presence. It's a calming and exciting presence. Ironically it's more so outside of the sessions than in the sessions. I can ask things from you explicitly, if not loudly, when I'm not with you. The other day, after I made love to this guy, well actually after he fucked me, there was nothing in it for me, I just lay there looking at the ceiling and silently screaming your name, "Please help." It felt as good as having an orgasm. But here, first of all, I have to be on my toes all the time; you kind of overwhelm me. I can silently scream "Please help me, help me" and you seem not to get my subtle request to be supportive. I think it was Erikson who said, "A girl may tilt her head for a kiss, but it would spoil the situation for her to verbalize her wish." Our therapy occasionally resembles supervision, which is fine, but my evolution as a therapist seems to require continual extinction of my neurotic personality. If I object to the process, I fear you'll consider that a breach of philosophical decorum, and see my weightlessness. At times sessions are too metaphorical and I become an observer to two reasonably intelligent people's duet, without any . . . ah, ah . . .

Me: Normative order?

[The Healer is one who provides deliverance from the imprisonment of mind.]

Carolyn: Yeah.

Me: Of course, musical compositions are supposed to contain, ah, ah . . .

Carolyn: Syntactic ambiguities and densities.

Me: Thank you.

Carolyn: But, you see, I mean, this is like the Charge of the Light Brigade: "It is interesting, but it is not a war." You are overextending the context. Even the music has disambiguating keys. I came here unavoidably uninstructed, and became an ad hoc witness. Furthermore, I'm behaving the same way with my patients, which puzzles the hell out of them. The other day, as an answer to one of my patient's questions as to why he may be having the symptoms of premature ejaculation with his wife, I replied, "Well, your symptoms may be a way of dealing with her." This just came out of me, totally improvised on the spot. He was very impressed. "You're right," he said. "She makes me feel inferior." Again I blurted, "Without your consent?" He was totally shook up, as if a revelation just visited him. These are not reheated versions of your statements, as you know. I do that too, though. The other day . . .

Either by evoking soothing memories or by becoming a soothing introject, the therapist promotes attachment, but also dependency. The latter could be the precursor, but they are not the same. One grows out of dependency, but never out of attachment. "Separation individuation is a lifetime process," say Colarusso and Nemiroff (1981), "because of the inherent threat of loss in every stage of life" (p. 24). They go on to say that attachment protects one against such losses and consequences of adult developmental arrest. The therapist must induce attachment with the patient, which is an important, if not essential, ingredient of successful psychotherapy. Researchers and theoreticians have approached this subject of how to induce attachment from different angles, from the perspective of biological innate behavior, that is, the fetal voice, to that of psychological induction hypotheses, that is, frequency of contacts. Some have dealt with it at a deep level of affective empathy and still others on the surface of the communication, such as using undifferentiating language. In this regard, Havens (1986) says that the therapist must be highly attuned, almost rapt, when trying to get at the patient's inner feelings. Here "adjectival exclamations [such as "awful!" or "wonderful!"] accompany the attention like punctuation marks" (p. 44). But one must be careful with nuances. For example, he also notes that accented adjectives are patronizing when used deliberately, which sharply increases personal distance, rather than bringing patient and therapist closer.

Another effective way of establishing the closeness of communication with the patient is with reverse cognitive empathy. Instead of reaching out to experience the patient's feeling state, the therapist brings the patient nearer to himself by recruiting cognitive empathy from the patient. Some persons can elicit such empathy without realizing that they are doing so. Havens (1986) tells of a British prime minister who stammered and, at the climax of his speech, was unable to complete the final word he wanted; he was only able to say its first or second syllable. Nonetheless, "The entire House of Commons, caught in the momentum of the Prime Minister's point, would join him in a mighty chorus to conclude the thought" (pp. 104–105).

Of course, the therapist need not simulate a stammer to induce cognitive empathy—just incomplete sentences followed by silences would do it. The clinician need not complete the thought, but rather should explore whether the patient would join him in a particular concept. Thus, metaphorically, his silence is like the prime minister's stammer. It reflects the tentativeness of a concept by which the therapist may be implementing a cognitive dialectic, a counterpart to Havens's (1986) "emotional dialectic."

From imprinting research, we learn that the longer the exposure to an object, the stronger the attachment to that object. With most patients, however, other dynamic forces enter the picture and interfere with the natural occurrence of attachment by exposure. One solution is to interpret those dynamic forces that are prompting the patient to flee, while gaining time for exposure attachment to occur. The problem is the anxiety-producing nature of interpretations, the very tool of psychotherapy, which promotes independence but also, paradoxically, interferes with attachment. Moltz (1960), for example, has concluded that imprinting (attachment) to an object results from a young creature's associating the object with a state of low anxiety. Likewise, the therapist has to tailor interpretations so as not to generate excessive anxiety, that is, to keep it at a relatively minimal level, even if he has to compromise their exactness and/or completeness. The matter is even more difficult because we are dealing with adults whose imprintability had already ended as a result of imprinting, when they were young. When these patients encounter a therapist's anxiety-lowering behavior, they get quite confused. They do not believe the possibility of such a relationship until many unfailing, repetitive confirmations. This is like the congenitally blind who become sighted in adulthood—they experience the world as an optical chaos until they develop the ability to categorize, organize, and interpret visual stimuli.

Only the hopeless can be omnipotent enough to stand abandonment. Adult attachment has a certain illusionary quality. Therefore, as Theodor Reik (1952) recommended, the therapist doesn't need to do anything to promote it, he only "must do nothing to disturb it" (p. 112).

The most accepted view of providing an attachable context without generating anxiety is to become an emotional extension of the person (a selfobject), even though some subgroup of patients experience this as too intrusive. Kohut (1977) describes the selfobject as an archaic object that would be nothing more than the embodiment of a psychological function the patient's psyche couldn't yet perform for himself. This is a precarious process. Those who form selfobject transferences are incompletely separated and integrated, in a desperate search to make themselves whole in others, and respond with undue dependency. Others are doubtful that they will ever be found, and thus defensively reject the therapist's primitive selfobject offerings in order to avoid the repetition of the pain of the past. According to Edwards (1982), only when one is helpless can one be omnipotent enough to withstand abandonment.

The undesired quality of clinging dependency is an unavoidable, albeit necessary, phase prior to the development of attachment. Although the analogy is flawed, we know that rhesus monkeys cling to anyone or any object before discriminating the mother. Closer to home is Bowlby's (1969) observation of an infant's relation to his mother. He says that it is the mother figure who takes all the initiatives to keep contact, and the infant must distinguish this object from other persons before he can cling to her or move actively toward her. So, I see my role as therapist to make all the initiatives to establish contact with the patient, while waiting for him not only to distinguish me from others and recognize me as a dependable attachable object, but also to experience our commonality. [**Cultivation of the awareness of being irrevocably separated is a spiritual misprision.**]

————◆•◆•◆————

Only redemptive relationships are transformative. All other relationships are subordinate to the redemptive one. While the therapist sustains the knowledge that each individual has an entirely separate experience and developmental differentiation, the redeemer seeks to confirm the "secret evidence of common destiny" (Seguin 1965, p. 28). This redemption is not geared toward sins, but to the redemption from one's mind. There is no blame, no fault, no punishment, no forgiveness. It is the rescue of self from the self, emancipation from the confinement of human entanglements, and deliverance from the imprisonment of mind. Redemption expands away from the self, and evokes harmony with one's self and the universe. It is not normative, but transformative; it extracts meaning out of meaningless; it seeks communal undifferentiation. It augurs not knowledge, but *puzzlement*—it is an irreducible communion.

11

If You Understand the Whole,
You'll Understand the Parts

THERE ARE NO RULES, UNTIL YOU BREAK ONE

Carolyn: I asked the old bag, sorry, Oldie, what are the ten commandments of psychotherapy? She sent me almost a dissertation. I brought you a copy. But let me read it to you, actually it isn't that long.

1. Don't move when the patient is talking. (This she got from the old axiom of the theater, that you don't move when the other actor is talking.)
2. Don't use sincerity as a technique. (This one from George MacBeth on the poet Anne Sexton.)
3. Don't throw stones at a barren tree.
4. Defer forever the closure.
5. Unsay yourself.
6. Fall short, rather than long.
7. Don't offer an unsolicited unconscious hand.
8. Don't disturb people's neurotic equilibrium.
9. Hide through an elusive presence.

10. Only a mediocre therapist is at her best.

P.S. This is just a sample. There are another 10,000. If you're interested, just lie down.

I had no idea that Oldie had a sense of humor and depth. So I have a new name for her too: Goldie. Do you think in her P.S. she was inviting me to her analytical couch or to her bed? Anyhow, whether she meant those ten rules to be funny, they actually made sense to me. I mean, there must be so much to know. How could they let me loose on innocent people with so little knowledge? Even if no man is a good judge of her case, there are at times clear cases. I have to get more supervision.

Me: Knowledge has a relationship to the knower.

[**For the Healer a person is not what he knows.**]

[**Not yet** her fear and wish of sexual invitation of the supervisor; **not** exploring the genetic source of her sense of inadequacy, **not** empathy with her sense of being overwhelmed.]

Carolyn: I know, I know I've got to grow up fast, experience life more, do more, feel more or be differently. Once you mentioned that one acquires degrees of being, so it's an accumulative process. It isn't just more supervision, more books or even more patients to be gotten, but the phenomena that are to be experienced. Otherwise, what seems to be mastered remains insecure. Oh goodness, am I lecturing? Just a few minutes ago I was talking about feeling totally inadequate to the job, not even knowing the basic rules of the game, now I'm . . .

What Somerset Maugham (1949) said about writing a novel is also true for psychotherapy: There are three rules—unfortunately, no one knows what they are. But even if these rules were known and explicitly stated, they still would not serve their purpose: the formation of the therapist. In fact, the focus should not be on rules that the therapist must follow, but on the therapist as a person. The statement "Drivers should stop at red lights," says Fierman (1965), should be replaced by "Drivers should be persons who stop at red lights" (p. 160).

In his often-quoted chess game analogy to psychotherapeutic communication, Freud (1913) said, "Anyone who hopes to learn the noble game of chess from books will soon discover that only the openings and end-games admit of an exhaustive systematic presentation and that the infinite variety of moves which develop after the opening defy any such description. This gap in instruction can only be filled by a diligent study of games fought out by masters" (p. 123). (And now it's done by computer!) Freud was emphasizing the limitations of the rules that can be laid down for practice, that only the beginning and ending of psychotherapy can be taught; in between, you are on your own. If at first you don't succeed, you are running above average.

In psychotherapy training, you'll frequently encounter trainees who have gotten colloquially caught "between the devil and the deep blue sea." This problematic position invariably occurs because they are presented with a set of rigid rules to which they must adhere, compounded by a complete absence of guidance. Young clinicians are either given a straitjacket in the form of strict theoretical dogma of a single school, or totally left to their own unbridled devices in the name of spontaneity. These two roads to psychotherapeutic learning, whether less or more traveled, remain opposing paths for the novice therapist (and even, sometimes, for the teacher or supervisor).

If you agree with the stand that in psychotherapy the goal is not just to undo what is already there and malformed but to newly create what never existed, then the notion of having no preordained rules can possibly apply. In this context, Spence (1982) has suggested that if the therapist functions more as a pattern maker than a pattern finder, then we may be faced with a glaring omission of general or specific guidelines. There aren't many other trades or professions that have such a determined ambiguity. Some consider this a useful confusion, for a creative science. Kohut (1977) makes a heroic attempt to differentiate the creative science of psychotherapy from the absoluteness of belief systems. He searches for the roots of the truth that might generate rules of psychotherapy:

> All worthwhile theorizing is tentative, probing, provisional— [it] contains an element of playfulness. I am using the word *playfulness* advisedly to contrast the basic attitude of creative science from that of dogmatic religion. The world of dogmatic religion, i.e., the world of absolute values, is serious; and those who live in it are serious because their joyful search has ended—they have become defenders of the truth. The world of creative science, however, is inhabited by playful people who understand that the reality that surrounds them is essentially unknowable. Realizing that they can never get at "the" truth, only at analogizing approximations, they are satisfied to describe what they see from various points of view and to explain it as best they can in a variety of ways. [pp. 206–207]

If the psychotherapist who lives in such a forever-unfolding relativity finds himself beleaguered in the middle of *no* road, he must consider himself another therapeutic trailblazer and make a path by walking. [**One composes music by inspirations, not by rules. But the musician, first, must know the rules. If his inspirations break any of the rules, his audience will be exalted.**]

PHYLOGENETIC SELF-KNOWLEDGE

Carolyn: I really have no serviceable model of what it is to be a psychotherapist. Goldie plays an empathic mother and not that successfully, because underneath she wants to be a friend as well. I guess all mothers do that with their grown-up daughters. I wish I could be a fly on the wall of her office to see what she actually does with her patients. Two of the therapists I had seen before you tried to ground me basically in analytical theory. In their operating silences they expected total doctrinal compliance and, in return, promised an internal structure to my mind as a remedy to all my conflicts and deficits. I kind of got there . . . all right, I suffered from the lack of maternal love and excessive if not deviant paternal love, and I search for an affectionate love in older men; then the incestual nature of the relationship generates guilt, and I run to young women. As my father did, in identification with him I played with them a torturous game, as I cannot bring myself to consume the substitute. I end up being isolated, alone, disconnected, ungrounded, and hating everyone. I end up digesting my own empty shell. You . . . you think I should better unground myself by liberating myself from the tyranny of my mind. But there is nothing concrete that I can hang onto. Like in your book, you deconstruct and bury the map of your treasured reconstruction under an impossible path, with a lame excuse that you're trying to avoid any kind of reductive and premature synthesis. But is there any? I cannot treasure what I cannot find. Even if I wanted to, and appreciated the wish to emulate you as a professional ideal, there is no supporting literature, school, organization, no lecture to listen to, just a vague concept of becoming a soulful and spiritual being. But how? If it isn't "let there be insight," as the inescapable Freud urges in other therapies, what is it? Let there be *what*?

Me: The voices of inner contentment.

Carolyn: To listen to my inner voice?

Me: And no other.

[**Not** rehashing or correcting the understanding of herself; **not** her caricaturization of the dynamic formulation, thus hostility toward analyses, analysts, and all therapists, including me.]

Carolyn: You see, that's not enough. What if I'm delusional, with auditory hallucinations, trying to fit the external world into my mind, rather than the other way around? For so many years I am adaptively trying to do that. I cannot persuade myself that my entire life is a dialogue between me and me and occasionally with you. From that little, I'll invent a new paradigm, which you claim will help me to sail into calm waters. What if yours isn't anything more than a hint of a process of nonsystematic institutionalization of "transcendental subjectivity," a plausible and seductive retailing, like religion, a kind of secular theology? Having dispensed with "the fiction of objectivity" with a leap of faith in you, what if I find myself shipwrecked to my inner voice of soliloquy?

Me: You'll be changing your way of being wrong.

[**Not** any promise that "I'll always be there for you," or "We are in this together," **not** "Believe me, this is the way" assertions, **not** yet that she is frightened, with her inner voice that she may go crazy, **not** yet her doubts about me.]

Carolyn: I have a vague sense of what you're talking about. But I'm not sure whether that's a sense of familiarity from the literature or real life, or just my eagerness to pin things firmly in some place so that I'm coercing my own inner voice. Or is it your outer voice? I feel like sinning against reason, if I were to say I am the ultimate author. I don't need a belief system to be a good therapist, but a centering on the knowledge of man. If I'm going to belong to a sect, it should be a scientific one. I don't want a concept of psychotherapy that seems to do away with psychotherapy. It has taken . . .

A therapist never truly has the opportunity to carefully observe another therapist at work in vivo (in part due to issues of privacy and confidentiality). The few exceptions are perhaps some short-term therapies, or being occasionally privy to behind-the-screen training exercises. The latter are invariably "one-shot" scenarios, conducted either by a novice trainee, or, at the opposite end of the spectrum, by a seasoned "star" of the field. Both are less than perfect as role models for reproducing "real" treatment. Whereas the student is too inexperienced, the charismatic luminary often errs in a different direction, such as dazzling his or her eager audience with some special effects that cannot (and should not) be copied. In both instances, the recipients may be left to pick up the pieces. Even the most scrupulous supervision is indirect, working from notes or second-hand reports of sessions, and, nowadays, selected segments of sessions on videotape. The bottom line is: One never gets to witness the complete and unexpurgated experience of actual treatment by someone else.

If the therapist has undergone his or her own course of psychotherapy, that may be another way of experiencing a senior clinician's work. But it's not really the same, as one can't be a patient *and* a dispassionate observer at the same time. Anyhow, not many would emulate their own therapist, at least consciously, or identify with the ambivalent experience of having been analyzed, then transporting its impact onto their own future practice—learning by default. Although his response may seem extreme, Jeffrey Masson, in his book *Final Analysis* (1990), told his analyst: "Look, here is what your analysis has taught me. I have used it to know what *not to do*" (p. 83, italics mine).

Perhaps in the subjective study of intersubjectivity there is no learning by seeing alone, anyway. Learning psychotherapy may parallel the development—and the formation—of the individual therapist. This means that, in keeping with the biological evolutionary principle, professional as well as personal "ontogeny recapitulates phylogeny." But if the accumulated archives that represent the history of clinical literature (psychotherapy's phylogeny) are composed of deficient, abortive, or false selves (its ontogeny), one cannot then give birth to an authentic self.

ALL PERFECTIONS ARE INAUTHENTIC

Carolyn: After I got enough encouragements from Goldie, finally I confronted Belle today about her frequent cancellations, her coming late to sessions, her not paying my bills on time, and her acting out erotic transference. I told her that she was shortchanging her own treatment. It was very bad timing, because she brought me an expensive gift, I assume as an apology. Do you know what pashmana is? Well, I didn't know either. It's a kind of Kashmir goat wool apparently, but only from the neck, under the chin of the animal, the ultimate softness. A shawl from it costs thousands of dollars. Incidentally, this is an endangered species, so there was a lot of controversy about it. I didn't know that either. Look, I don't travel in those circles. Pashmana, mashmana, what do I know? Anyway, last evening I wore it to Goldie's supervision. I thought I was bringing first-hand material; she was flabbergasted. Obviously she knew it, the old bag, what that was and began tearing into me. She wanted to know how I could accept such an expensive gift. "And it wasn't even your birthday." I thought that was really funny. If it were my birthday, would that have been more acceptable? And how did the old goat know my birth date? Wait, it gets even funnier. Having been sufficiently punished, I went home only to realize that I left the shawl in her apartment. No, this doesn't even deserve any interpretation. I didn't call her about it later on and neither did she. I thought she took the pashmana and ran out of town. Anyhow, if I knew that it was such an expensive gift I would have definitely said something to Belle. But otherwise I don't make too much fuss about little gifts. I give my patients gifts also. Yes, it's all "countertransferentially contained." I don't want to hurt my patients. If I can't help them much is one thing, but I dread inflicting further pain on them, which I seemed to be inadvertently, or unconsciously, doing.

Me: Only the capacity to wound has the potential for healing. [**The Healer never draws emotional blood.**][**Not yet** to indulge into the sexual triangulation between the therapist, the patient, and the supervisor; **not yet** why she needed so much encouragement to confront the patient's behavior, the obvious timing—the patient must have given the gift at the beginning of the session (countertransferential aggression as a flight from the intimacy of the gift?)]

Carolyn: I can't take my shortcomings always to the point of good faith. Keeping a vigilant eye on my countertransference is necessary, but not sufficient. I don't know how one converts a good human relationship into a therapeutic one, even though I tell everyone that one need not be concerned with such technicality. "Psychotherapy is what psychotherapists do," I say, with a verbal sleight of hand. This is like Forster's arresting story of a young man who declares one day that he's a writer. That's very well, says his aunt, but what will you write about? "My dear Aunt," says the young man, "one doesn't write about something, one simply writes." That's only the outer dissolution as to my . . .

Therapists should not aspire to be perfect, but to be authentic—even if it means that their reactions to their patients exceed the well-known garden variety of countertransferences. At times such authentic imperfection would border on countertransferential neurosis, that is, the patient becomes excessively important in the therapist's life. Well, the transference is a matter of equal rights both on and behind the couch. Dewald (1964) elaborates:

> The emphasis must be on the therapist's willingness to accept the occurrence of counter-transference without undue guilt or shame, and on his honesty in self appraisal in attempting to identify and understand such reactions. As with the patient in treatment, the therapist must then attempt to use such newly gained understanding and awareness to change his reactions and behavior in the current situation. Unless the therapist is willing to face issues of psychological truth within himself, regardless how disturbing it may be, he is hardly in a position to request this from his patients. [p. 261]

Besides attendance and appropriate fee, all other demands of the therapist on the patient are countertransference driven, which the therapist must watch. It is believed that if one establishes an adequate fee, there is less temptation to desire other compensations from the patient. The therapist who is adequately paid for his services is less likely to need positive transference manifestations, gifts, and other tokens of love. The therapist should be straightforward about that compensation, that he is paid for his service.

As Sheldon Roth (1987) has further emphasized, "One's financial arrangements should not be presented to a patient as if they were motivated by the patient's therapeutic needs" (p. 249). Nor should they be influenced by the therapist's personal needs, for example, for love, gratitude, appreciation, praise, patient compliance, or dependency. All of these motives, if unexplored and perpetuated, are deemed to undermine the therapeutic endeavor.

Countertransferential demands on the part of the therapist tend to get intensified toward the termination of treatment, such as reducing the fee, and new justifications for continuing. The concept that the therapy never ends is intended to signal the therapist to maintain an appropriate distance from ex-patients who might need his or her help again in the future. The permission of natural friendship, never mind the sanction of a sexual or marital relationship after a period of termination, betrays the patient. Discussing what is left after the therapy is over, Freud (1937) said, "What remains of the transference may, indeed should, have the character of a cordial human relationship" (p. 213). I think that before and during treatment, as well as posttreatment, the therapist should maintain a cordial human relationship. What remains *after* the therapy has terminated is future potential therapy. Transferences and countertransferences never get completely resolved anyway. These enduring displacements (both the therapist's and patient's) are eventually simply integrated into patterns of living. They are unconsciously repeated patterns of relationship, thus parts of living that gradually lose their intensity along with everything else in one's life, as long as the therapist keeps his eyes fixed on his countertransferences. **[They say that fixing eyes on a stable point prevents sea sickness.]**

THERAPEUTIC MISALLIANCE

> *Carolyn:* I'm in real trouble. I got a call from Belle's mother, who wants to come to talk to me. "I don't think you're helping my daughter," she says. She's skipping classes and smoking cigarettes and marijuana. Did I know that she contracted genital herpes? Oh my! "No, I didn't. But I know that it's a lifelong problem, with child delivery complications!" I said I felt terrible and angry at Belle. Now it all makes sense. Bitch. I collected myself and asked her whether she had her daughter's permission to call me or visit me. Now she was furious. "My daughter is a minor. I have the full privilege and responsibility for her well-being. I initially agreed not to contact you

without her knowing, but look what this got us into. You don't even know that she's in trouble in every possible way. Have you ever seen her report card?" No, I didn't. Damn. She continued, "Incidentally, did you say to my daughter that I may be jealous of her relationship with my husband?" she asked. Oh shit. "Well, not exactly," I said. I told her, "You know, it's the kind of oedipal stuff that families go through, especially when the daughter is between the ages of 4 and 7. And you know she is still a little immature for her age!" Oh, fuck me! What am I saying? Finally I managed to promise her that I'll call her as soon as I discuss the matter with her daughter, and hung up. Boy! She must be some fucking mother. Total emotional annihilationist. So I saw Belle the following day. She was not only half an hour late, but in a rage: "Did you tell my mother that I was as immature as a 4-year-old?" "Listen," I said, "let me explain." "No," she replied, "you talk to my mother behind my back? Me, who mistrusts trusting. How can I talk to you about my problems if you're going to betray me, and lying on top of that. I never told you that my father loves me more than he loves my mother! How do you know that herpes is a permanent condition and that my kids will all be born blind? My doctor never told me anything like that." I just gave up. You know they're both right and I don't belong in this profession. I can hardly handle my own life. I should have been in the advertising business, or something like that, where being right or truthful or correct or healthy didn't register. Here I totally failed.

Me: What is crucial is your attitude toward it.

[**For the Healer the only pain insurance is possessing a passionate inner presence.**]

[**Not** to soothe her by trying to show her both mother's and daughter's distortions, **not** in interpreting how her unexplored anger toward her patient allowed her to act out; **not yet** that her permissiveness was a vicarious living through her patient.]

Carolyn: I know, I generalize. I'm so demoralized that I don't even want to get into your "anchoring in depth" stuff. Believe me, this isn't just a low self-esteem issue. I'm incompetent. Neurosis is not always a substitute for legitimate suffering. I'm actually suffering from the inadequacy, not from the sense of inadequacy. No matter how I try, I'm always back to myself, and there I find the intolerable abyss of myself yawn at my feet, myself with all its inner inquietude.

Me: And in the end you'll experience only yourself.

Carolyn: What? To experience the depths of my ignorance, on top of my "non-self."

Me: And bind yourself to yourself.

Carolyn: I cannot believe that you say things like that with a straight face. Yours and your colleague Yalom's failures have gone to your heads. He says, "If a way to the Better there be, it exacts a full look at the worst." You both believe in a veritable cult of suffering.

The therapist makes most common mistakes not when he is anxious or angry, but when he forgets that even in individual therapy there are more than two people in the room. As Peter Kramer (1989) says, "Individual therapy is family therapy with one person" (p. 164).

I sometimes receive unsolicited but significant information from the relatives of my patients—a spouse, parent, or child who has some concern about me, the patient, or the psychotherapy process. As a clinician who practices individual psychotherapy, I generally avoid contact with other parties, including family members. I do this primarily for reasons of protecting the integrity of the intersubjective field and of maintaining privacy and confidentiality (except, of course, in life-threatening situations).

Within this context, if my patients need couples therapy, I refer them to someone else.

Nevertheless, I occasionally accept a request to see someone who is intimately involved in the life of my patient, specifically to secure their cooperation in the treatment. I do this only with one proviso—the full consent of the patient. Before meeting with outside others or family members, I discuss with them the purpose and inform them that I will be disclosing the nature of our session to the patient. Usually, that displeases the family members and they leave relatively dissatisfied with the outcome of these meetings, which I generally consider a good gauge for measuring whether I have been at least relatively able to maintain my priority—the integrity of the individual treatment.

There are other counterproductive aspects of therapists' outside contacts, in particular two potential traps: treating relatives as patients, and, perhaps worse, recruiting them as cotherapist/informants. It seems that one or both of these susceptibilities is likely to occur not within an explicit special engagement with members of the family, but rather, through mismanagement of transference that has been extended beyond the boundaries of individual psychotherapy.

More specifically, there is a natural tendency to underestimate the family's needs and expectations of the encounter with the therapist of their relative. Most of the time I hope that these concerned parties will not compound the problem, that they themselves will be healthy and helpful. Very often, this is wishful thinking and family members have their own agenda. In any event, if you don't deliver what they want or need, you may not only lose their cooperation, but also find obstacles placed in your path. In difficult cases, I try to refer family members to another therapist. This doesn't have to be a serious problem if it is done gently.

Out of this potential entanglement of meeting with a family member can come a special complication that is quite serious—the relative divulging important information to me that I never received from the patient. In fact, the need to reveal some family secret, to "tattle" about the patient is frequently the motive, or ulterior motive, for wanting to meet with the therapist. Therefore, simply agreeing to see a spouse (or other family member) is like soliciting, or actually asking for personal revelations that would otherwise remain unknown. This is a no-win situation.

Agreeing to see someone as a primary patient doesn't mean being obliged to conduct couples therapy for each person who happens to have marital problems. Obviously, there are special criteria for family treatment and specific strategies for benefiting from the support of the spouse, the way that cognitive-behavioral therapy (CBT) and interpersonal therapy (IPT) do in the treatment of depression. In CBT, for example, the patient's spouse is utilized as an objective reporter, gathers data, and provides positive reinforcement for compliance with homework assignments.

On the other hand, if the role of the spouse is exaggerated in treatment, the therapist may end up giving an excessively burdensome message, such as the notion that patient and spouse are each other's keepers. Equally burdensome is IPT's implying a pathological role of the spouse in the patient's problems, for example, that the partner may produce depression as a concomitant or consequence of their marital difficulties. IPT may even imply that the marriage is the *cause* of depression, although this is not as witty, through equally irrational, as asserting that marriage is the cause of divorce.

The other reason I tend to avoid contact with a spouse is to maintain the patient's individuality. One's problems are never exclusively marital. Each person unwittingly repeats the past, and the selection of one's spouse is largely determined by earlier intrapsychic events. It then follows that ambivalence or discord in marriage may not be more than another expression, or recapitulation, of already existent internal struggles. These are best approached individually, insofar as the real source of marital conflicts involves each person's unconscious attempts to master his or her original family conflict, using current intimates as stand-ins.

I also think that there is a somewhat simpler and more relevant argument against seeing the spouse or other significant members of the patient's family. It has something to do with the exclusivity of the relationship between therapist and patient. This special connection requires the clinician's acceptance of the patient's subjective experiences exactly as he presents them, real and valid, whether they are complaints, recriminations, or resentments. Wright (1991) has described the dyadic relationship as one that can "freeze the recipient's subjectivity. The subject becomes no more or less than what the other sees" (p. 229). [**Is this good-enough otherhood?**]

The fidelity of this process must not be tempered by a third party's objectivity, or worse, subjectivity. Listening to any challenges of the patient's presentation would be perceived as interference, attempts at devaluing the justification of the patient's complaints. These contradictions, in turn, would only slow down the therapeutic process (even if they were true). In important ways, the marital couple may be mirrored in the therapist–patient pair. Thus, any attempt on the part of therapist to be empathic with the spouse, or even just to be objective, could compromise the development of a resonant and intersubjective dyadic bond. In such relations everything will be known that is worth knowing, and anything that a family member could bring will be totally expected. [**Only the echo contains the unexpected.**]

WIZARD OF ID

> *Carolyn:* I woke up in the middle of the night with a hellish dream. I was in a car, as a passenger. I don't know who was driving, but it was, I think, a man. I couldn't see his face. He was driving very fast, downhill with lots of curves, steep alleys. A few times we almost fell off the

cliff, but he seemed not too disturbed. I wanted to say, "Slow down, stop it," but no voice was coming out of me. I knew that we were going to crash any time soon because he kept speeding even more, and the roads were getting narrower and narrower. I was clutching my bag as if it were a safety instrument, and I must have been squeezing it hard because whatever was in it began to leak all over my lap and flooded down to the road and made it slippery. Now we were just gliding down. "We're going to die," I want to scream, but again no sound came out of my mouth. I woke up drenched in sweat. In the foul rag-and-bone shop of the heart, as Yeats would say, as much as I am terrified about where you might be taking me, I'm also obviously very excited to the point of flooding the road. Am I right or am I all wet as a result of my strenuous inwardness?

Me: The fruit is located at the end of the branch.

Carolyn: Is this one-downmanship? You mean, if I hang in there with you, I'll eventually get the fruit at the end of the road. Yours is more pedantic than my dream. How about this: The dream signifies my "inner bitch." I wet the floor and blame you for my slipping on it. Or what if the man in the driver's seat is my father or she is not a man but a woman, Old Bag Goldie, or Belle? I know that each story can easily become a self-legitimizing mental promiscuity. But to respond to my specific dream with a generalizing old saying has a dismissing quality of the dreamer. Weren't you supposed to individualize the dream material by using some symbolic code? Like if I dream about a spider, you would think that I'm saying something about my mother. From the general to the specific. Not the other way around. I don't think Jung meant that by his concept of collective unconscious. What you did derailed me totally from my focusing on the meaning of the dream for myself. If you're going to do that, you better be careful with your aphorism. You know there are "non-fruit" trees, and if you go to the end of their branches they'll break and you'll fall on your ass. Let's use another generalizing aphorism closer to home: "The interpretation of the dream changes the dream." What would that mean—don't interpret the dream? Or do, and have it change, or you keep interpreting as it changes? Is the dream interpretation terminable or interminable? And you get yourself a gravy train! Basically by generalizing my dream material, you're saying to me that I'm not that special or unique, that I'm unimportant and insignificant and my fears are irrelevant.

Me: In fact, you are very much a part of the whole and your fears are universal.

Though psychopharmacologists say dreams are more likely the result of strong cheeses than anything else, for most people dreams have always been events of great curiosity, mystery, and prophecy. Even Diogenes thought that we are more curious about the meaning of dreams than about things we see when awake. Night dreams and daydreams are Janus-faced; they are fallacious but also telling. They may be attempts at finding solutions to conflicts in one's present or past, or rehearsals of anticipated ones.

Psychotherapists took Freud's "Dreams are the royal road to the unconscious" a little too literally. They expect that the patient reports dreams. Most patients get frustrated if they cannot remember their dreams. They get more troubled by *not* being able to recall. This gets compounded not only by having disappointed the therapist, but also by being interpreted by him as having repressed the "unacceptable content." There starts a struggle, if not an impasse, between therapist and patient, not unlike the one between King Nebuchadnezzar and the psychics and astrologers—the therapists of their time. The king of Babylon, Nebuchadnezzar, during his second-year reign of Jerusalem had some dreams. He was troubled, but slept. The king sent for the magicians, psychics, sorcerers, and astrologers so that they could tell him what he had dreamed. So they came to the king.

The king said to them, "I had a dream and I'm troubled by it. I want to know what the dream was." They spoke to the king, "Your Majesty, may you live forever! Tell us the dream, and we'll interpret it for you." The king answered, "I mean what I said! If you don't tell me the dream and its meaning, you'll be torn limb from limb, and your houses will be turned into piles of rubble. But if you tell me the dream and its meaning, I will give you gifts, awards, and high honors. Now tell me the dream and its meaning."

Once more they said, "Your Majesty, tell us the dream and we'll tell you its meaning." The king replied, "I'm sure you're trying to buy some time because you know that I meant what I said. If you don't tell me the dream, you'll all receive the same punishment. You have agreed among yourselves to make up a phony explanation to give me, hoping that things will change. So tell me the dream. Then I'll know that you can explain its meaning" (God's Word 1995, p. 1105).

One needs not take King Nebuchadnezzar's story literally either. He simply wanted them to identify what may be bothering him at that time, which was obvious to everyone (i.e., famine, destruction). The stubborn psychics, however, most likely considered it a compromise to the integrity of their profession if they were to short-circuit their method. The king wanted someone to articulate his anxiety, and even comfort him. The psychics would have none of it. They were as dogmatic as some orthodox Freudians, who are more Freudian than Freud himself. They insisted that the king tell his dream before they would tell him its meaning. Most likely the king couldn't remember the content of the dream; he only experienced its horrifying affect.

The analysis of dreams may sometimes seem like a form of wizardry, in which the psychoanalyst has some secret code to each dream's symbols. The Talmud says that the dream is its own interpretation. All the modern therapist has to do when the patient is stuck with the problem of recollection is just to ask for the affect of the dream, not the content, and then to search his awake life for a corresponding context. Then the therapist will be given "high honors," positive relations, and will deserve the "gifts and awards"—a good hour.

Different psychotherapeutic schools have their own templates for dream analyses and for the messages they impart. A Freudian analyst may be looking for libidinal conflicts with a fixed symbolic code [**priapic preoccupation?**], while a Jungian analyst may identify archetypical patterns as harbingers, or guides, for the future [**the communal road to the unconscious**]. Therefore, what a patient actually dreams may itself be a product of therapeutic influence. Ehrenwald (1966) has referred to the general phenomenon of "doctrinal compliance" (i.e., accepting a therapist's belief as if it were fact and behaving in a way to verify it). This is exemplified in the remarkable observation by Calestro (1972) that patients in Freudian analysis reported forbidden dreams of oedipal passions, sexuality, and rivalry, whereas those in Jungian analysis had a different type of dark dream, about primordial archetypes, legendary spirits, and demons.

Some elements in another's dream seem so easy to understand. Even the patient at times will say, "Well, this is very obvious" or "How ridiculous that I dreamt about X; it's so transparent." But then there are the others with highly disguised material because of its unacceptability to the patient. Still other dream content is utterly undecipherable and, at least according to Lacan (1977), is not meant to be deciphered. He says that the interpretation of dreams is analogous to the decipherment of ancient pictographic script, such as Egyptian hieroglyphs. In both cases there are certain elements that are not intended to be interpreted (or read). Instead they are only designed to serve as "determinatives," that is, to be utilized to expressly establish some special meaning beyond themselves. [**Therefore, you'll understand the parts, if you understand the whole.**]

THE TEACHER OF SANITY: ONE REPAYS A THERAPIST BADLY, IF ONE ALWAYS REMAINS A PATIENT

One repays a teacher badly, if one always remains a student.

—Friedrich Nietzsche

Carolyn: I don't know whether I should stop seeing "Beau B." He's a bore—Beau "BB." Last weekend he made dinner for us in his apartment and invited another couple that we recently met. The guy works for an ad agency, and the woman for cable TV. Very lively, playful couple. BB is a very good cook. "Chef," sorry. He grilled Chilean bass over risotto. It was delicious. But he was otherwise a nonparticipant in the conversation. These poor people made every possible effort to engage him, to no avail. It was painful for me to watch. He's not absent. In reality, he isn't as uninteresting as he comes across, either. I mean, he is a college graduate, reads enough, successful, seems not anxious, so what the fuck is the matter with him? I think he's just too concrete. He's concretely present. That's it. The woman gamefully asked, "What book would you have with you if you were stranded on a desert island?" Her husband said, "The swimsuit issue of *Sports Illustrated*." Tongue in cheek, I gave Chesterton's reply: "A guide to shipbuilding." The Bore says, you cannot build a ship with a book, you should take tools, not the book. Mercifully, the phone rang. Their babysitter asked them to come home because their 4-year-old was vomiting.

After they left, I didn't want to talk to him. Just went to bed. He, totally unaware of my reaction, did the dishes, put the food away, came into the room quietly, and got under the covers and hugged my behind. I was playing dead. He began to rub my shoulder, which I love, and kissed my neck. I came alive. We had incredible sex. I actually had a vaginal orgasm with him, I mean during regular intercourse. Never happened with anyone else. Other guys either had to play with my clitoris or I had to do it myself. Anyway, the next thing I remember is a tray on the bed with freshly brewed coffee, toasted English muffins, and strawberry marmalade. He's a sweet man. He's loyal, I don't mean just sexually, and reliable, considerate, generous, potent, and hardworking. I'm not bored with him usually when we're alone, but when we're with other people he's just insufferable. So I really don't know what to do. I don't want to lose him. It isn't that there are guys beating down my door, as you know. But I don't want to be unfair to him either. He wants to get married and have a family. I love him, but I don't enjoy him. Does this make sense to you? Would it be a lie for me to marry him? If so, would I ever come to terms with my lie? And not torture both of us for the rest of our lives?

Me: Presence is not reciprocal.

[**Not** that she is ambivalent about the boyfriend; **not** the search for her ambivalence in early childhood; **not** whether this is a sexual orientation conflict. **Not** whether she fears commitment.]

Carolyn: You don't believe in mutual orgasm? Oh, I know that isn't what you mean. Oh, here's an example of concreteness, if there ever was one. This therapist asks his patients in couples treatment: "Do you have mutual orgasm?" The man replies, "No, we have Mutual of Omaha!" Ha, ha, ha. Especially these days everyone is more concerned about their insurance coverage than covering up. I know that in some areas I may be absent. He isn't a complaining type, but if he were he could say that I don't reciprocate as he may wish me to do. I return one out of three of his calls. When I'm reading I cannot

be talked to no matter what the subject is. Of course, I
don't cook or clean; I leave my clothes all over the
apartment, mostly on the floor. He actually collects and
neatly folds or hangs them up for me. Are you suggesting by your statement, "The presence isn't a reciprocal
thing," that I should marry him?

Me: You want to see a fully grown oak and are not content to
be shown an acorn instead.

[The Healer believes in the practice of patience.]

Carolyn: What are these tree analogies? Do you have any idea
how long it will take an acorn to become a fully grown
oak? Sorry, I don't mean it. Occasionally, I think it's
primarily with you that I become as concrete as BB is
with our friends. I think it's geared toward sobering us.

Me: From abstract drunkenness?

Carolyn: No, it's actually to tame your conceptual bewitchment. Maybe that's why BB behaves that way in the
company of the literate people—to tame their verbal
bewitchment. At times I wonder whether I bore you,
then I end up entertaining you by my stories, my
quotations from philosophy. Those are the moments I
know we're most engaged, the total opposite of what I
have with BB. But I doubt that you'll pick up my clothes
from the floor and wash the dishes. So am I saying . . .

The therapist must not only help the patient to increase his
capacity to suffer and enjoy, but also to learn. In fact, psychotherapy may be defined as a subtle form of education. Even Freud
(1910a) wrote, "You can, if you like, regard psychoanalytic
treatment as no more than a prolongation of education for the
purposes of overcoming the residues of childhood" (p. 48), the
kind of learning that increases differentiation. Unfortunately, at
times, the therapist carries this out too concretely, finding himself
unwilling or unable to resist the temptation to teach, give explicit
direction, or specific advice, either cognitive or behavioral guid-

ance. The possession of wisdom doesn't justify its dispensing, even outside of the sessions. Lord Chesterfield says the wisdom is like carrying a watch. Unless asked, you don't have to tell everybody what time it is.

No amount of advising a patient, counseling him or her, would do any good. "Advice is free," says Colby (1958, p. 12) (and "worth it"). What Johnson (1989) says about the semanticist is true for the therapist as well: "The after-dinner speaker's quaint specialist, who came to know more and more about less and less until he knew everything about nothing, serves well as a model of what a therapist is not. Ideally, a therapist comes to have fewer and fewer misconceptions about more and more things, until finally he no longer has any delusions about anything" (p. 169). Anyhow, independent of a therapist's agenda—if he should have any—the patient does not want to receive any instruction that may threaten the stabilizing adaptation he or she has managed to make, no matter how maladaptive it may seem to an outsider. Furthermore, should anyone give advice to a patient, that person acquires a feeling of superiority over the recipient, whether the advice is accepted or not. Furthermore, says Langs (1973), most patients respond to direct advice with some degree of mistrust. They feel manipulated, and wonder why the therapist's objectivity and neutrality have disappeared. They also get frightened of passive and submissive wishes in themselves. Beyond that, not only do we know that anything that is worth learning cannot be taught, but in the psychotherapeutic setting, as Chessick (1980) points out, resorting to an educational posture may represent an expression of therapeutic despair.

Psychotherapy at its best operates on the patient's experience, not on some existential or abstract experience. Even then, some patients will be receptive, and others resistant, depending on what method the therapist adopts. For rare individuals, being a patient is like studenthood—therefore they may have to be instructed. For some, it is like childhood—therefore, their needs must be taken care of. And for still others, it is a sort of loyal companionship to be reciprocated—therefore, their woes must be listened to without undue criticism. The therapist, at times, may have to be a surrogate parent (maternal or paternal), teacher, friend, or all of these. To help troubled persons adapt and actualize themselves, express authentic affect, lessen defenses, and correct distortions of reality, the practitioner may play many roles on the complex path to each patient's mental life.

It has been said that the mutual recognition between mother and infant may be the model of some of the most exalted encounters in life. The therapist–patient relationship is no exception. As Orlinsky and Howard (1987) emphasized, "The patient has to have a sense of self relatedness, that is, he/she being both the subject and object of experience. He should be able to be both an I and a me" (p. 6). As their therapists tend to move forward, such patients are able to delve deeply, while at the same time take a certain distance from themselves. They are considered the most promising patients. With the less developed or less desired patient, a therapist has to reach out—both metaphorically as well as realistically. [**Can we consider these as "step-patients"?**] Here the therapist has to reverse his preferred position, by meeting the unappealing or underdeveloped patient more than halfway. In short, to be truly therapeutic, the therapist must move closer to such patients. Yalom (1980) has traced this paradoxical process as follows: "I listen to a woman patient. She rambles on and on. She seems unattractive in every sense of the word—physically, intellectually, emotionally. She is irritating. She has many off-putting gestures. She is not talking to me; she is talking in front of me. . . . My thoughts wander. My head groans. What time is it? How much longer to go?" (p. 415). Yalom goes on to engage with himself (I-me engagement), realizing that whenever he thinks about how much time remains in the hour, he recognizes that this is a very telling event with critical implications. Alas, he knows what it means—"I am failing my patient."

Instead of being a setback, this realization should propel the clinician forward. Thus, like Yalom, the therapist does not stop there. He attempts to rectify, and reverse, the situation by trying to touch the patient with his thoughts, and further, to understand why he avoids her. He does so by asking himself not only how he as the recipient feels, but also how *she* feels. He thus ventures outside of himself to ask the following questions: What is her world like at this moment? How is she experiencing the hour? How is she experiencing me?

Yalom not only poses to the patient those very questions, but admits to the other how he experiences her. He tells her that he has felt distant from her for the last several minutes, and he wonders whether she too has had similar feelings. The two of them talk about that together and try to figure out why they lost contact with one another. This difficult and otherwise solitary experience soon becomes not a one-way or a two-way, but rather a three-way engagement—I, me, and you. Then a surprising thing happens: "Suddenly we are very close. *She is no longer unattractive* (italics mine). I have much compassion for her person, for what she is, for what she might yet be. The clock races; the hour ends too soon" (p. 415). [**Only direct experiences are self validating.**]

THE MIND CANNOT BEAR TOO MUCH REALITY

> *Carolyn:* It isn't totally ethical, but it isn't illegal either. I know a few therapists who married their patients. As to supervisors, you can't even figure that out. In your own school, two well-known training analysts, I mean *training analysts*, married their analysands.
>
> *Me:* Life requires widening rings, not narrowing.
> [**Not yet** are you delaying the decision about BB by wishing that that may be true for us, too?]
>
> *Carolyn:* This is a well-beaten path. Actually I would be scared to marry you. A long-distance and infrequent affair would be just right. Also I think my self-destructive traits have reasonably disappeared, wouldn't

you say so? You're married, much older than I am, you're
my therapist, and you've given me no hints that you're
available—a woman can tell, you know; a man seems to
have no clue—plus you didn't get where you got
without some restraints. I like Ayn Rand's statement that
facts cannot be altered by a wish, but they can destroy
the wisher. Furthermore, what have I to offer to you
anyway? (Long silence.)

Me: Hmm.

[**The Healer experiences the patient's painful unveil-
ing.**]

Carolyn: Are you upset about my delirium of desire? You're
never so silent for so long. Where did your deeply
consoling intelligence go? My love for you is just the
means of entry into a profound relatedness. It isn't
intended to be a transgression, unless, of course, you're
affected in a way that I don't understand. Well, *Fiat
Mihi,** man.

Me: The divine relatedness may be an epiphany, rather than
an understanding.

For Wright (1991), uninterpreted transference is a form of
living within the pattern or symbol, a means of perpetuating a
relationship with the original object that has been lost. Interpreting the transference is a way of moving the person out of a lived
relationship to an external position where the pattern can be seen
and disengaged from the lived structure, to create a representatial
symbol. Interpretation is also a means to an end, uttered in the
expectation that it will lead to additional clinical material. It is like
a metaphor, creating the world afresh. Its truth lies more in the
present and future than in the past; that is, it may become true for

---

*The Virgin Mary says to the Angel, "Let it happen to me, even though
I don't understand," in response to the Angel's demands of faith that she be
pregnant with a divine child.

the first time just by being said. There lies the most dangerous potential of interpretation, especially since interpretations tend to favor the id, which arises from the biological furnace of the body, therefore encouraging the patient to act out.

There are other not as dangerous, but equally harmful, aspects of interpretation. Pine (1990) has warned against interpreting defects and deficiencies, because "interpretations that make the patient see . . . defects in the subjective self (low esteem, shaky boundaries, discontinuity) pose the danger of rubbing salt in wounds or of eliminating hope or of merely causing pain" (p. 250). Although interpretations foster differentiation, they can also frustrate the unprepared. This is so to the extent that they necessarily rob patients of their childhood illusions, which have been formed as armor against harsh reality. This is why all interpretations may be construed as deprivations, as Tarachow (1963) has suggested.

Wile (1984) says that interpretations often have a blaming or pejorative quality, whether direct or veiled. At times they are simply aggressive, if not retaliative. According to Strupp's (1960) research on the nature of the psychotherapist's contribution to treatment, it is surprising how many respondents, and not merely inexperienced ones, reacted with retaliative responses to their patient's anger, hostility, or demandingness. They tended to punish, to moralize with interpretation.

There are few cautions that a therapist can take in interpreting in order to be useful, at least not traumatic. For example, technically they must be given sparingly and stay close to the patient's current understanding, in order to be assimilated as experience slowly and over a period of time. Interpretation is not like jazz or bananas, meant to be consumed on the spot, says Kramer (1989). Rather, interpretations are to be used to build on each other. This is reminiscent of Frieda Fromm-Reichmann's (1950) famous dictum that in order to come to terms with a troubled past, what is effective in therapy is that patients *experience* the therapy as a helpful and constructive human relationship, not as an interpretation of how and why they became the kind of people they are.

More importantly, the accumulative integrity of the interpretive process requires equally a cumulative effect of this human relationship, as in all other human relations. Therefore, I avoid interpretation in the early stages of treatment, or I begin with "incomplete" or "inexact" interpretations that dilute interpretive impact, either by utilizing only a small or superficial part of the clinical material, or by deliberately offering a temporary substitute for the dangerous and intolerable complete truth. "Humankind cannot bear very much reality," says T. S. Eliot in *Murder in the Cathedral*, especially the one who is already traumatized with other external realities. I wait for some sign of the consolidation of my connection to the patient. One of the early signals is the emergence of a kind of private vocabulary between us. Once a deeply engaged bond has been established, I worry less about the alienating or depriving effect of any interpretation. [**Both speech and silence can transgress.**]

LOOK AT THE SAME THINGS AGAIN AND AGAIN, UNTIL THEY BEGIN TO SPEAK

> *Carolyn:* From a few questions that you asked and statements you've made, I have a feeling that you want to marry me off to BB. Are you a member of WAM? According to Betty Friedan (1963), this is a school created by dead white men. It stands for wanting women to be "Wives and Mothers." Unless you're a little tempted, thus off with the temptation, or worried about my relations with Belle. I can't tell. Because you don't ask much about her or women at large, and I don't volunteer, either. I think you're a little embarrassed by my explicit sexual recitations. I restrain myself from talking about my imagina-

tion so as not to make you uncomfortable. The other day you asked whether it's because of you that I'm not marrying BB. It isn't just the marriage. I'm not content being with him because of you, if you want the truth. Storr writes about how the imagination robbed man of contentment. The more I'm conscious of you, the less content I am. My consciousness and unconsciousness both escaped their origins.

Me: Conscious means "a knowing together."

Carolyn: Well, it's a consolation prize, but thank you. The fact that you're also learning by being with me gives me enormous courage to co-author my life. I have, right now, a "helper's high." OK, now I can talk easily about women. First, let me just preface it by saying that regardless of how I feel toward women, I'm still going to get married and have a husband and children. That has nothing to do with the fact that I really, truly enjoy being with other women. I don't mean just sexually, I like men also. But I love being in women's company, talking with them, shopping together, and eating together. I never get tired of being with women. I am more myself with them than with men, as if the female interpersonal synchrony generates self-synchrony. For me, you're the only man I've felt the same way about. I know so little about you, but just by being with you, or even thinking about you, I feel attuned to myself. You occasionally disturb that by one of your heightened self-decenteredness remarks, which manifest in variations of intuitive dissonance. Then other times you mutter something without any emphasis, which pulls me into a drunk satellite existence toward you. Like the other day when I asked, "How do I know whether I love BB?" you quoted Nietzsche, something about life "from love of man, one occasionally embraces someone at random." That day I felt like

I loved everyone. My psychic inertia disappeared, I was full of ideas, interests, energy, and tolerance. . . . Sorry, let me get back to the girls, I mean women, ah girls . . .

Some contend that a therapist's questions are a type of therapeutic intervention in and of themselves; they can act to open space for client explanations and possibilities previously restrained. In this way, according to White and Epston (1990), questions if posed with a communicative synchrony and intimacy, may serve to recruit, liberate, and even circulate alternative knowledge that would have been otherwise inaccessible. For Freedman and Combs (1993), they are thus a form of invitation—which, of course, the patient can conceivably accept or decline, or be surprised by.

However, even the most seemingly tactful queries can represent a form of uninvited interrogation, or even resemble an inquisition because of the natural reluctance to face the truth. The therapist's intent is what distinguishes a therapeutic interview from other interviews. It taps the unconscious. Due to the patient's ambivalence about answering, these efforts at gathering guarded information can easily produce unauthentic answers. Such problematic responses are largely attributed to the fact that direct inquiries reawaken the repressed memories residing behind all of the questions that could not be answered before, because the true responses were too disturbing, dangerous, or shameful to acknowledge. Thus, the clinician may compound the problem of needing to understand the patient by the very act of trying to solicit information, instead of simply focusing on the patient's spontaneous offering. Freud (1914) urged the therapist to look at the same things again and again, until they themselves begin to speak.

Others caution the therapist, for different reasons, against actively questioning the patient and incurring the undesirable side effects of the interview format. The major concern here is not the issue of resistance to inquiry; rather, it relates to an excessive *expectation* on the part of the patient—that once all the presumed pieces of information asked for have been amassed, the clinician will come up with some useful, even "perfect" solution.

All questions posed by the therapist are inherently restrictive. They are bound by each respective clinician's own set of cultural, contextual, and theoretical constraints, which in turn involve his or her particular personal, political, and professional beliefs. Every system of knowledge simultaneously involves systems of power and rhetoric, including the socially supported value systems that reside behind the clinician's questions. Thus, according to Foucault (1984), all expressions of therapist language, as well as the practices and techniques of these expressions, are attempts to rhetorically persuade the listener of something that is based on the clinician's culturally influenced knowledge system. As Madigan (1993) concluded, "Questions are then never viewed as *rhetorically liberated*, but rather as evidence of what kind of rhetoric the speaker is choosing to bring forth and for what purpose" (p. 222).

What's more, since all therapeutic conversations, narratives, or structured speech acts are necessarily restrained (Ricoeur 1983), it has been suggested that the linguistic structure of the question itself can also act to oppress and obstruct the search for solutions. This is especially applicable to the issue of repressed material in psychotherapy. It raises Tyler's (1990) concern that the very question a therapist selects to propose may paradoxically place an emphasis on questions *not* asked.

The purpose of getting to know patients is geared toward understanding their ways of being special. But this cannot be learned from superficial, structured, or forced forms of question-and-answer. Technically, the interview approach is faulty because its modus operandi is interrogation. One does not get to know the patient via specific information received through direct investigation, but rather by a sentient waiting that follows the lead of the patient. It is not steered by the curiosity or insistence of the therapist. Furthermore, as Arieti (1974) has said, the patient "should leave the session with the feeling that he has been given something, not with the feeling that something, even diagnostic information, has been taken from him" (pp. 550–551).

Anna Freud has made a comparison between the eyes of a preverbal child in the observation of events around him and the psychoanalytical eye, letting itself be led, whatever the phenomenological consequences. Similarly, such sensitivity also meant the special use of a different sensory modality, the analyst's inner experience aided by additional auditory equipment—Reik's "listening with a third ear." [**The way of non-inquiry: The contemplation of the other reveals the self.**]

TO UNDERSTAND SOMETHING, ONE MUST ALREADY BE FAMILIAR WITH IT

Carolyn: Then the question is, If I enjoy women so much, why don't I just declare myself a lesbian, find a partner, and settle down? I think I was closer to that conclusion before I began therapy with you. Don't ask me why.

Me: A fake question?

Carolyn: Yeah, I guess so, but it may also be a fake content, because whenever I get too close to a woman, I manage to kill the relationship.

Me: Aborting the substitute?

Carolyn: Not sure. Well, here you may be giving yourself a tad too much significance. You're also spoiling the story with your interpretation. What's the matter with you? You're behaving like a genuine imitation therapist. Stop it . . . OK. Where was I? God, you got me totally off track. You know I didn't get a parentectomy for nothing. They were very intrusive people. Maybe I need to have a therapistectomy as well. You don't have to do or to say something, just be there. Oh, I get it, you're trying to stop me from talking about women, right? Is it again the

discomfort of the subject for you, or do you think that if
I talk about my relations with women, it would fan my
neuroses? One way that Laing advises therapists is not
to let a schizophrenic talk to them. He thinks it
aggravates their psychoses, and hear this: it's like giving
a laxative to someone with diarrhea. As in a bone
fracture, he says you've got to immobilize the fractured
minds. So that's what's going on here. You are immobi-
lizing my mind. Come on, yes? . . . Now you seem to
be in a frenetic passivity.

Me: Follow *me* not, but you.

Carolyn: Chicken! I thought by following you I'll experience
the dilemma of life, as lived once by you and processed
over time. Your false modesty isn't becoming. You know
everything, at least about me, you just don't share it
under the guise of the idea that knowledge is infinite.
There is a cap on the knowledge about the human mind.
After all, this isn't astrophysics, and you've reached
where one can on the subject.

Me: George Leonard tells a story of a man with a black belt in
Judo, who asked that he be buried in his white belt so
that he could go on learning.

Carolyn: So learn, but let me have at least a little trickle-down
wisdom. I don't know any other way to become. My
relationship with women is a significant dimension of
my life, about which you ask no questions. If I were in
treatment with a woman therapist, especially a lesbian
one, that subject would have been the main topic. You,
at best, treat it as a counterfeit subject, that I'm this
liberal heterosexual chick, who is also extracting some
perverse pleasures out of gayness. On the other hand,
just to be fair to you, you don't ask that many questions
about any other subject either. Why? You're definitely a
curious person—are you afraid of engaging? Afraid that
if you ask questions, I may reply, or worse, I'll ask

questions in return to you? For example, have *you* ever
had any homosexual relations?

Me: No.

[**For the Healer man needs to be taken in.**]

[**Not** silence; **not** why such a question; **not yet** "If I
didn't have, do you feel I wouldn't understand you?"]

Carolyn: It shows, so you may be homophobic. Ha! This is
where the deer pounces on the lion. Do you have latent
homosexual dreams?

Me: The pot drips only what's in it.

Carolyn: So you're not going to tell me what's in the pot. I
should just wait and watch what might drip from it.
You're a sad sack. Sadness is about your untapped
homosexuality. You are a homotriste.

Me: A homotriste is someone who cries after orgasm.

Carolyn: You're kidding? Thank you. So I've been misusing
that term. Goodness, how embarrassing. I guess a little
Latin is dangerous. Well, a lot of it may not be any
better. I better request that I get buried with my M.A.
degree so that I'll keep learning. . . . I don't know how
we got here, but let me reassure you that we shall not
cease from exploration.

Me: And at the end of all our exploring . . .

Carolyn: You son of a bitch! "We will arrive where we
started."

Me: And . . . ?

Carolyn: And know the self for the first time. Now that we
butchered Eliot . . .

Don't say to the patient, "Can you?" because that implies that
maybe he cannot, suggests Masterson (1983). Equally, *why* must
we always ask *why*? Despite—or perhaps because of—its unparalleled power in the minds of children and therapists alike, we
need an alternative to that classic interrogative word. It may
sound very simple because it is only a single syllable. At the same

time, however, it is too emotionally loaded. While conferring with the patient and trying to comprehend his motivation, I have become totally disenchanted with the word. Therefore, I find myself increasingly disinclined to start any sentence with such a seemingly useful word. After all, in the therapist's task to explore the psyche of another, it's so tempting to ask: Why are you late? Why do you think you dreamt about your mother? Why did you feel angry at your husband? Why don't you like your son's new girlfriend? Why have you been looking at the clock? Why are you bringing up the subject of money now?—ad infinitum.

Why do I feel as I do? Because "whys" are deceptive in their simplicity and can easily signify something other than their obvious informative motive. Might this be because of the persecutorial tone of the word as an accusatory inquisition, instead of an innocent inquiry? Is it then a matter of reminiscence of earlier parental control and invasion of privacy, the earliest voice of authority toward the guilty or shamed confessor? I suspect so. Brenner (1976) further suggests that the word *why* implies an immediate or known answer that the patient is expected to have. It obliges the unprepared person to rationalize thoughts in order to deliver more than he or she feels able to. This pressure to reply, of course, may in turn generate hostility in the threatened patient toward the prying therapist.

More specifically, the word *why* can imply an inequitable form—it does not give to the other, and at the same time it demands from the receiver. It is not a fair exchange. In a Lacanian sense, language, before signifying something, signifies "for someone." Thus, the query "Why?" targets the patient and fails the communication by disturbing the balance of the relationship. The interpersonal function is the hallmark of any dialogue.

Therefore, it has been suggested that rather than asking why, substitute the question "What are your thoughts or feelings?" As an improved alternative, the latter is more congruent with the definition of the therapist as an empathic scientist, not a curious moralist. In such a context, both therapist and patient can be considered as reciprocally exploring and explored instruments. This is consistent with Lacan's thesis that it is the *exchange* of words and not their content that is important, especially since most of what we say consists of redundancies rather than information. He could have said "sounds," instead of words. [**Intellectual debris.**]

The issue of *why* notwithstanding, there are four overriding questions that are intricately related to any interpretation and to each other: When, What, How, and Who. The issue of *when* involves the timing of familiarizing the patient with the general content of his particular psychodynamic without alienating or overwhelming him. It requires anticipating the patient's receptivity at a particular moment in order for the interpretation to have maximum effect (even though the defensive rejection of an interpretation can itself be interpreted).

The *what*, or specific content, must already be in the patient's preconscious or brought to it. A hermeneutic perspective, for example, accepts the reality of "thematized understanding" (Merleau-Ponty 1962); such understanding is grounded in the person's prior involvement with the matter, a form of prereflective understanding. In short, to know something, the subject must be already somewhat familiar with it.

As to the issue of *how*, opinions are conflicted. Some believe that there is no reason for total interpretation, which invariably means gratifying the total narcissism of the therapist combined with undue aggression. Others, like Alexander (1935), who described the total interpretation as one that connects the three elements of the *actual life situation* with *past experiences* and with the *transference situation*, believe that "the more interpretations approximate this principle of totality, the more they fulfill their double purpose: they accelerate the assimilation of new material by the ego and mobilize further unconscious material" (p. 609). To me, this completeness is more like what in the trade is called a "double-breasted interpretation." Never mind the totalness. As Tarachow (1963) recommends, "An interpretation should rarely go as far as possible. It should, by preference, fall short even of its immediate intended goal. This gives the patient an opportunity to extend your interpretation, gives him a greater share in the proceedings, and will mitigate to some extent the trauma of being the victim of your help" (p. 49).

Children who receive the answer before they framed the question never grow up, says Dorsey (1976). Similarly, the best approach is to "onion peel," to go from the outermost surface toward the deep and complex. I, like most therapists, also try to gradually prepare the patient to make the interpretation himself, not deliver it in such a neat package as to soften its impact. The interpretation not only means deprivation, but separation, as every interpretation is a separating experience. Very frequently simple clarification may lead to a patient's making his own interpretation, being responsible for the separative steps, and gaining self-confidence. This may seem too slow—a long distance, indirect process. Well, as Freud suggested, when it comes to human encounters, the shortest distance between two points is not a direct line. In fact, by the time an interpretation is made, it should be almost superfluous. Furthermore, by making partial interpretations in preparation for the more advanced interpretation, I also get a chance to verify and make midway corrections along the way. Interpretations, like all other creative activities, endure best in installments.

Another point: How would the therapist know for certain whether the patient has accepted the interpretation, or is just tolerating it? A common yardstick is to see whether the intervention will prompt further elaboration on the part of the patient, more associations, or new material, although these are not the only measures. Sometimes a long silence may validate the therapist's interpretation, insofar as it may be a reflection of an incubation period, which is one of the formal characteristics that precede insight. Moreover, in a negative transferential context, paradoxically, the rejection of a particular interpretation may prove it to be the salient one. It is covertly accepted by the patient in spite of the manifest protest.

On the other hand, what gets even trickier is knowing the effect of an interpretation on those patients who are in positive transference with the therapist. Such a patient's superficial acceptance and indiscriminate noddings of apparent approval could easily be misleading. It can get the gratified therapist to proceed in an incorrect direction. All these ambiguities prompted Parloff (1981) to sardonically suggest that there is no way to measure whether a patient has swallowed an interpretation or is holding it in his cheek.

Finally, the *who* issue—who is making the interpretation and to whom—gets even more complicated. Malan (1979) has offered this dictum: "You must not make interpretations until you have found out what kind of patient it is that you are talking to. And yet, . . . you may not be able to find out what kind of patient you are talking to without making interpretations" (p. 212). By such a twist, Malan is not simply creating a witty impasse. Needing to find out what kind of patient you are talking to also ipso facto refers to knowing the speaker. It is the patient in relation to yourself that you have to find out about; a patient may be "found out" differently in a different relationship by a different therapist. Although every interpretive comment is presumably personal, it is also intersubjective; it reverberates between both parties. [**"I keep six honest serving-men. They taught me all I knew; their names are what and why and when and how and where and who. I send them over land and sea, I send them east and west; but after they have worked for me, I give them all a rest" (Rudyard Kipling,** *Just So Verses***).]**

FELT COGNITION: THE INSIGHT IS MORE CAUGHT THAN THOUGHT

Feeling unsays itself.

—Anonymous

Carolyn: You know there isn't much more insight I could gain here. This "process of quarrying" brings out no more marbles. If life has to be understood backward, it must be lived forward. You know who said that. I've understood it and felt the dynamics of my family, if that's the source of my sexual ambiguity, the changing of my profession, and my ambivalence about it. Psychotherapy as a profession is intellectually not a challenging field. The average vocabulary used in sessions, including its jargons, must be no more than about five thousand words. The best part of the profession is through understanding the mind, and no longer being afraid of it. I can also help others to come to the same place. To take it to the next step, I have to return to academia. I feel every day that I'm impoverished as an intellectual. I've gained access to my emotions, for sure. Now I'm angry if need be, affectionate and empathic, assertive and anxious, or depressed as I live a fully felt life. But that's it. There isn't going to be some earth-shattering discovery about me that will make me take a gigantic leap to somewhere not yet known. I don't even want to. I overlook BB's shortcomings and my own; my "unworthiness" doesn't stop me from continuing to live my life. My mood goes up and down, but not drastically. It's just at this level of fluctuation. Maybe I'm getting older also. As they say, the mills of God grind slowly when you get long in the tooth. The only thing that has to rush a little is having a child. So what's pathological right now is self-evident. One is my still deep-down own superficiality, which ceased to be of concern to me as it became clearer, but a little sad . . .

Me: The grape never looks like wine.

Carolyn: I hope that the sedimentation you imply will occur. Right now I'm neither a grape, a juicy, sensual, tasty, frivolous thing, nor a full-bodied, intoxicating substance. Even the best knowledge that I would obtain would be brought to that superficial base. It's like a stream that can form its bank only within the natural configuration of the land. I wish I were born to a different family, brought up in Boston, went to Harvard. I wish I were beautiful and tall, with straight blond hair, that we were a normal family, my mother was a loving competent housewife, my father a solid citizen of the community, respectfully affectionate and a disciplinarian, that they were generous souls, that we all remained very close, that I got married to a classmate of mine, had three children, and that my wonderful parents became even better grandparents. . . . Why do you let me go on like that? These fantasies depress me, and then I find everything I have, I do, is a compromised life; I'm dealing with life at second hand. Instead of feeling better as I'm maturing, and knowing more, I live a dysphoric life.

Me: Once you stand up, your shadow lengthens.

Carolyn: Thanks a lot. I really would like to sit down for a while—hah! Once I saw a witty sign on a bumper sticker. It said, "Welcome to Idaho, you can leave now." This one is "Welcome to maturity; now you can no longer leave." As much as I complain, I wouldn't want to go back where I was a year ago. Actually it's hard for me to think that . . .

Interpretation, says Schafer (1976), is a story, which to be effective must comply with the four "C" criteria: coherence, consistency, comprehensiveness, and common sense. But even the best told story doesn't end well for the patient and therapist, unless it leads to insight. Therapeutic insight occurs only if the interpretation brings about a consciousness that combines cognitive and emotional experience with personal and social consequences in one's everyday life. Consciousness, as a symbolically mediated awareness, is simply an intellectual exercise. At best you'll have a professional patient who can cite all the intricate dynamics of his or her neuroses—without any signs of change. In fact, the patient may glorify his neurotic state with irony and wit, which serves to rationalize and sustain the psychopathology. Such a person may even gain secondary or tertiary benefits, but not the primary one.

Nor can insight be equated with the effects of abreaction. An affectively charged event or situation may facilitate learning, but first there has to be something to be learned. Heightened arousal will unfreeze chronic pathological attitudes and make the individual accessible to alternatives, and these alternatives are best assimilated with such charged emotional states. The therapist must be careful, however, because it is precisely these states that also facilitate regression in patients, reducing their critical faculties and making them vulnerable to suggestion. It is a thin line that lurks between the assimilation of insight and the influence of brainwashing.

It has been said that a flash of insight is more "caught" than thought, emphasizing the felt rather than understood aspect of this experience. At times, the impact of an insight is so powerful that it may trigger a feeling of transcendence, which often involves an unintended mystical leap. But, in the real world of psychotherapy, "Eureka!" experiences of insight rarely occur. Even such a sudden sense of enlightenment, if it ever does happen, must be received with some scepticism. A well-known Zen story tells of a student being taught to meditate on his breath. The student rushed to his master, saying that he had seen the images of a golden buddha, radiating light. Ah yes, said the master, but don't worry; if you keep your mind on the breath, it'll go away.

Even the most superficial insights are obtained in a drawn out, attenuated form over a sustained period of time. Freud talked about the time lag for assimilation of interpretation. All learning is accumulative; it draws on previous ones. The development of true and lasting insight ideally goes through a succession of stages: preparation, incubation, inspiration (careful here), and elaboration. Each fully developed insight is an independent entity of treatment by itself, even though it is part of the yet unexplored whole. In fact, within the larger phenomenon a single particular insight may lose its value, or can even be considered completely false. That is why the insightful experience is a slow, evolving process, if it is to lead to authentic and lasting change. As Freud (1937) pragmatically put it, "Experience has taught us that . . . the liberation of a human being from his neurotic symptoms, inhibitions and abnormalities of character—is a lengthy business" (p. 253), and one must try to attain it approximando. [**Friedrich Nietzsche said: Hail, dear drudge and patient fretter, more drawn out is always better.**]

COGNITIVE RESONANCE: YOU UNDERSTAND, IF YOU ARE UNDERSTOOD

Carolyn: Well, we got engaged. It was a quiet and lovely ceremony with a few friends. BB looked very elegant in his tuxedo. Incidentally, BB now stands for Best Beau, no longer an ambivalent name. We got really wonderful gifts, all toward the household. You know a toaster, a clever can opener. Goldie gave us a portable kitchen TV. Oh, speaking of TV, BB is what he is. He just couldn't help being stupid to the point of holiness. Everyone knows that by now and loves him anyway. What happened is that Goldie said she wasn't sure about her gift and made a little witty remark, that she pondered "TV or not TV? that is the question." Everyone laughed. BB jumped in and said, "No, it's 'cable or not cable.'" Now he knows that much of Shakespeare, everyone does. He just doesn't . . . I don't know. Everyone laughed at that, too. It was really a wonderful event.

Me: Congratulations!

Carolyn: Thank you, I wish you were there. You would have witnessed how your lunatic is beginning a normal life. The question is, How far do I have to carry this normalcy? I don't want to be totally normal. It's a boringly demanding existence.

Me: The tyranny of normalcy!

Carolyn: Now you're telling me! It requires not only undoing the past, but also catching up with the past. The present demands so much that I'm willing to have gilded rear windows as well as a gilded windshield. I think that's what normalcy is, to cover up everything potentially disturbing, making the best of the worst. But you see, underneath is lurking my psychological DNA, that sooner or later I'll be found and exposed as a crazy person. I'll, of course, happily confess my crime and my guilt. The night of our engagement, after everyone left, I felt horribly depressed. Is that all my life is going to be? BB was so happy that I didn't want to spoil it. But I stayed up long after he fell asleep, I thought about taking a few clothes and so forth and leaving for another city, if not for another country. I even thought about turning on the gas in the oven and killing us both.

Me: Making the worst of the best?

Carolyn: Make your mind up. You're supposed to be either for normalcy or against, not both, and what are these "telegraphic" messages? Are you concerned whether there's enough time in our sessions for you to elaborate on your theories, like Fermat's last theorem? He found the margin of his notebook too small to contain his wonderful and ultimate ideas. Get another book, man. Well, whether I'm making the worst of the best, I also decided to quit my job. I've been selling my soul to these people who are only interested in how many billable hours I had. They even mock my concerns for the patients. These abusive and arrogant bureaucrats who are well paid, in return pay us, the clinicians, very little. "In for a penny, in for a pound," as they say. So, whatever I make in private practice, I'll live with that, and if I get married to BB, it'll be more comfortable. Do you see how middle-class you made me? I'm talking about comfort. You converted an interesting, lusty, inwardbound cunt into a boring upward nonbeing bourgeois, someone like yourself.

Me: Lust rhymes with dust.

[**Not** her anger and insults to me; **not** her postdecision ambivalence.]

Carolyn: Everything rhymes with dust eventually. Sometimes you are so subliminally irrelevant that someone may mistake it for brilliance. I think you feel responsible and bad for where I am, for I've forfeited my potential. I should have seen a Jungian. But the idea that I have to make myself understood all over again is just intolerable. So I'm stuck with you. Tell me that we were wrong. Do we have to be loyal to our mistakes? I can restart life from an entirely new angle. I can go back to teach English literature, and live the life of an utterly free person. No pretension of sageness, normalcy, helpfulness, seriousness, meaningfulness, all that shit, and become a veritable wizard of id. Even talking about abandonment of this "life as therapy" and/or "therapy as a life" brings an exaltation of freedom.

Me: We've got to stop.

Carolyn: In more ways than one, I guess. OK, see you next week.

Short of "emotional resonance," the affective synchrony with patients, I attempt to establish some cognitive meeting of our minds, at least as a foothold for an evolving relationship. Whereas such a cognitive alliance may not be as valued as an affective encounter, it is a preparation for a deeper experience, except that such cognitive engagement occasionally serves to disengage me from my own emotional state. The therapist's rational presence structures the sessions, lowers the tension, helps to contain the unexpected, and thus reduces the chances of making mistakes. Most mistakes occur when the therapist is anxious or overwhelmed and begins to make self-revelatory experimentations. Any departure from an established structure and routine procedures, says Dewald (1964), should be scrutinized as possibly related to countertransference. Nevertheless, the therapist's emotional self is in his countertransferences, with which the therapist is handicapped.

There are times when I sense definite discrepancies between the verbal communication of the patient and the reaction he arouses in me. When this occurs, I invariably wonder whether I should focus more closely on the patient's communicative attempt, or on my own felt, but noncommunicated response. Some therapists believe that therapists had better suppress all of their own reactions in the name of neutrality. In fact, they are expected to make a concerted effort to distance themselves so that they are not tempted to bring their emotions into play.

To really resonate with the patient, however, the therapist should neither impose nor suppress how he or she spontaneously feels. Basch (1980) has suggested that the therapist's reaction to what the patient is saying or not saying provides the best, if not the only, clue to what to do. This means simultaneously listening attentively to the patient's communications as well as to one's own inner voice. Both are essential and need not preempt or cancel out the other. It is neither necessary nor ever advisable to keep the therapist's reactions under wraps. It is natural, for example, to feel aroused by a seductive patient, paternal to a deprived patient, frightened by an aggressive patient, burdened by a demanding patient, or jealous of a successful patient. Therapists who are out of touch with their own feelings are of limited help to those in pain. Thus, real resonance requires individuals who are themselves responsive to their own and others' emotions. These

internal cues provide special sensory information that is the raw
data of psychotherapy.

———————◆:◆:◆———————

The simple application of technique in relation to another
person is a bad faith, only serving to promote inauthenticity in both
parties. If deliberately pursued, it generates a philosophy of discontinuity, alienating all involved from the world.

12

Authentic Communication Is Neither Verbal Nor Silent—It Is an Irreducible Communion

LINGUISTIC QUARANTINE: THERE IS NO ESCAPE FROM LANGUAGE

Carolyn: I've got nothing to say. I thought about what I should talk about on the way up here; nothing came to my mind. No, I'm not angry at you, or depressed. It may be just a Monday crust; I'll recover. Maybe I feel a little guilty about my ravings last time against my family, BB, you, the profession. Besides the fact that I'm a certified bitch, which may explain my behavior toward people in my present life, the past is a bit more suspect. Therapy is a telescopic process. Your Pine says it's in an optical instrument. In such a distant look, the depth of field is ordinarily lost. I'm sure my parents took care of me, loved me their own way. I mean, how else would I have made it? They paid for college and graduate school. I never had to work like most of my friends to pay for my expenses. I have no early memories, like under 5. I see some of the home videos, I look cheerful, playful, a little chubby but happy. It looked like my parents were trying to do something with me. I seem relatively impervious, just doing my thing, whether running around or jumping into the pool, obviously aware of the camera, acting on an outer state. But I wish I knew what my inner state was like. I remember the first day of kindergarten. I didn't want to go and I think it was a struggle to get me to stay there. My mother had to come and stay there all day with me. Was that an attachment to a loving mother, or the clinging of a deprived child? Why do I feel unloved by her? I also accuse her of my lack of sense of continuity, though she was always there, however passively, never punished me, or anything like that. I was obviously well fed, I never lacked anything, you know, outfits, shoes, toys. At one time my friends were rather surprised how many Barbie dolls I had. I think psychotherapy itself is partly responsible for my having such a negative image of her. In my adult years, I beat on her more than she could have ever on me, to the point that I disorganized her internally, and she actually became the severely neurotic selfish woman that I accused her of being. Have I blamed her for all my failings in life? Or is she really responsible? From an adult perspective the latter sounds totally ludicrous, but if you're trained to see the present through the lenses of the past, you end up living out of time and carrying a tragic view of life, believing that everything in the present has been preempted by the primary process. This may be a useful view for maintaining a self-image, until it carries onto the delusional—because where we start isn't necessarily where we end up.

Me: The end where we start from.

Carolyn: I wonder whether that's what Eliot meant. The semantic self-reflectiveness tips the balance in favor of reshaping and rewriting the past. So, in some ways, the more one stays in treatment, the less truth she'll be facing. I have this strange image of . . .

The Heideggerian notion, "You are what you say," makes man a finder of substitutes. The self, thus conceived by the mind, attempts to comprehend itself through dialogues with others, potentially reducing the life to a series of conversations. Man has "an overwhelming temptation to settle for a story," says Friedman (1988, p. 400). Thus, the therapist and frequently the patients themselves cannot tell the facts from the unconscious elaborations of their fantasies, dreams, wishes, and fears, or even from the tales told to them in their early years. Where does the authenticity end and the reconstruction—if not construction—begin? The therapist straddles between taking these memories literally, or memories of memories, and just spoken representations of memories to be deciphered symbolically, as Lacan (1977) suggests. The word constitutes the truth, even if it is destined to deceive. In talking about the nature of memory, Maurois (1962) says, "For every man and for every woman it makes the recollection of his or her life a work of art and an unfaithful record" (pp. 65–66). Schafer (1954) puts it, "How a patient . . . represents his past tells us how he needs to see that past *now*" (p. 144). The fact is that this very need may change, thus altering the presentation of earlier recalled events. The truth gets blurred, if not perpetually revised as time goes on, to the point that it no longer even remotely resembles the real past.

Maybe there is no absolute originality, or even truth, but all are time and circumstance dependent in the creation of some semblance of believable "facts." Postformal thinkers assume that since change is a basic characteristic of reality, there may be no finite truth. That is why patients may seem to be receptive to different truths at different times, in turn related to stages of their own development as well as maturational phases of their relationship with the therapist. According to Spence (1982), by helping the patient to interpret the past (i.e., historical truth), the clinician constructs a new understanding (i.e., narrative truth). Jerome Frank's (1974) classic exploration of persuasion and healing suggests that such presumed truths (or more aptly, mutual belief systems or myths) may endure not so much for their evidentiary value as for their rhetorical appeal.

According to Aristotle, the rhetorician persuades by winning the confidence of the listener, by emotionally engaging the listener, and by providing apparent truth, which may not be more than a "mobile army of metaphors, metonyms, and anthropomorphism," as Nietzsche insists. For a therapist it should not be difficult to accept that degree of ambiguity. Our profession necessarily requires tolerance for distorted perceptions, cognitions, and self-presentations, and we take enough philosophical distance to accept the idea, as the adherents of Goethe might, that only what is fruitful is true, or even to take comfort in believing that the truth is an arbitrary punctuation in relationships and only relevant if it is in the service of self-coherence.

Psychotherapeutic truths are further restricted because they must be "sayable." This is the first of four criteria for what constitute clinical facts: they are capable of being said; they must be said to another person; they must represent a piece of psychic reality; and they are capable of entering into a story or narrative.

There are also other dynamic forces that shape the presentation of past events in psychotherapy. Schafer's quote above suggests that the past may be used to justify the present state of mind, or to explain it. Goffman (1959) speaks of the patient's past history as an "apologia" constructed by selective memory to create "an image of a life course . . . which selects, abstracts and distorts in such a way as to provide him with a view of himself that he can usefully expound in current situations" (p. 133). In therapy, according to Frank (1987), patient and therapist collaborate to recall and reorder the former's past experiences in order to create an apologia that sustains a better self-image and a more hopeful future. [Yet the past deprives itself, and the future is used, misunderstood, or even understood in terms of the present.]

NARRATION-EDITED TRUTHS

Carolyn: Now I realize that both my mother and my brother were frightened people. My father's intellectual snobbism and aggressive diminishing presence forced them into cowering to every demand of his. My mother, before she married my father, seemed to have had a full, assertive life. She came from a middle-class Baptist family in South Carolina, was a cheerleader, homecoming queen, and even won a citrus-queen contest in Florida. She was a nice, self-effacing southern belle. Oh, no! You aren't going to make a case out of this, are you? The Belle Bitch is neither a southern belle, nor a citrus queen. She's a Jewish-American Princess. Anyhow, my father, who came from a Jewish, intellectual, atheist, and communist New York family, bulldozed her. Why she would have married him is beyond me. He even interfered with her going to church. Poor woman. She used to secretly tell us about "the little Jesus," and that He was always there to protect us. Even though we were prohibited from celebrating Christmas, she would manage to give us gifts and read us stories of Santa Claus. I remember as a young child, maybe 6 or 7, she would plead with him to let us go caroling. She used to say to him, "Look, the kids should learn something about religion and God. If you like, we'll all go to the synagogue, I don't mind." He would laugh at her naïveté. I thought he was laughing because she didn't recognize that *he* was God. I did. My brother, of course, was always hiding, literally. For him, Dad might have been a god, but a dangerous one, or at least one with a bad temper. I loved it. I loved him as much as I disliked him. Is that possible? Is that the source of my ambivalence toward BB?

We all need our past as an organizing framework for our present experiences and as building blocks of our sense of self. Some of the distortions are deliberate reconstructions, if not autobiographical fabrications. Recent social theorists have proposed that it is the narrative, or story, that provides the major framework for making meaning of one's life. More specifically, not only is it through these narratives that persons make sense of their experience, but these stories also largely determine which aspects of experience are selected out for expression. Most significant, these stories create *real* effects in terms of the shaping of lives. This perspective, however, should not be confused with the comparable notion that stories function as a reflection or mirror of life. Instead, the narrative metaphor proposes that persons actually conduct and shape their lives on the basis of stories and which have real, not imagined, effects.

As the individual matures and stabilizes his self in the present, he may revisit his past presentations, says Schafer (1954): "Often it is only late in treatment before certain vital corrections are introduced into the patient's initial account of his past. The case history at the beginning and end of treatment may therefore read quite differently" (p. 144).

One of the unstrung pearls of Freud, notes Modell (1990), is the concept of *Nachtraglichkeit*, which refers to the idea that memories are cyclically retranscribed over time into new cognitive and affective categories based on later life experiences. Thus the therapist can continuously rely on hearing what is not said, or what is not yet said, or even what is not yet there. "Knowledge of a life story is acquired in the course of attempting to tell it," say Schacht and colleagues (1984, p. 69). Only the simultaneous

edition of historical and transectional memories give the individual a frame and a sense of his life. [The orchestra score derives
its value from the fact that it is read both vertically and
horizontally.]

RENTED MEANINGS: MEANING RESULTS FROM
INTERPERSONAL NEGOTIATIONS

> *Carolyn:* If all this sounds to you as if I'm rewriting my past,
> I wouldn't be surprised, because it does to me. How
> could I sit here empathizing with my "poor mother,"
> whom I have blamed all my life as a coconspirator with
> my father? Now I'm saying that she was a co-victim with
> me and my brother, another poor schlemiel. You must
> know that much Yiddish.
>
> *Me:* The memories of truth evolve.
>
> *Carolyn:* You mean these are only the truths of my memory,
> that they may not be the truth? Are you one of those
> who believe that memory distorts the facts? Are you
> insinuating that my father didn't give me wet kisses on
> my neck, but I wish he did?
>
> *Me:* You'll acquire your past in your attempts at remembering
> it.
>
> *Carolyn:* I don't understand. I'll be making up my past as I
> keep trying to remember?
>
> *Me:* And as you attempt to tell me.
>
> *Carolyn:* Are you trying to drive me crazy? Not only will I be
> making a bunch of lies about my past under the disguise
> of "the truth of the memory," but further embellish it as
> I would tell it to you? Are you basically telling me that
> all this time I've been talking to you, I've been telling the
> "truth of my memory as I told it to Dr. K."?
>
> *Me:* Yes.

Carolyn: Yes! Yes to "I'm a liar"? Or yes to "You're driving me crazy"?

Me: Yes to the former.

Carolyn: Does that mean "No" to the latter?

Me: No.

Carolyn: Listen! Not just in psychotherapy, but even in the ordinary interpersonal context, linguists agree that any conversational postulate requires that, at least on the surface, what you say relates to what I just said.

Me: And hopefully, what you just said is related to what you think, and ultimately, what you mean.

Carolyn: Are you now saying that I don't say what I think, and furthermore I don't make much sense?

Me: You were telling me that now you remember your mother as a co-victim with you and your inadequate brother, and I'm saying that you came to recognize this memory while you were telling me.

Carolyn: Why didn't you just say that you were trying to drive me crazy?

Me: No, I wasn't trying.

Carolyn: You mean, you don't have to try too hard? I can't believe that my own therapist thinks that I'm a total lunatic. I'm kidding, I'm kidding. Incidentally, a schlemiel is not an inadequate person, professor. It's . . . well it's best described with this story. Once, in the old country, there was a schlemiel. His father was a schlemiel, so was his uncle, and his paternal grandfather. There was no question about his schlemiility. But the man severely protested the designation. So he went to see the rabbi and complained to him about his ordeal. The rabbi sympathized with his plight and told him that there is only one way of finding out whether he was a schlemiel or not. This ultimate test was how he buttered his toast. So the rabbi invited the man to dinner and watched him butter his bread. As he did, the slice of bread fell to

the floor, the buttered side down. The rabbi looked at
the man and said; "Yes. There is no question, you are a
schlemiel."

Me: (Laughs.)

Carolyn: So, I really feel sorry for him and my mother. What
kind of person would think that these two utterly
helpless people were setting me up?

Me: A *meshuga.*

Carolyn: (Laughs) A *meshugana*, please! At least I got some
therapy. These two pathetic souls are totally left to their
own devices. Of course, my brother is now completely
out of it. For my engagement he sends me a book; *God's
Prayer*, that me and BB should read a section of it every
morning together before we leave the house. It's elaborated Bible stories. He knows that BB is Christian, so I
guess he thinks that I should go in that direction. He
doesn't call me to ask where I am in my own world,
never mind faith. It's at least his first assertive behavior
against our father. Oh, my father, if he knew this, he'd
kill him. Speaking of killing . . .

There is no pure observational language, says Kuhn (1970);
rather, listening is actively construing an intervening language, so
that each therapist naturally hears the patient's words in his own
idiosyncratic way. Therefore, there is no such a thing as the zero
or null context, and we can only understand meanings against
background assumptions. The therapeutic situation casts an
"unpleasant light" on the patient, as Friedman (1988) suggests,
which is designed to make the patient insecure about his meanings and assumptions, thus making him susceptible to change his
maladaptive paradigm.

In that sense, patient–therapist communication succeeds if
the therapist is also an expert linguist. In de Shazer's (1993)
intriguing essay entitled "Creative Misunderstanding: There Is No
Escape from Language," he contrasts three very different ways of

approaching language in broad context, with which a therapist must be familiar:

1. In traditional Western thought, language is usually viewed as representing reality. This leads to the idea that language can represent "the truth," which leads to the further notion that a science of meaning can be developed by looking behind and beneath the words.
2. From an Eastern point of view, Buddhists, for example, would say that language blocks our access to reality. So, this leads them to the idea of meditation, which is used to turn off language.
3. Language *is* reality. In sum, contemporary philosophers look at how we have ordered our world in our language and how our language has ordered our world. Furthermore, the patterned linguistic form imposes itself on current and past perceptions, which, combined with the multiordinality of the language, create a highly flexible world.

If words such as *yes, no, true, false, fact, fantasy, cause, effect, agreement, disagreement, love,* and *hate,* can be applied to a statement, they can also be applied to a statement about that statement, and so, ultimately, applied to all statements, no matter what their order of abstraction is. Terms of such a character are called *multiordinal terms,* according to Korzybski's (1941) concept. The main characteristic of these terms is that on different levels or orders of abstraction they may have different meanings, with the result that they have no general meaning; for their meanings are determined solely by the given context, which establishes the different orders of abstraction.

Accidentally, our vocabulary is enormously enriched without becoming cumbersome, without such exactness. Thus, *yes* may have an indefinite number of meanings, depending on the context to which it is applied. A blank "yes" represents, in reality, "yes"

("yes unlimited"), but this includes "yes$_1$," "yes$_2$," "yes$_3$," and so on, all of which are may be different. All speculations about such terms in general, for instance, what a fact or reality is, are futile, and, in general, illegitimate, as the only correct answer is that "the terms are multiordinal and devoid of meaning outside of a context" (Johnson 1989, p. 156). [**Is "is" is?**]

Holquist (1982) suggests that the problem of differentiating views about the acquisition and understanding of language can be clarified by posing the question, "Who 'owns' meanings?" In answer, he proposes three primary positions: *I* own meanings, *no one* owns meanings, and *we* own meanings. The first position, called personalism, is deeply rooted in the Western humanist tradition that extols the individual as unique. The second view, which is said to exist somewhere out there in the culture, is impersonal, even nihilistic. The third view, which he calls dialogism, is an interpersonal position, in which ownership of meaning is mutually shared. It is a way of being with another. He insists, "If we do not own it, we may, at least, *rent* meaning" (p. 3). In psychotherapy, as Stern (1985) says, "Meaning results from interpersonal negotiations involving what can be agreed upon as shared. And such mutually negotiated meanings (the relation of thought to word) grow, change, develop and are struggled over by two people and thus ultimately owned by *us*" (p. 170). The thought-to-word meaning *is* an interactional mental process between two people, which also has a phylogenetic and ontogenetic grounding. Although all human nervous systems contain genetically determined archetypes, which leads us to attach the same meanings to certain stimuli, the therapist is especially concerned with particular, local, and highly personal and interpersonal meanings. Whether unique or universal, in the deconstructionist Jacques Derrida's (1978) terms, when certain narratives are taken apart to make room for alternative understanding, there is a *coconstruction* of meaning that characterizes therapeutic conversation.

The search for meaning is insidious, but it always succeeds, says Spence (1982). As Zerubavel (1991) surgically put it:

> Islands of meaning are generated by analytic thinking, which presupposes a mental scalpel that allows us to carve "things" out of their context. Such a scalpel, however, inevitably violates the integrity of our experience. When analytic thought, the knife, is applied to experience, something is always killed in the process. What is usually killed in the process is context. By searching for laws that are independent of context and relying on highly decontextualized laboratory research and statistics, science, for example, ignores the fact that meaning is inherently grounded in particular contexts. Our analytic ability to decontextualize is admittedly a great intellectual achievement (we could not have developed algebra, geometry, or formal logic, for instance, without it), yet it clearly also entails some "context blindness." Being able to focus, for example, inevitably presupposes wearing mental blinders. As such, it entails a tunnel vision and, since tunnels are necessarily narrow, narrow-mindedness as well. [p. 116]

As a therapist, I try to be guided by what Havens (1983) calls "perceptual empathy," seeing something for the first time—experiencing it without presuppositions or expectations and without the habitual baggage of perceptions. With such a disposition, I let the patients take the lead and I reflect on their productions, and as Freud said, show them primarily what is shown to me.

The therapist has the primary responsibility to provide the ground. As Haley (1973) suggested, the person "who does not know what to do and is seeking help should be expected to determine what happens in the session" (p. 17). It is the therapist's role to provide a context and to help to restructure the patient's experiences on an ongoing basis. He does this by responding to what is *living*, in Gendlin's (1964) words, "to the functioning experience" (p. 132), no matter what those experiences are and how they are presented. [**The bee makes the same honey from every flower.**]

GROUNDING IN DIALECTICAL AMBIGUITY

There is a story of two Vermonters, one of whom was hard of hearing, who were standing one day on the edge of a crowd listening to a soapbox orator. The one who was hard of hearing nudged the other and asked him what the speaker was talking about. After listening closely for another moment or two, the other replied, "He don't say."

A third party listening to a therapist's comments to his patient could easily have the same reaction. Such "not saying" by the therapist for the purpose of preserving neutrality and ambiguity has been praised and encouraged for decades. He was only to search for meanings in the patient's narration, independent of the context. If, by any chance, the patient dared to ask for a clarification of what the therapist just said and meant, he only received an *obscurum per obscurius* (the alchemist's phrase for the method of explaining the obscure by the more obscure). The neutrality of the therapist needs to be only a dialectical neutrality, not a content neutrality.

There is also a linguistic neutrality that the therapist conforms to, by reading the ambiguity of "signs" (Lacan 1977), both within and independent of the patient's content production. The therapist, as a quasi-linguist, would interpret such signs by focusing, defocusing, differentially alternating, or applying some other idiosyncratic combinations. Lacan goes on to say that there are two possible interpretations of the sign, one referring to the code, the other to the context of the message: both processes are continually operative. Their joint goal, as is the function of language, "is not to inform but to evoke" (p. 86). However, using consistently ambiguous interpretations can also be a manifestation of the therapist's own countertransference. Honestly acknowledged, as Richard Isay (1977) says, it is an attempt to disguise a lack of understanding of the patient.

Have you noticed psychotherapists have a very limited vocabulary, especially within the session? Some of them are so theoretically restrained that they are at best repetitively ambiguous. How can a patient have an authentic exchange with someone who never takes a clear position? This is not unlike the observation in *Alice in Wonderland*:

> "It is a very inconvenient habit of kittens [Alice had made the remark] that, whatever you say to them, they *always* purr. If they would only purr for 'yes,' and mew for 'no,' or any rule of that sort," she had said, "so that one could keep up a conversation! But how *can* you talk with a person if they *always* say the same thing?" Hmmm!

EXPERIENCE IS THE PRISONER OF LANGUAGE

Carolyn: I asked my mother whether she ever saw my father in any way inappropriately relating to me. She didn't get it, until I made it unavoidably clear. "Did he behave towards me the way that a man would behave toward a lover?" She was mortified. "Definitely not," she said. "Where is this coming from? Is that the reason you've been so aloof the last few years? Your father loved you, the way that a father would love his daughter. You two were alike, you roughhoused a lot. He treated you a little bit as if you were a boy, because your brother was a shy and reticent boy. You were tomboyish in those years. So I don't know what you're talking about." Now, what do I do with this? Is it really possible that there was nothing sexual going on, in his mind? I mean, he never said anything that can be construed as suggestive. So I can't quote a sentence, a word, but a feeling of his Aqua Velva cheap perfume on my neck, brushing a wind of his breath to my hair, my ear, could all these be hallucinatory memories? Could I have wished them all to happen to me, unconsciously? Or did they happen in a non-sexual context, like roughhousing, and then titillated me to sexual sensations? And did he get stimulated himself? I can't visualize him when I talk about him, and when I visualize him I can't talk about him.

"The act of talking *about* something which one is feeling, rather than simply feeling, is the first step toward control," said Storr (1979, p. 26). Sometimes it is very much needed, such as during acute anxiety. Sooner or later, however, the therapist and patient have to settle with less need of control through the use of language's expressive mode. This is because, in Lacan's (1977) terms, language is a process of the degradation of the symbol into sign. It is valuable insofar as it communicates the sense of the experience and not the experience itself (but might also degrade the experience in the process). In his "Note Upon the Mystic Writing-Pad," Freud (1925b) commented on the idea of a double inscription (fleeting vs. permanent), surface and deeper engraving, a conscious "word presentation" and an unconscious "thing presentation." The latter—the primary material—is mute because the linguistic marker has not been superimposed upon.

If the patient is truly veridical in his reporting, as Spence (1982) insists, he cannot be understood; if he is understood, he is not freely reporting. Empathy permits us to perform a silent translation of the patient's language as he is speaking, so that we are, in effect, his dictionary, and in general, come a bit closer to seeing his world as it looked in the split second before it was transformed—and distorted—into language.

The very act of verbalizing is fundamentally incompatible with feeling and experiencing. How can you subject visual, tactile, and olfactory data to verbal analyses without losing, or at least sterilizing, the very nature of the experience? Sound, touch, and smell disengage themselves from sensory events, as one attempts to use spoken language to describe them. Experience precedes language. What we see never resides in what we say, declares

Foucault (1973). The unconscious, where the experiences are also registered, does not use recognizable linguistic codes.

The acquisition of language simultaneously represent a loss, says Lacan, who also considers the unconscious a language. The unconscious is the nonverbal sediment of experience. Whereas language itself can be construed as one of these experiences, it is not the best translator of other experiences. This is because the process of putting such elusive emotional events into language culminates in losing them. To put a mental picture into words, says Spence (1982), is to run the risk of never seeing it again. Then there is the danger of providing the wrong lexicon. As the map is not the territory, so verbalization is not the experience. According to Ricoeur (1977), it is at best a *report* of the experience. To the extent that psychotherapy concerns itself primarily, if not exclusively, with what is "capable of being said" (p. 836), there is an inherent restriction in reliance on words.

After all is said and done, if the equation between words and true feelings, or between what is spoken and what is unspoken, is flawed, how then can one continually translate from the private language of experience into the common language of speech? Spence suggests that one does so by speaking in half sentences wrapped around incomplete thoughts. He could have added "and complete silences." [**Language scrambles the purity of the phenomenological voice.**]

NON-ARTICULATION OF EXPERIENCE

> *Carolyn:* My father flew to New York after my mother clumsily told him my conversation with her. He was devastated. He said he'd rather commit suicide than be living with my conviction that he sexually abused me. I couldn't bear to watch him suffer. I told him that I had no such conviction, it was a stage in my analysis where the father–daughter relation was examined. It's a kind of

a romance that prepares the child for future loves, etc. He was a little relieved. That night he took me and BB out to dinner. I smelled the Aqua Velva and almost vomited.

I can't for sure tell whether he is innocent or not, whether he abused me. Actually "abused" isn't the word, sexually something, "played" with me? Why would he desire an ugly tomboyish girl, when he had this beautiful wife, anyway? What do you think? You've been awfully silent. Do you have daughters? Do men do that? If you watch Oprah, you would think that every family is incestuous. I smell no perfume here. I see in your face a little pain whenever I describe my feelings, or rather, my sensation. I believe that you sense my agony at not putting this matter to rest. Is it that important that I do? Incidentally, does it have a final answer? I want to feel safe with my father, the way I feel here. Not that he would ever do anything inappropriate now, just the feeling of having been betrayed, just violation of trust. But if it never happened, what if I'm accusing this man totally unjustly? The more I talk about this . . .

Though any verbalization itself may interfere with one's experience, it is especially so when one is struggling with early memories. This is more so for the patients who don't feel at one with their own words. As Balint (1968) advocates, in order to have access to preverbal material, the therapist's role in certain periods of new beginnings resembles in many respects that of the primary substances or objects. He must be there; he must be pliable to a very high degree; he certainly must be indestructible, and he must allow his patient to live with him in a sort of harmonious interpenetrating mix-up. Realizing that what he is insisting on may sound rather comical, Balint pleads for the practitioner's forbearance because "I am trying to render into words experiences that belong to a period well before—or beyond—the discovery of words, and largely even before the emergence of objects" (p. 136).

Early childhood memories, like dreams, are akin (though not identical) to artistic symbols and cannot be explicated. As Langer (1979) put it, in her study of the symbolism of reason, rite, and art:

> Many presentational symbols are merely proxy for discourse; geometric relations may be rendered in algebraic terms— clumsy terms perhaps, but quite equivalent—and graphs are mere abbreviated descriptions. They express facts for discursive thinking, and their content *can* be *verbalized*, subjected to the laws of vocabulary and syntax. Artistic symbols, on the other hand, are untranslatable; their sense is bound to the particular form which it has taken. It is always *implicit*, and cannot be explicated by any interpretation. [p. 260]

The phase of childhood that occurs before the emergence of objects in a strict sense of the word may represent the selfobject phase of the relatedness. This transition from selfobject to object relationship transpires through a mini-interpersonal process encompassing process units of primarily sensorimotor or affective experiences in the internalization process. In describing early human interactive behaviors, Stern (1977) defines such units as not necessarily the smallest unit of perception in any modality, but as the most finite unit in which a temporally dynamic interactive event with a beginning, middle, and end can occur. In short, it constitutes the briefest incident or vignette that can contain an element of experience and, accordingly, have signal value as an interpersonal event. Examples would be a vocal utterance, formation of a facial expression, or a discrete head movement. Each of these events occur within the same virtually imperceptible duration, from approximately a third of a second to a little under a few seconds. These interpersonal process units, he feels, may be the units of sensorimotor-affective experience that are initially internalized as the separate representation of another person.

The therapist's role in dealing with such experiences is a way of being with the patient. Patients whose childhood selfobject had failed traumatically in this area will require long periods of empathic holding and containing, gratifying without challenging needs, and simply being present in the unity with other. [**One day the Zen master, climbing a mountain, saw a man fall down in the snow, hands stretched out, crying out for help. The master came toward the man and lay down beside him. Then they both got up and walked away.**]

STOP TALKING SO THAT YOU CAN BE HEARD

"Speak," said Socrates, "so that I can see you." But the words can also camouflage the speaker. Reik (1952) observed that the therapist hears not only what is in the words; he also hears what the words do not say. He listens with the "third ear" in order to hear not only what the patient actually speaks, but at the same time his or her inner voice that emerges from the depths of one's own unconscious. It has become a metaphor for the way in which the clinician must tune into the patient as well as his own noiseless, pianissimo self. Freud (1912b) earlier stressed the importance of such attunement, using the commonplace analogy to a telephone receiver: the "doctor . . . must turn his own unconscious like a receptive organ towards the transmitting unconscious of the patient. He must adjust himself to the patient as a telephone receiver is adjusted to the transmitting microphone" (p. 114). Lacan (1977) has elaborated on Freud's concept, suggesting that just as the telephone receiver converts back into sound waves the electric oscillations in the telephone line that were set up by sound waves, so the therapist's unconscious is able, from the derivatives of the unconscious that are communicated to him, to reconstruct that unconscious.

This electronic process, however, is not that easy to transmit into human terms. First of all, the therapist must experience his self, with another, and resonate. Based on his intricate study of the interpersonal world of the infant, Stern (1985) concludes that there are many ways that the phenomenon of self with another can be experienced, "including some of the most widely used clinical concepts, such as merging, fusion, a haven of safety, a security base, the holding environment, symbiotic states, self objects, transitional phenomena, and cathected objects" (p. 100).

Once such a state is achieved, the therapists may receive different signals from the frequencies of each patient and hear different tones at different times. They even develop a private vocabulary between them. The therapist trains his ears to hear multiple notes simultaneously. Every statement that a patient makes will have a series of overtones, and the therapist must be able to resonate with all the tones without losing the fundamental note. As Thomas Moore (1994a) points out, "If you go to a piano and strike a low C rather hard, you'll hear, whether you know it or not, a whole series of tones. You hear the 'fundamental' note clearly, but it would sound very strange if it didn't also include its overtones—C's and G's and E's and even B-flat" (p. 234). Communicative intimacy requires establishment of a parallel processing so that the therapist may receive, think and give in dual, if not multiple, channels. He must be able to hear two not yet attuned instruments simultaneously. Free attention, says Spence, is not an automatic decoder of free association. The clinician, as a finely tuned therapeutic instrument, must resonate not only with the whole series of a patient's notes, but also with his own fundamental notes and all under- and overtones. [**The ultimate attunement is the resonance with the intransmissible.**]

REVELATIONS IN SILENCE

> The notes I handle no better than many pianists. But the pauses between the notes—ah, that is where the art resides.
>
> —Artur Schnabel (1958)

Carolyn: At dinner, I was watching my father interacting with BB. He was grilling the poor guy, "What do you think of Ignatius of Loyola, the Spanish aristocrat and founder of the Society of Jesus, and his spiritual exercises?" "Is theosophy the property of the faithful only?" "Why do you go to Kabbalah readings when even most Jews wouldn't?" "Did you get to read the Zohar, the canonical text? It was written by Moses de Leon, a Spanish Jew of the thirteenth century in ancient Aramaic." "Do you agree that a beautiful woman could be a daughter to a man, a lover to another, and just a good meal to a wolf?" Poor BB was totally lost. He kept dropping his utensils, his napkin, eating bread and drinking beer incessantly, nodding his head approvingly, occasionally glancing at me, like coming to my rescue, what is this thing?

My father, unfazed, continued: "The fact that you are a practicing Christian and my daughter is an agnostic Jew, you two must join the ecumenical spirit. You know, the fate of Judas. You should really read Anatole France's story of the Pious Abbé Aegger. My daughter underwent analysis to have Telos, to give her life a value. Teleology is Telos with an added 'ology,' her analyst couldn't figure that out, never mind pulling herself toward any goal."

Finally BB was drunk enough to open his mouth: "I believe all religions teach the same thing: brotherly love." I added, "Where no one fucks or eats the other." Wait, it gets funnier. My father, totally dismissing my intrusion, turned to him and shouted: "Omega!" A dead silence ensued. My poor BB replied: "No! Citizen." My father for the first time looked puzzled; he couldn't figure out whether this guy is a total ignoramus or what. "Citizen love?" my father asked. "The Omega point," my father said, irritated, "where brotherly love would reign supreme." My BB thought Dad was asking about his watch. It would have been hilarious, if it weren't so painful. As I was listening to him, I was becoming totally convinced that I really loved my BB and I was the luckiest woman in the world to find him. I would never marry someone like my father. I also decided that I'm going to convert to Christianity, well not even convert, my mother was Christian anyway. Agnostic! My ass. He's the one. I want my children to have Christmas and go to church every Sunday and I'll do my best to be a good wife and mother. Or was it a good-enough wife . . . ?

The dinner was a crucial point in my life. I don't even care whether he physically abused me or not, his mind is abusive, brilliant but abusive. He is so busy with his cranial equivalent of overeating that he couldn't get involved in relationships, even an incestuous one. I accuse him now, not for his wet kisses, but for his obese and evil mind. The evilness, BB thinks, is simply the absence of God. My father cannot complain of the absence of God in his life, for his is the culprit party of the deicide, like the fellow who kills his parents and then asks for mercy because he's an orphan. All other behavior of my father's stems from his godlessness. His morality is secular, mundane, legal, and I must give him credit, ecological. He taught us in our younger years never to harm nature, for nature is the real cathedral. He asserted that ecomorality is the highest morality and our reciprocation to Nature an expression of the purest goodness of man. The only thing he appreciated about BB was his engagement with the Hudson River Project. I recently joined that volunteer group for cleaning the waterways of pollutants. I know you're also involved. Did you read last week's *New York Times*, that bass is coming back, and even edible? I was so excited. We're going to buy a little cottage in upstate New York by the Hudson. We've been renting it. We enjoy not only working on the Hudson, but the area itself. It's so quiet, we go there now every weekend. I don't miss all those New York activities a bit—galleries, concerts, ballet, lectures. I have enough of them on weekdays. We have a little garden in our backyard, we cook together and join our Hudson River friends for long walks, hike and just sit, watch the birds. All this beauty of nature has been there for generations . . . I was taught in analysis that learning is a process of recollecting what one has forgotten. But that recollection must extend to all preceding generations—otherwise the self remains an encapsulated impostor.

My father kept drinking and BB, out of his politeness, was attempting to accompany him, and getting drunk. In spite of his seeming understanding, my father wasn't really accepting my marrying BB, especially because of BB's belief in religion. So he was trying to instill his ideas in BB very subtly: "You see religion is a matter of faith, a blind faith in fact. Therefore, whatever you love is your faith. That could be Jesus or that could be the Hudson River. God's DNA has not yet been deciphered, so his physical existence is less relevant than what he represents. One's nearness to God isn't going to a church or synagogue, but nearness to goodness. That is the supra-celestial place." I've heard my father's dialectical gymnastics in his customary negative labor so many times, I can almost recite it word for word. Now that I have some psychic infrared access into the human mind, I see that he's less interested in the content of his recital than in his desire to maintain his centrality. The supra-celestial place is what he used to occupy, but as he's getting older now and he lost his pulpit in literary circles. I can see he can't even drink as much. The doctors told him that his liver was enlarged and in a precirrhotic state, and that he must stop or at least severely curtail his drinking. I think I recovered from my parental fallacy. They are neither good nor bad. Hillman's idea that we are less the victims of parenting than of the ideology of parenting definitely applies to me.

"Dad," I said, "You remember the doctor's advice?" "Listen, I'm also a scientific agnostic," he replied. "They say if I don't drink anymore, I may live a long time. Well, if I don't drink, it may seem like a long time. You see, BB, death doesn't bother me at all, dying does. I've seen enough, I eat enough, I slept enough, I drank almost enough, so if I live another ten years it'll be like the movie *Groundhog Day*. There is nothing that I regret not having or having done, there is nothing about my life that I have to apologize for to anyone except to you, and you as a generic patient listener whom I have most likely bored too often."

I paid the bill, as neither of them was aware that we were the only ones left in the restaurant and the waitress was about to push us out. As we were walking out, I saw my father putting his head on the waitress's shoulder and loudly whispering: "Do you ever get to Florida?" You would have been proud of me. I saw him giving her his card. It didn't faze me. I said; "What one loves may be one's faith, but definitely one's character is one's fate," and walked away peacefully to our apartment. BB took him to his hotel.

Me: And?

Carolyn: And? I guess even growth, maturation, and transformation all are at some level comfortably disappointing. I want to reengage in my profession. I accepted the offer to be part-time faculty at the school and also teach at the institute. This would mean some loss of income, but I'm very excited about the possibilities. I want to write again. Most likely, this also will be somewhat disappointing, but I'm counting on your reassurance that the disappointments bring freedom.

We have overdone the use of silence, says Leston Havens (1986), in a historical anecdote about one of his own principal teachers: "When he [Ives Hendrick] had begun teaching psychiatry in the 1930s, the great task had been to keep doctors from talking too much in the therapeutic situation. This was so successfully accomplished by the 1950s that it was necessary to revive the use of speech and get them talking again" (p. 4).

Well, now I believe that some psychiatrists may again be talking too much, thus concealing themselves unsuccessfully. Every thought of the therapist, no matter how brilliant it is, need not be stated. One of the criteria of being grown up, never mind being a therapist, is "to stop saying everything loud," says Schafer (1976). The therapist must be careful not to be interruptive of and intrusive in the patient's narration, like the Japanese who worry about upsetting other people in coming or going. Spence (1982) considers silence a baseline condition of the mind; it is empty of words until one makes an effort to find them. Furthermore, the less the therapist says, the greater will be the impact when he does say something. There *is* still a place for the phenomenon of therapeutic silence and ways of implementing it. [**Talk is no breast.**] I like Bugental's technique; he says "What else?" in his silence and that there is always more information to be obtained, so whenever a patient pauses, he says, "And . . . ?"—although he makes a special point of not starting a session that way.

Not only the words and their meanings, but their sounds, have an effect on the relationship. When the sound structure holistically adheres to an exactness of one-third of a second (e.g., sixteen notes with the metronome set at 60), we experience that as music, the lyrical tenderness, says Edelson (1975), a sound structure that may require holistic adherence to an exactness of one-third of a second. Patients respond to general sounds of the language of the therapist. These sounds are presented in periodic and aperiodic subpatterns, the boundaries of which provide clues to the patient. Each therapist does this in his own way by a falling inflection at the end of words, phrases, and sentences, as well as by strategic pauses and accents.

Harmonic cadences, note/tone durations, and dynamics (e.g., to stress loudness, attack) are forms of musical punctuations. Some sound structure can be quite disturbing to the receiver, and by compounding the verbal structure can also disrupt one's own internal rhythm as well as the word's additional reactive effect on the speaker. The sound can make words more conscious and/or suppress further the unconscious material. The adherence of musical structure will give communication the same quality that Robert Frost gave to poetry: "The poem must ride on its own melting, like a piece of ice on a hot stove." Haiku verses, with their 5-7-5 consecutive syllables, are perfect examples of the pleasant sound structure of words without any cohesive meaning. And each one can be recited in less than 30 seconds:

Unhappy woman
I pedal my bike today
Through puddles of rain

A therapist need not always make sense when he speaks. He can put his words between brackets, as long as he adheres to the sound structure and keeps it short. "Anything that cannot be said in 30 seconds is not worth saying," goes an old wisdom. In contrast to the politician who is never to open his mouth unless he has nothing to say, the therapist opens his mouth only when he has something to say, and very briefly.

Elie Wiesel (1990) tells the story of Rabbi Mendel of Worke, who established a school of silence, and people would come there simply to be silent with him. Once the Rabbi of Kotzk, who was known for his anger, met Reb Mendel, and he said, "Mendel, Mendel, I know that you are trying to do something important in heaven. You are trying to achieve something with silence—to elevate it, to transform it. Tell me, where did you learn the art of silence?" And the holy man didn't answer. But silence is not always holy, not even golden. It can be misused by the therapist and misunderstood by the patient. "Silence is only as worthy as what we can bring from it," says Layer (1993, p. 74). The idea is to reduce noise and amplify signals. Here the gold of silence can be tarnished by the therapist who overrates its usefulness, and by the patient who misinterprets its intentions. It isn't best appreciated, like all other things, in its relative absence. For example, can it be a form of withdrawal or passive aggression, especially in less healthy hands and minds? Examination of the psychology of silence has revealed that there are many meanings, for the clinician as well as for the patient. The range is so great that the messages silence send are actually antithetical. In Zeligs's (1961) words, silence can mean

> agreement, disagreement, pleasure, displeasure, fear, anger, or tranquility . . . a sign of contentment, mutual understanding, and compassion. Or it might indicate emptiness and complete lack of affect. Human silence can radiate warmth or cast a chill. At one moment it may be laudatory and accepting; in the next it can be cutting and contemptuous. . . . Silence may mean yes or no. It may be giving or receiving, object-directed or narcissistic. Silence may be a sign of defeat or the mark of mastery. [p. 8]

The therapist remains appropriately silent while the patient is working. Such silence helps the therapist to resist the temptation of understanding too quickly or to make serious mistakes. As they say, "A closed mouth gathers no feet."

Lacan (1977) asserts that the therapist remains quiet so that the Other can speak. Fink (1997) explains:

> The analyst must shift from being an other person to being an other. . . . In other words, the "person" of the analyst must

disappear if he or she is to stand in for the unconscious. He or she must become a more abstract other, the other that seems to speak inadvertently, in the slips and cracks in the analysand's discourse. In a word, he or she must stand in for what Lacan calls the Other with a capital *O*: that which the analysand considers to be radically foreign, strange, "not me." [pp. 31–32]

Thus, silence, like the rest of the language, is not an inert intermediary between men. As Lacan (1977) has further pointed out, language is itself a mediator in the formation of objects. He makes a distinction between thought and sound, with language serving as an intermediary. Gill (1979) is less lofty and more practical when he says that the therapist's silence is "an indication that analyst is listening" (p. 277). "The active power of silence makes small talk transparent," says Reik (1952, p. 24). With these opposing vantage points, it is possible that the therapist's silence is meant to facilitate the therapeutic process, whereas the patient's silence may wittingly or unwittingly resist it. Both are useful. At bottom, perhaps, silence is simply a wish to be understood without verbalizing.

At times, I find myself in drifting away in silence. This is frequently in simultaneous regression with the patient, during which I may not pay attention to each and every part of the communication between the patient and myself, but maintain the full dynamic picture in my mind. By not casting the net narrowly, I keep my eyes wide open on the landscape, taking in everything I can. The French impressionist Paul Cezanne reportedly said that he wanted to paint the entire picture at once, because each part changed every other part and the meaning of any segment could only be discovered in the whole.

The primary function of language is to establish a relationship, says Lacan (1977). It is metaphorical and a form, not the substance. Silence, on the other hand, forces the substance. That is why the intersubjective silent space is murkier than the subjective one. That is also why all trained therapists are quite similar in their handling of interpersonal verbal communication. The silences within intersubjective space, ah, that is where *the* art, if not the holiness, resides. That is why Herman Melville says that silence is the only voice of God.

Authentic communication is neither verbal nor silent, it is an irreducible communion. All we can know in others stems from what we cannot articulate about ourselves. Words and thoughts generate systematic misinformation. The microanalyses of the mind bring subjective impasses. The knowledge that we need resides in the sediment of experiences, with the others manifest as silent revelations.

13

Ontological Attunement

Back to the T'ehom [primal waters].

—Carl Gustav Jung

THE ONLY MASTER YOU FIND ON THE TOP OF THE MOUNTAIN IS THE MASTER YOU BRING UP THERE

There is no structured school of the art of healing. The spiritual existentialism is a way of being—it frames other therapies, but is itself frameless. This means that it cannot be contained by the human mind, just as the mind may comprehend something about itself but does not reach the ineffable depths of self. The mind is not only composed of conscious and unconscious forces, but also spiritual ones. It carries the remembered oneness and the sacred belonging. As the philosopher Karl Jaspers (1954) observed in his *Way to Wisdom*, man is fundamentally more than he can know about himself, because the way to self-knowledge is twofold: the person "as object of inquiry, and as existence endowed with a freedom that is inaccessible to inquiry" (p. 63). It is the latter that is both the subject, and the object, of the art of healing. As such, the art of healing does have its own tenets, not as principles of treatment but as principles of *existence*. Moreover, although certain nonspecific therapeutic practices may emanate from its precepts, healing at best becomes not what the healer does, but what he *is*, in Lasch's (1978) words, a virtuous man who has little to repent of or apologize for at the end of his life.

How does one arrive at this exalted state of virtue? According to the fourth of Chopra's (1994) seven spiritual laws of success—the Law of Least Effort—such an individual tries to do nothing; he just is. He accepts people, situations, circumstances, and events as they occur, life as it unfolds. He does not struggle against the moment, in the same way that "Grass doesn't try to grow, it just grows. Fish don't try to swim, they just swim. Flowers don't try to bloom, they bloom. Birds don't try to sing, they just sing" (p. 53). For the therapist who aspires to such a soulful and spiritual existence, it reflects a natural and quiescent state, a union with nature characterized by the principles of fewest words (i.e., profound silence) and least actions (i.e., inner harmony).

Venturing beyond the boundaries of science and medicine, life of the spirit and soul is directed toward devotional belief in the influences of the ethereal, incorporeal, and immaterial aspects of beings, as distinguished from the influences of one's physical, concrete, and evidential existence. Comparing the essence of both of these perspectives, the sacred and the nonsacred, it can be said that spirit is to the soul what blood is to the body. More specifically, the art of healing conceptualizes care and compassion within the dual contexts of love and belief beyond oneself. In this context, a clinician who belongs to any school of psychotherapy or profession can become a healer, *if* regardless of his own ardent allegiances, he conducts his practice according to the six tenets of transcendence: three on the way to soulfulness—love of others, love of work, and love of belonging—and three on the way to spirituality—belief in the sacred, belief in unity, and belief in transformation.

An overview of the vast variety of psychotherapies of the last century reveals their attempts to resolve the individual's past and present conflicts and remedy his or her deficits by three major change agents: cognitive mastery, affective experience, and behavioral modification (Karasu 1977). Yet even when this entire armamentarium is applied, psychological conflicts are relatively resolved, deficits filled, and defects corrected, ultimately patients still experience posttherapeutic dysphoria, a loss of meaning or sense of emptiness, a nonluminous hollow. These diverse strategies have shed limited light and left patients bereft, because in the process of treatment (if not the psychopathology itself) the person's soul has been neglected and spiritual connections severed.

Of course, all therapies may provide at least transitory relief simply by the presence of someone who is interested in the patient, provides an explanation for his or her condition, offers some semblance of comfort and support, and even expressly teaches coping mechanisms in the form of alternative modes of thinking and behavior. However, traditional approaches eventually reach an impasse, a place where the therapist himself resides and in which he and his patients can become irretrievably trapped. [**Psychology alone made us something less.**] This invariably occurs when an overly confident clinician, regardless of his respective school, presents himself as a prototype of health and salvation for his recipients to emulate. Alas, Chessick (1989) says, the therapist is limited by an inherent constraint: [**The therapist can take his patients only as far as he himself has reached.**]

NIGHT MAKES THE DAY: SOUL AND SPIRIT ARE DAYS AND NIGHTS TO EACH OTHER

The soul and the spirit are frequently used interchangeably as equally rarefied concepts. Although they reside neither in consciousness nor unconsciousness, they may be "found" in objects and events from the sacred to the secular, from the divine to the ordinary. They are related as transpersonal abstractions, but are also quite different. According to Hillman (1992), the soul calls one "down and in" whereas the spirit calls one "up and out" (p. 26). The soul immerses itself within the world through intimacy, relationships, pleasure and pain, and aspires to egoless attachment and engagement. It views human suffering and illness with reverence, by "honoring symptoms as a voice of the soul" (Moore 1994a, p. 3). It is personal as much as transpersonal to the extent that it cultivates depth and sacredness in everyday life. Alternatively, the spirit aims for the impersonal and toward detachment. As Kovel (1991) has pointed out, *spirit* is the more general term, connoting a relation between the person and the universe, while *soul* is the more self-referential term.

Moreover, the soul is the seat of human emotions and sentiments with all its lowly limitations and descents, whereas the spirit is the repository of the moral and religious; it has the highest inspirations and can soar. In addition, the spirit's road can be straight and well paved, while the soul's road is more rough and roundabout. Moore (1994a) refers to the latter as meandering, likened to "the odd path of Tristan, who travels on the sea without oar or rudder, making his way by playing his harp" (p. 259). Based on the myths of the ages, Campbell (1949) suggests a more difficult and demanding route, referring to "a dangerous journey of the soul, with obstacles to be passed" (p. 366). Moore (1994a) clearly contrasts their dual courses: "In spiritual literature the path to God or to perfection is often depicted as an ascent. It may be done in stages, but the goal is apparent, the direction fixed, and the way direct. Images of the soul's path are quite different. It may be a labyrinth, full of dead-ends . . . or an odyssey, in which the goal is clear but the way is much longer and more twisted" (p. 259).

In sum, they are both archetypally distinct entities from the physical body and physical world. They are immaterial in nature, but can make their appearance in all earthly matter. The soul penetrates the plain particulars of life, the spirit transcends them. The soul gazes at life inwardly, while spirit gazes beyond it. The discovery of our true self is only possible by allowing our soul to wander and wend its way, and however circuitous, bring us closer to our spiritual selves. Whereas the soulful and the spiritual each may be pursued separately, one opens the door for the other. In tandem, they form a divine union.

The therapist must tend to the patient's soul as well as his own. In early Christianity, tending needs of people was known as *cura animarum*, the cure of the soul, and the role of the curate was to maintain the individual in a religious and spiritual context, to sustain him for the inevitabilities of fate. The care of the psyche and soul thus began as a sacred act by its practitioners and priests. Then medicine and psychology as secular science started to differentiate the two. In fact, these sciences removed the soul from their vocabulary by objectifying subjective experiences. They even went one step further, emphasizing the individuation of the person at the expense of belonging and believing. Thus modern man was subjected to the demise of his soul-making connections. As a result, not only did the original illnesses not disappear, but they were compounded by the individual's lack of spirituality and faith. The colloquial cure was worse than the disease itself. In ancient Greece, "therapy" meant service to the gods. In modern psychology, however, it has more often meant coming to terms with the death of God and its success has brought with it the impoverishment of the soul, becoming the worst illness of the twentieth century.

The ways to soulfulness and spirituality inhere in our basic ontological disposition. Yet these fundamental capacities tend to get overlooked, if not destroyed, in contemporary living. Thus they need to be cultivated if they are to be preserved, bearing in mind that they are separate, albeit often overlapping and, at times, even contradictory roads. More specifically, the way to soulfulness is achieved by transformation of the extraordinary to the ordinary—and its only required ingredient is *love*. Comparably, the way to spirituality is achieved by transformation of the ordinary to the extraordinary—and its only required ingredient is *belief*. Taken together, they respectively comprise the six tenets of transcendence cited above.

THE WAY TO SOULFULNESS IS LOVE

Love of Others: Love Is the Only Constituting Medium

The love of others is, first, a matter of self-differentiation. Love demands attachment, yet requires a healthy distance. Here the subject is separate from the object, heading toward subjective selflessness. For such love to occur, one must make sure that the other's separateness is secured independent of one's own. As the poet Rainer Maria Rilke so eloquently advised, each person has to protect the solitude of the other. As explorations of intimacy inevitably reveal, it is only by being separate that one can truly be together with another; enmeshment is not intimacy. Love that strips the other person from his or her sense of self, in which privacy is invaded and boundaries are blurred, is not real love. Indeed, getting to know and love someone deeply may require not seeing too clearly or being too close. In this sense, the magic of any loving relationship is in part maintained by taming one's desire for fusion, not obliterating the other through merging—in short, honoring each member's freedom. In revering the wonders of love and relatedness, it has thus been wisely proffered that "the soul . . . needs flight as much as it needs embrace" (Moore 1994b, p. 21).

Love also means forgiving. The soul soars when one concedes to one's loved ones their freedom and cherishes what they are willing to give without asking more. There is no categorical goodness or badness, and one must expect failings, betrayals, and (if one is fortunate) expressions of contrition. Then one must forgive. After any ethical transgressions, the slate must be wiped clean and the relationship permitted to continue as if the wrongdoing never existed. Humanness, we know, is always imperfect, relative, and tainted by sin and folly. This view might help us to tolerate our own shortcomings and many uncertainties, including interpersonal, moral, or religious waywardness. Forgiving would free us from the corrosive effects of anger, hate, humiliation, and embarrassment. It would allow us to save otherwise unsalvageable relationships among spouses, parents and children, and friends. At bottom, love means totally accepting the other. As Adam was formed out of the mud of the earth, so are the rest of us. Any attempt to destroy the impurities of nature also removes the fertile soil that can be nourished to grow.

Love of Work: The Love that Goes Out into Our Work Comes Back as Self Love

Work is *liber mundi*, monks said, a life literacy, whereby their religious duties were highly intertwined with daily labors. Both activities could be paths to divinity, provided that they were carried out with the same profound regard. Although contemporary secular work is far from early monastic life, it could be equally sacred if we were to accept its special calling. Every act of labor, no matter how seemingly commonplace and trivial, if attended to with a depth of devotion, can open the path to soulfulness. In this sense, God is not only in the details of prayers, but also in details of everyday chores. Not only through the rituals of the temple, but through the hard work of ordinary tasks, does one enter a higher plane. Rituals of the church (liturgy literally means "the labor of laity") and the divine acts of the worshiper need to be transported to the commonplace. The ultimate purpose is not to differentiate between the sacred and the secular, but to bring a reverence to everyday living.

One cannot search for soul only from within; it cannot be divorced from one's relations in the outside world. In the quest for coherence of the self, Storr (1988) has suggested that work in the form of creative acts, such as making art, music, or literature, or other human interests and labors that may be more mundane, can also serve as substitutes for good objects. They may function as reparation for early losses or later difficulties in fruitful interactions with others, in Eagle's (1981) words, "interests as object relations" (p. 527). One of the indispensable ingredients of the transmutation into soulfulness is the sheer love of work, through which the self and other can be unified. In cultivating depth and sacredness in everyday life, "The love that goes out into our work," says Moore (1994a) in his *Care of the Soul*, "comes back as love of self" (p. 187).

Love of Belonging: Love Is Congregation

Belonging is living together; it is outer communion—*convivium*, celebration of "the sweet communion of life—the demonstration of love and splendor, the food of good will, the seasoning of friendship, the leavening of grace" (Moore 1994b, p. 104). Conviviality requires some degree of sacrifice of one's self-centeredness and being part of communal life. It means focusing not on one's own success, but on that of the society at large; not striving to possess things individually, but viewing all of life's riches as shared. It means appreciating the simple life, honoring basic virtues, and, above all, promoting selflessness. One does not lose one's self by such conviviality; in fact, it is the only way that one can truly find one's self. As Kovel (1991) has pointed out, "The group is the larger being from which individual being emanates and to which it returns. . . . The group, be it family, clan, tribe, class, nation, or church, becomes the intermediary representation of being to the self, a way station between the isolated particle of consciousness and the universe" (p. 78).

Belonging means believing together. It provides communal meanings and finds faith through kinship and mutual accord. Expressions of faith, however, need not always be strictly religious. In his book *Gods and Games*, which aspires toward a theology of play, David Miller (1973) describes faith as being gripped by a story, by a vision, by a ritual. It is being seized, being gripped by a pattern of meaning that affects one's life pattern, that becomes a paradigm for the way one sees the world. It is difficult for every individual to formulate such a personal paradigm, and religion provides a ready-made one. Such a shared worldview is more likely to facilitate an identity of universal being, embodying the spiritual power of belonging to the group.

Kovel (1991) further suggests that religions always engage spirit, but to differing degrees; they are particular historical ways of binding spirit and socially expressing it. To the extent that they are an institutionalization or regimentation of spirit, they ipso facto become less than fully liberating. Although religious institutions, at least superficially, serve the process of belonging by believing, at bottom spirituality has the capacity to transcend religion in that "the quality of spirituality, religious or not, . . . depends . . . on the social relations it advances" (p. 4). Thus, religious congregations can perform the role of communal cement, a shared belief system serving to establish and reinforce cohesiveness relationships. As Rabbi Harold Kushner (1981) concluded, "One goes to a religious service, one recites the traditional prayers, not in order to find God (there are plenty of other places where He can be found), but to find congregation, to find people with whom you can share that which means the most to you" (pp. 121–122).

THE WAY OF SPIRITUALITY IS BELIEVING

*Believing in the Sacred: Whosoever Feels Doubt in His Heart
Is a Secret Believer*

By believing in the sanctity of everything around us, ordinary
things are experienced as truly extraordinary. Seeing the luminos-
ity of nature transports all of our experiences, including health
and illness, pleasure and pain, joy and sadness, gain and loss,
success and failure, birth and death. They become life events that
are not dualistic, but reflect a dialectic of the ineffable, equally
worthy of veneration. Such a sense of sacredness demands
detachment from worldly possessions, yet endows them with the
wonder of life. As in the poet Pablo Neruda's famed exaltation,
Odes to Common Things, one looks at everyday objects as one
might at stars in the sky. It is a beholding of the universe in all its
majesty. It is an epiphany that may come as a form of revelation,
not as a matter of logic, just as God surpasses logos and is exempt
from proof or disproof, "distant, hidden, and undemonstrable."
Rather, God is accessible not through thought, but through faith.

The sacred experience demands some detachment from
others. As soulful as belonging is, it does not mean never being
alone. Man also needs solitude for his spiritual growth. Being with
people for long periods of time, no matter how loving, wonderful,
or interesting they might be, interferes with one's biopsychological
rhythm, with one's synchrony with nature, with one's own
authenticity. Solitude synchronizes the body with nature and
reinforces man's belonging to a larger presence. Private religious
devotion provides similar harmony, in that the person who prays
in private feels himself to be alone in the presence of God.

Storr (1988) posits a return to self through solitude, which is
a way of putting the individual in touch with his deepest feelings.
In a reciprocal process, the more we are in contact with our own
inner world, the more we will establish connections with the
sacredness of the outer world. It is only by becoming a part of the

sacredness of nature that we may unearth our spirituality. It is there waiting for transformation. In his attempt to transform the everyday into the sacred, the visible into the invisible, Rilke wrote in a letter to a young poet that our task is to stamp the earth into ourselves deeply, so that its being may rise again invisibly in us. Similar is existentialist Albert Camus's (1995) wise words on the road to discovering the magic of ordinary existence—if there is a sin against life, it consists perhaps not so much in despairing of life as in hoping for another life and eluding the implacable grandeur of this life.

Believing in Unity: Paint the Picture at Once

Believing in unity means a sense of being undifferentiated from the outside world—natural and supernatural; in Buddhist terms, a feeling of oneness. This unity brings meaning and serenity to the self, as life's burdens become too heavy to bear if can find no universal meaning. Universal meaning, of course, is not a quantifiable and measurable entity. As Jaspers (1954) noted, unity cannot be achieved through any rational, scientific universal. Nor does unity reside in a universal religion. Unity can be gained only in boundless communication. It is a sense of responsibility for all, a sense of total commitment, a selfless way of relating to the world around us. Moreover, believing in unity ultimately reflects the seamlessness of mind, body, and spirit. As Kovel (1991) put it, "If mind-body is a unity, then spirit can be read as the coming-to-be of that unity. And this coming-to-be depends on the way we act and on our relationship to the world" (p. 20).

Rinpoche (1994) refers to an unfolding vision of wholeness, a sense of a living—and implicitly loving—interconnection with humanity. The glue for that mysterious unity is a kind of love that dedifferentiates ourselves from other persons, other things, and finally, from the universe, extending our limits, a stretching of our boundaries. The more and longer we extend ourselves, the more blurred becomes the distinction between the self and the world. We become identified with the transpersonal, and we begin more and more to experience the same sort of feeling of ecstasy that we have when we fall in love. Instead of having merged temporarily with a single beloved object, we have merged more permanently with the universe—a primordial unity.

Such transpersonal love is the source of compassion and praised by religions. It is exalted as the ultimate goal to be attained, surpassing one's knowledge, skills, power, and all worldly possessions. Believing in unity is the undifferentiated base of love from which other variations spring. This love is not possessing, not capturing; it isn't *doing* something. Love is a way of existing, a way of being with people, animals, nature, and God.

Believing in Transformation: There Is No Self, There Is No No-Self

Believing in transformation is believing in spiritual continuity and rebirth. We may be finite in our presently expressed form, but eternal in our true nature. As Rinpoche (1994) concludes in *The Tibetan Book of Living and Dying,*

> In death all the components of our body and mind are stripped away and disintegrate. As the body dies, the senses and subtle elements dissolve, and this is followed by the death of the ordinary aspect of our mind, with all its negative emotions of anger, desire, and ignorance. Finally nothing remains to obscure our true nature, as everything that has clouded the enlightened mind has fallen away. And what is revealed is the primordial ground of our absolute nature, which is like a pure and cloudless sky. [p. 259]

We inherit spiritual as well as physical and psychological elements from our parents as well as from the previous generations. Similarly, each generation is endowed by the experience and knowledge of all the prior ones. Whereas our physical and psychological qualities carry the assimilated elements of past lives, wherever and with whomever they have been, they are relatively limited to genetics and familial life. When these are inhabited in us, they give us our unique physical and psychological essence. Our spiritual essence, on the other hand, possesses the assimilated elements of past lives of the community, history, arts, cosmic world, and beyond. When these spiritual elements are inhabited within us for the duration of our corporeal life, they give us our soul.

The soul evolves in a particular existence. After the death of the person, the soul fragments again to its spiritual elements and coalesces again in someone else. Every culture is rich with the telling of this process of transmutation. Their mythology, their songs, their religion, their rituals gravitate toward that spiritual realization. The Chinese tell of a crossing of the Fairy Bridge under guidance of the Jade Maiden and the Golden Youth. The Hindus picture a towering firmament of heavens and a many-leveled underworld of hells. The soul gravitates after death to a story that assimilates the whole meaning of its past life. When the lesson has been learned, it returns to the world, to prepare itself for the next degree of experience. Thus gradually it makes it way through all the levels of life-value until it has broken past the confines of the cosmic egg. Dante's *Divine Comedy* is an exhaustive review of the stages: Inferno, the misery of the spirit bound to the prides and actions of the flesh; Purgatorio, the process of transmuting fleshly into spiritual experience; and finally, Paradiso, the degrees of spiritual realization.

Transformation starts by coming to terms with one's ending. Coming to terms with one's beginnings is difficult and ambiguous; it may occur in different ways (analysis, self-reflection) and mean different things (forgiveness, charity, or simply the end of an addictive litany against the past). Coming to terms with one's ending, one's finiteness, is clearer but even harder. Socrates said, "Practice dying," to youngsters asking for wisdom of life. Rinpoche (1994) speaks of the necessity of "letting go of attachment" (p. 224). In fact, Moore (1994b) paradoxically views loss of love and intimacy as a form of initiation, suggesting that although initiation means beginning, the most powerful initiations always involve some sort of death.

At bottom, all endings are potential beginnings and all beginnings have an end. To the soul, death is the ultimate beginning, for all the particulars of precious ordinary living creatures, famous or not, human or not, are still are transformed into another form. As Chopra (1993) says, in nature "death is part of the larger cycle of birth and renewal. . . . Our atoms are billions of years old and have billions of years more life left in them. In the remote future, when they are broken down into smaller particles, they will not die but just get transformed into another configuration" (p. 303). Similarly, our body is programmed to cease as a specific functional unit, but its elements are capable of taking quite different physiological forms: animals, flowers, ice, salt. Substances that make up living and nonliving things are one and the same. We are not diverse from things, from space, from light, from time, but one product. This ultimately reflects the reanimation of life, finding the soul in everything, *anima mundi*.

Full joyful living now and in eternity nonetheless requires understanding of this nothingness, in Rinpoche's phrase, "living in the mirror of death" (p. 3). In fact, only "nothingness" can become everything. And one cannot enter into this nothingness without giving up everything. The spiritual self is obtained by the negation of the ordinary self; letting go of the subjective sense of being. This subjective selflessness is not an absolute state of non-being or non-existence. Rather, it is a state of nondifferentiation from overall existence and reflecting deeply on impermanence. It is giving up differentiating self-awareness from the universe. It is living everywhere and in every thing. It sees our own flesh in continual exchange with the whole of nature.

To reconcile "being" and "nonbeing" simultaneously, to live within the external world while striving for inner transformation, and to search for the grail while not grasping its nature, provides a transcending state. Salvation for ordinary mortals isn't radical negation of living, nor is it waiting for a better life. Rather, it is an embodiment of the contradictions. [**It is life and death as a transformative harmony.**]

THE HEALER

Even Meditation Is Obscured with Meditation

The healer status is bestowed upon the individual by his or her society. Professional degrees for the practice of psychotherapy, including their credentialing and academic requirements, are forms of social sanction. However, too much attention is often paid to the professional training of therapists and not enough to their personal formation. Maybe this is because there are so many teachers eager to teach. It has been sardonically said that psychotherapy cannot be learned—but thank God it can be taught.

The formation of the therapist as healer encompasses personal growth, a broad education that goes beyond psychotherapy per se, and a life philosophy. It is for the therapist—as it is for everyone else—the issue of being and becoming, insofar as the therapist can help a patient grow only as much as he, himself, has grown. That is why what really matters is not schools of therapy but the psychotherapists themselves. Although one's theory is generally reflected in the particular modality he or she chooses to practice, the person of the therapist overrides both the theory and the school to which one is attached. In fact, therapists' technical skills are contextually tailored manifestations of their personality, although the therapist's self can be in danger of getting lost in the quagmire of polarized theories and allegiances. These theories have often replaced philosophy, and even religion, in extreme cases. For example, those who believe in Freud's "Where id was, there shall ego be," themselves behave like an alter-ego to their patients, whereas those who believe in Fritz Perls's, "Where ego was, there shall id be," become an alter-id to their patients. Similarly, the traditionalists value the mind over the senses, while the experientialists say that you should lose your mind and come to your senses.

Either way, both traditionalists and experientialists set man against himself (i.e., neurotic), or for himself (i.e., narcissistic), because they compartmentalize man and do not view him as part of a whole. The psychotherapists of the past have frequently thought of parts of the whole—religion—as a mass neurosis, if not a communal delusion. A single exception was Jung, who embraced spirituality, but considered religion a defense against the experience of God. Religion, however, will always remain a common ground toward spirituality; religion is also part of the *it*.

Those therapists who become overcommitted to the science of psychology, biology, or sociology invariably end up under-playing man's ethical and spiritual dimensions. Other therapists, by overemphasizing specific techniques, whether analyzed or behaviorally manipulated, also make man impersonalized, com-partmentalized, calculated (and most recently, "managed"), and thereby diminished. The contemporary therapist needs to regain his innocence by not being too scientific or too regimented about people, love, and pathology. He must maintain a certain free margin, an openness, credulity, and even ignorance.

The healer is one who is concerned with man's anguish of isolation and alienation, sense of meaninglessness and existential guilt over forfeiting one's potential. Real pathology is "human diminution," says Maslow (1970), and this is especially the case regarding the spiritual diminution. Thus, the healer is one who must himself transcend into a universal consciousness. He must do so in order to practice a psychotherapy that itself opts for such a higher state of consciousness and growth, and that targets the spiritual center of man. That target is approached by fertilizing one's self with broad curiosity and engagement, by expanding interest while seeking informed simplicity, by anchoring the self within solitude and without intimacy, by belonging and believing, and finally, by grounding one's soul in the serenity of spirituality.

The healer is also someone who identifies past and present conflicts and deficits, not to resolve but to *transcend* them. He accepts the person with all his limitations, and at the same time does not settle for that as an end in itself. Moreover, the healer doesn't just apply various techniques toward the resigned acceptance of human dilemmas, but helps the person toward harmonious emancipation from them.

Spiritual existence is a spectrum state. At the near end (earthly and accessible), it is a theology of secular man; here the therapist is a minister of everyday life. At the far end (celestial and inaccessible), it is a theology of cosmic man; here the therapist is a knight of sacred faith. He is at one with the numinous, a part of the incorporeal continuum. At both ends of the spiritual spectrum, the therapist cultivates a set of values, beliefs, and practices in veneration of the divine in life. He relates to the world with an ethic of conviction, and like the advice given to physicians by Paracelsus, shall have the courage to "speak of that which is invisible, unnamed and immaterial" (Moore 1994a, p. 165). [**Such a man is the enlightened man who is a reverent and devout believer of the impenetrable existence of the supernatural. He lives a godly life, has a tender composure. He cultivates a set of values, beliefs, and practices in veneration of the divine and in a state of objectlessness.**]

The Uninitiated and the Unfound

For the healer, there is no "patient" or "client," but rather an uninitiated human being. The healer rejects dualistic terms and discriminatory labels, like normal-abnormal, sane-insane, and all other diagnostic attributes in the form of binary categories. When such duality is transcended, its form disappears. This is the wisdom of nonduality, which is the foundation of the healer's philosophy. He thus opens all unrecognized direction and sees the person not with psychopathology, but with human frailty. Implicit here is a predisposition for growth and strength, wherein our best potential resides not at the pinnacles of our accomplishments, but at our breaking points. These are the fractured places at which we may begin to mend anew.

Moreover, the healer exemplifies two overall orientations or attitudes toward the patient that reach beyond diagnostic limitations. This refers to a

> dual search for the *unique* (selective) and *universal* (shared). The former looks for what makes the person singularly special, at his or her worst and best; it seeks those individual qualities that define and distinguish the person from all others. The latter orientation takes a seemingly quantum leap in the other direction to locate what he or she has in common with others, not . . . within the framework of psychopathology, but on the larger level of what fundamentally binds or connects him or her to all humanity with similar struggles. [Karasu 1992, p. 16]

Beyond this, the clinician's knowledge is independent of his own experience of reality; it is Kantian "a priori knowledge" not supplied immediately by the senses. For the healer the person is as he is because the "whole universe is as it is" (Chopra 1993, p. 157). [**He must show, and not just tell.**]

Statis Descendi

After all is said and done, human beings are really incomprehensible, that is, by the human mind alone. The art of healing considers all theories about the human mind as temporary attempts to fill the gaps of knowledge and, at times, justification of their therapeutic techniques. Nevertheless, even contradictory techniques that is, the resolution of past and present conflicts (when there is no before and after), or the remedying of deficits and strengthening the individual's capacity to cope, are all potentially useful—provided that one recognizes their relativity. The healer thereby sees no contradictions among various schools. In fact, such conflictual polarities invite an offering of faith. Then psychopathology, as defined by all these schools, becomes merely the surface reading of the human condition; similarly, symptoms of conflicts and deficits thus become manifestations of problems at the deeper levels of the soul—*spiritual* arrests, conflicts, and deficits.

Similarly, for the healer, the mind is composed not only of conscious and unconscious forces (the prohibitive superego, the impulsive id, or the executive ego), but also of collective spiritual forces that are prestructured to love and to believe. This makes our mind not a simple mechanical mind but a spiritual one. It carries with it a remembered oneness, a sacred belonging. [**There is no royal road to it, simply a sacred one.**]

One Who Expands to Seek Other, Finds "It"

The therapist's relationship to the individual in the art of healing at times carries some elements of that of doctor to patient (or client), teacher to student, friend to friend, parent to child, or lover to lover, but most of the time it has none of these. The healer's therapeutic role is not that of transference figure, cognitive structurer, behavioral trainer, supportive counselor, or empathic selfobject, although at times it may resemble any or all of these alliances.

Rather, the healer's type of relatedness is primarily a redemptive one and superordinates all other forms of relationship, that is, two persons mutually confirming each other's underlying sense of common destiny without blame or debt. Such redemption is geared not to common sin and guilt, but to a more benevolent restitution and liberation. There is no finding of fault, no punishment, and, in effect, no need for forgiveness. It is the rescue of self and other, an emancipation from the confinement of ordinary human attachments and entanglements, and deliverance from the imprisonment of mind and body without soul. It is a peaceful and restorative union.

Let Your Concerns Be Plundered

The healer has no preset techniques of his own. Like Matisse's students, he must go out and see a flower for the first time, again and again. Moore (1994a) states, "Its rituals are effective *ex opere operato*—from the things done—rather than because of the intentions of the performing the rite" (p. 227). The healer considers the application of specific strategies to another person, especially engaging in deliberate measures to change the other, as an exercise of bad faith, an inauthentic act. Nonetheless, he may borrow from any or all schools of therapy as a basis for "technique." He can utilize interpretation, confrontation, cognitive training, hypnosis, catharsis, role playing, encounter, free association, dream analysis, regression, meditation, or praying. The healing is a way of *being with* someone in a soulful manner that targets the spiritual center of man, independent of any technique to be used for some specific purpose.

The healer doesn't treat an illness, or try to cure a person who has an ailment; instead he remains with a person who is in the process of becoming. The healer and the uninitiated person are a contextual unit—a single entity, and although this single entity can have external and internal dialogues, it relies primarily on

what is not said. This is consistent with Jaspers's (1954) two paths
of philosophical life: the path of solitary meditation and the path
of communication with men, a "mutual understanding through
keeping silence together" (p. 122). If words are also deeds, as the
philosopher Wittgenstein proposed, then by plumbing the depths
of spiritual solitude, silences are also words.

To Reach the Source One Must Swim Against the Current

The healer is not a religious counselor. The Church and its religious
counselings typically represent a structured and organized form of
spirituality with highly specific traditions, proscriptions, and rites
that impose God as a separate theological conception, accompanied by required rituals of seeking His hand. By contrast, the
healer rejects strict formality and substitutes flexibility and freedom. His approach embodies a contemporary religious view that
is universal and nonsectarian, best portrayed as perennial wisdom
or philosophy or the transcendent unity of religions. Accordingly,
it warrants neither piety nor worship. Rather, in Campbell's
(1949) words, "The contemplation of life thus is undertaken as a
meditation on one's own immanent divinity" (p. 319). In short,
the divine being is viewed as a revelation of the omnipotent self
that dwells within everyone. Sheikh and Sheikh (1996) put it as
follows: "All of us have the potential for transcendent experiences.
The great saints and sages of human history are said to differ from
the rest of us by virtue of attainment and realization, not by some
unsurpassable God-given ontological divide that forever sets them
off from us as a separate order of being" (p. 546). Similarly, the
healer makes no godly claims beyond man's own human realization. Spirituality is a path of quiet contemplation, in which we
find the divine in the given world and within ourselves. Spiritual
existence is a journey; one makes the way by going.

The healer is not a typical existential psychotherapist, although both consider technique as bad faith and believe in the importance of real encounter. Existential therapy's fundamental negativity, anguish, doom, and sense of man's finitude are diametrically opposed to spirituality's emphasis on beauty, rebirth, and reanimation of life. In addition, with its phenomenological reduction to immediate experience as the only valid data, existentialism deliberately doubts all notions that are inferred, invisible, or carried over from the past—those that are easily embraced by spirit. Since it believes that human living is a distinct departure from the un-self-consciousness of objects, plants, and animal existence, it construes consciousness as making human life qualitatively different from that of any other species, thus setting man apart from the unity of nature. And although its method of doubt is intended for the ultimate arrival to create freedom from the meaning of meanings, instead it generates existential isolation and freedom from faith. In contrast, the healer is a perpetual beginner, whose uninitiated positivity generates hope and creates harmony with one's self and continuity with the universe.

The healer is not like an analyst. Analysis is founded on the model of sickness. It is pathomorphic, it makes diagnoses, and it seeks cure of patients' illnesses. In addition, it is deterministic (if not overdetermined) and is concerned with etiology and cause. In particular it has a mission; it seeks to crack personal unconscious codes in linear time. In its most orthodox form, analysis is an artificial induction of therapeutic illness by transforming form (the transference) into content. It aims at knowing, that is, insight, and such self-knowledge is its end point. Thus any puzzlement or obscurity must be undone. Furthermore, as the analyst induces transference in the patient, he paradoxically creates an iatrogenic hothouse that itself cultivates psychopathology.

By contrast, the healer believes in a model of health, which is normative and transcends (if not eliminates) diagnoses. It is interested in salvation and healing. It is undetermined, transformative, and noncausal, a transpersonal journey in omnidirectional time. In its most ardent form, spirituality is the induction of stillness, the cultivation of quiescence and harmony between mind, body, and soul. The healer aims not at "knowing" but at enlightenment, whereby self-knowledge is not the culmination, but the starting point. In so doing, it seeks the regaining of lost innocence in order to experience—not *answer*—the eternal riddles of life. In fact, the healer stays observant, until things gradually become obscure. He knows that puzzlement is a necessary state that precedes enlightenment.

The healer is not like academic psychotherapists. He doesn't follow standardized procedures in operational manuals that homogenize all treatment. His work is not based on large-scale bureaucratic research requirements, efficacy, efficiency, or cost-effectiveness. He does not steer in shallow water; he does not prescribe and predict. Rather, the approach used is highly improvisational and fully accepts (if not promotes) heterogeneity. Its N equals 1 and is, by definition, both unique and immeasurable. It is *not* a matter of science and proof, but of belief and faith. He steers in deep waters.

Healers do not practice New Age therapy. New Age psychotherapies promote search for the self—but never get beyond it. They are geared toward self-actualization, self-protection, and self-love (in the smallest sense of the word). They primarily offer quick-and-easy answers that derive from pleasure, not insight or enlightenment. In seeking instant gratification, they are indulgent, excessive, and exalt only the immediate moment, even if they get there by riding others.

In contrast, the healer seeks the self beyond itself, in order *not* to be self-preoccupied; in short, he is egoless. His approach is geared toward self-transcendence, the love of others in a universal, timeless, and spaceless field. Healers help their recipients to relinquish self-serving actions, to express compassion and forgiveness. And they get there by carrying others.

ZENDUST: MASTERING STUDENTHOOD

"I have come empty-handed," said the student.

"Lay it down then," said the teacher.

"But I have brought nothing; what can I lay down? asked the student."

"Then keep on carrying it," was the reply.

—Chao Chou

There is an "ontological primacy" of meanings (Waelder 1930) and the basic human motivation is toward finding compatibility among them and put them into a formally coherent context. This is because the incompatibility of meanings is a basic threat to the human mind. As the mind cannot know itself in an absolute sense, any attempts to do so leave man with the anxiety of the discontinuous. Man must transcend his own mind.

Zen means enlightenment by intuitive insight, a non–self-reflective awareness. It is unknown knowing—but it is a humble perennial studenthood. It never portends to have arrived; that would be a spiritual misprision. Zen knowledge is ultimately reduceable, to be strewn in or to be sprinkled with one's subjective experiences, like the dust. Enlightenment is the redemption from the theories of mind, which regards the mind as an object, a recognition of the hollowness of the search for context. It is reaching a postformal stage of thinking, that understanding itself is an old, outdated model. For the pilgrims of the mind, it will remain just as it is within its own innate ideas. One only begins to comprehend the inner life by a discipline of diminishing one's self and a deliberate resignation.

What is said for the monks is true for therapists: the vocation of a young therapist is to become an old therapist. This implies some transcending maturation and growth as a person as well as a professional. Wisdom, unfortunately, doesn't come automatically with old age. As the outspoken author of "Dear Abby," Abigail Van

Buren, once said, "It's true that some vines improve with age, but only if the grapes were good in the first place." In short, in order to transcend, one has to have something to transcend.

The healer has to cultivate the fourth ear, not only hear the unconscious of the patient with his third ear, but also to hear the transpersonal, transgenerational, and transmaterial in ontological space. The mind is not just a collection of forces and agencies, as Freud formulated, or collective memories, as Jung conceived, but also the seat of soul and spiritual endowments.

To enlighten, the therapist must give up his idealized self for himself and others, to cultivate a willpower of desirelessness, to seek salvation through vulnerability. Enlightenment is a dynamic inactivity, not doing something special. It is a way of being, and the work is never finished. It is recognition that a life is full of joy and sufferance. One need not indulge or eliminate them but simply acknowledge, bear, and put them in perspective and transform them to an enlightened state, dissolving them in wisdom.

In the consolidation of a soulful and spiritual existence, the therapist continues to come closer to an authentic self. Only such authenticity contains really meaningful therapeutic tools, because what endures ultimately emanates from within. The healer seeks innocence and harmony, cultivates an inner and outer stillness, and partakes of unclassified wonderings. He is decentered, a continuous figure behind the ground. He is with the pilgrims of eternity all the way to the altar and beyond. He has only one aspiration: to deserve to be one with the sacred and immortal, a port of the incorporeal continuum.

Finally, alas, the therapist must recognize that this is not a field for spectacular successes (if any field is); as Freud early warned us, every therapy is a relative failure. The tranquility of the therapist largely depends on the ability to live with optimum disillusionment and still maintain profound faith in all persons, with all their vulnerabilities and strengths. Then healing becomes not so much a profession as a way of being in a harmonious relationship to man and infinite nature, a unified quality of mind and heart and soul.

———————◆•◆•◆———————

The turning of one's mind into God is losing both. It isn't "Where ego was, there shall I be," but it is "Where ego was, there shall soul be." It isn't "Where id was, there shall ego be," but it is "Where it was, there shall I be." It is the whole, the collective us, comprising nature and the supernatural.

References

Adler, G. (1986). Psychotherapy of the narcissistic disorder patient. *American Journal of Psychiatry* 143:430–436.

Alexander, F. (1935). The problem of psychoanalytic technique. *Psychoanalytic Quarterly* 4:588–611.

American Psychiatric Association Commission on Psychotherapies. (1982). *Psychotherapy Research: Methodological and Efficacy Issues*. Washington, DC: American Psychiatric Association.

Anderson, H. (1997). *Conversation, Language, and Possibilities: A Postmodern Approach to Therapy*. New York: Basic Books.

Arieti, S. (1974). *Interpretation of Schizophrenia*. New York: Basic Books.

Atwood, G. E., and Stolorow, R. E. (1984). *Structures of Subjectivity: Explorations in Psychoanalytic Phenomenology*. Hillsdale, NJ: Analytic Press.

Bachelard, G. (1971). *The Poetics of Reverie*, trans. D. Russell. Boston: Beacon.

Baker, H. S. and Baker, M. N. (1987). Heinz Kohut's self psychology: an overview. *American Journal of Psychiatry* 144:1–9.

Balint, M. (1968). *The Basic Fault*. London: Tavistock.

Basch, M. (1980). *Doing Psychotherapy*. New York: Basic Books.

———— (1987). The interpersonal and the intrapsychic: Conflict or harmony? *Contemporary Psychoanalysis* 23:367–414.

Beck, C. J. (1989). *Everyday Zen: Love and Work*. New York: Harper Collins.

Beier, E. (1966). *The Silent Language of Psychotherapy*. Chicago: Aldine.

Benjamin, W. W. (1998). *The Magical Years: A Boyhood Remembrance*. Edina, MN: Beaver's Pond Press.

Berzins, J. I. (1977). Therapist–patient matching. In *Effective Psychotherapy: A Handbook of Research*, ed. A. S. Gurman and A. M. Razin, pp. 222–251. New York: Pergamon.

Bion, W. (1967a). Notes on memory and desire. *The Psychoanalytic Forum* 2:271–281.

———— (1967b). *Second Thoughts: Selected Papers on Psychoanalysis*. London: Heinemann.

Bowlby, J. (1969). *Attachment and Loss, vol. 1: Attachment*. New York: Basic Books.

Bradshaw, J. (1990). *Homecoming: Reclaiming and Championing Your Inner Child*. New York: Bantam.

Brenner, C. (1976). *Psychoanalytic Technique and Psychic Conflict*. New York: International Universities Press.

Broyard, A. (1992). *Intoxicated by My Illness and Other Writings on Life and Death*. New York: Fawcett Columbine.

Brussat, F., and Brussat, M. A. (1996). *Spiritual Literacy: Reading the Sacred in Everyday Life*. New York: Touchstone.

Buber, M. (1937). *I and Thou*, trans. R. G. Smith. Edinburgh: T. and T. Clark.

Bugental, J.F. (1987). *The Art of the Psychotherapist*. New York: Norton.

Calestro, K. (1972). Psychotherapy, faith healing and suggestion. *International Journal of Psychiatry* 10:83–114.

Campbell, C. H. (1941). Presentation at Central States Speech Association, Oklahoma City, OK.

Campbell, J. (1949). *The Hero with a Thousand Faces*. New York: Pantheon.

Campbell, R. (1989). *Psychiatric Dictionary*. New York: Oxford University Press.

Camus, A. (1955). *The Myth of Sisyphus*. New York: Knopf.

Carroll, L. (1981). *Alice's Adventures in Wonderland and Through the Looking Glass*. New York: Bantam.

Charleton, J. (1980). *The Writer's Quotation Book: A Literary Companion*. New York: Pushcart.

Chessick, R. (1980). *Freud Teaches Psychotherapy*. Indianapolis, IN: Hackett.

―――― (1989). *The Technique and Practice of Listening in Psychotherapy*. Northvale, NJ: Jason Aronson.

―――― (1993). *A Dictionary for Psychotherapists: Dynamic Concepts in Psychotherapy*. Northvale, NJ: Jason Aronson.

Chopra, D. (1993). *Ageless Body Timeless Mind: The Quantum Alternative to Growing Old*. New York: Harmony.

―――― (1994). *The Seven Spiritual Laws of Success: A Practical Guide to the Fulfillment of Your Dreams*. San Rafael, CA: Amber-Allen & New World Library.

Colarusso, C. A., and Nemiroff, R. A., eds. (1981). *Adult Development: A New Dimension in Psychodynamic Theory and Practice*. New York: Plenum.

Colby, K. (1958). *A Skeptical Psychoanalyst*. New York: Ronald.

Cumming, R. D. (1992). *Phenomenology and Deconstruction: Method and Imagination*. Chicago: University of Chicago Press.

Derrida, J. (1978). *Writing and Difference*. trans. A. Bass. Chicago: University of Chicago Press.

de Shazer, S. (1993). Creative misunderstanding: there is no escape from language. In *Therapeutic Conversations*, ed. S. Gilligan and R. Price, pp. 81–90. New York: Norton.

Dewald, P. (1964). *Psychotherapy: A Dynamic Approach*. New York: Basic Books.

Diagnostic and Statistical Manual of Mental Disorders, Fourth

Edition (DSM-IV). (1994). Washington, DC: American Psychiatric Association.

Dorpat, T. (1977). On neutrality. *International Journal of Psychoanalytic Psychotherapy* 6:39–64.

Dorsey, J. S. (1976). *An American in Vienna.* Detroit: Center for Health Education.

Druck, A. (1989). *Four Therapeutic Approaches to the Borderline Patient.* Northvale, NJ: Jason Aronson.

Eagle, M. N. (1981). Interests as object relations. *Psychoanalysis and Contemporary Thought* 4:527–565.

——— (1984). *Recent Developments in Psychoanalysis: A Critical Evaluation.* Cambridge, MA: Harvard University Press.

Edelson, M. (1975). *Language and Interpretation of Psychoanalysis.* Chicago: University of Chicago Press.

Edwards, D. G. (1982). *Existential Psychotherapy: The Process of Caring.* New York: Gardner.

Ehrenwald, J. (1966). *Psychotherapy, Myth and Method: An Integrative Approach.* New York: Grune & Stratton.

Eysenck, H. J. (1959). *The Uses and Abuses of Psychology.* London: Penguin.

——— (1966). *The Effects of Psychotherapy.* New York: International Universities Press.

Fairbairn, W. R. D. (1954). *An Object Relations Theory of Personality.* New York: Basic Books.

Felperin, H. (1985). *Beyond Deconstruction: The Uses and Abuses of Literary Theory.* New York: Oxford University Press.

Ferenczi, S. (1928). The elasticity of psychoanalytic technique. In *Final Contributions to the Problems and Method of Psychoanalysis,* ed. M. Balint, pp. 87–101. London: Hogarth, 1955.

Fierman, L. B. (1965). *Effective Psychotherapy: The Contribution of Helmuth Kaiser.* New York: Free Press.

Fink, B. (1997). *A Clinical Introduction to Lacanian Psychoanalysis: Theory and Technique.* Cambridge, MA: Harvard University Press.

Fliess, R. (1942). The metapsychology of the analyst. *Psychoanalytic Quarterly* 11:211–227.

Foucault, M. (1973). *The Order of Things.* New York: Vintage.

——— (1984). Space, knowledge and power. In *The Foucault Reader,* ed. H. Dreyfus and P. Rabinow. New York: Pantheon.

Frank, J. (1974). *Persuasion and Healing: A Comparative Study of Psychotherapy,* rev. ed. New York: Schocken.

——— (1987). Psychotherapy, rhetoric, and hermeneutics: implications for practice and research. *Psychotherapy* 24:293–302.

Freedman, J., and Combs, G. (1993). Invitations to new stories: using questions to explore alternative possibilities. In *Therapeutic Conversations,* ed. S. Gilligan and R. Price. New York: Norton.

Freud, S. (1910a). Five lectures on psycho-analysis. *Standard Edition* 11:3–58.

——— (1910b). Observations on wild psychoanalysis. *Standard Edition* 11:219–227.

——— (1911). Psycho-analytic notes on an autobiographical account of a case of paranoia (dementia paranoides). *Standard Edition* 12:3–82.

——— (1912a). The dynamics of transference. *Standard Edition* 12:97–108.

——— (1912b). Recommendations to physicians practicing psychoanalysis. *Standard Edition* 12:109–120.

——— (1913). Papers on technique: on the beginning of treatment. (Further recommendations on the technique of psycho-analysis I.) *Standard Edition,* 12:121–144.

——— (1914). Papers on technique: remembering, repeating and working-through. (Further recommendations on the technique of psycho-analysis II.) *Standard Edition* 12:145–156.

——— (1916–1917). Introductory lectures on psycho-analysis, part III. *Standard Edition* 16.

——— (1925a). An autobiographical study, part 4. *Standard Edition* 20:40–47.

———— (1925b). A note upon the mystic writing-pad. *Standard Edition* 19:227–234.

———— (1937). Analysis terminable and interminable. *Standard Edition* 23:209–254.

Friedan, B. (1963). *The Feminine Mystique.* New York: Norton.

Friedman, L. (1988). *The Anatomy of Psychotherapy.* Hillsdale, NJ: Analytic Press.

Fromm-Reichmann, F. (1950). *Principles of Intensive Psycho-therapy.* Chicago: University of Chicago Press.

Gendlin, E. (1964). A theory of personality change. In *Personality Change,* ed. P. Worchel and D. Byrne, pp. 102–148. New York: Wiley.

Gill, M. (1979). The analysis of the transference. *Journal of the American Psychoanalytic Association* 27(supplement):263–288.

———— (1982). *Analysis of Transference, Vol. 1.* Psychological Issues, monograph 53. New York: International Universities Press.

Glover, E. (1955). *The Technique of Psycho-Analysis.* New York: International Universities Press.

God's Word. (1995). *Today's Bible Translation That Says What it Means.* Grand Rapids, MI: World Publishing.

Goffman, E. (1959). The moral career of the mental patient. *Psychiatry* 22:123–142.

———— (1967). *Interaction Ritual.* Chicago: Aldine.

Goldberg, C. (1977). *Therapeutic Partnership.* New York: Springer.

———— (1992). *The Seasoned Psychotherapist: Triumph Over Adversity.* New York: Norton.

Green, A. (1977). Borderline concept in borderline personality disorders. In *Borderline Personality Disorders,* ed. P. Hartocollis, pp. 15–44. New York: International Universities Press.

Greenacre, P. (1954). The role of transference. *Journal of the American Psychoanalytic Association* 2:671–684.

Greenson, R. (1967). *The Technique and Practice of Psychoanalysis,* vol. 1. New York: International Universities Press.

Guntrip, H. (1971). *Psychoanalytic Theory, Therapy, and the Self.* New York: Basic Books.

Gurman, A. S., and Razin, A. M., eds. (1977). *Effective Psychotherapy: A Handbook of Research.* New York: Pergamon.

Haley, J. (1973). *Uncommon Therapy: The Psychiatric Techniques of Milton H. Erickson, M.D.* New York: Norton.

———— (1981). *Reflections on Therapy and Other Essays.* Chevy Chase, MD: Family Therapy Institute.

Hanly, C. (1985). Logical and conceptual problems in existential psychiatry. *Journal of Nervous and Mental Disease* 173:263–281.

Harris, F. (1967). *I'm OK—You're OK.* New York: Harper & Row.

Hartmann, H. (1939). *Ego Psychology and the Problem of Adaptation.* New York: International Universities Press, 1959.

Havens, L. (1983). *Participant Observation.* New York: Jason Aronson.

———— (1986). *Making Contact: Uses of Language in Psychotherapy.* Cambridge, MA: Harvard University Press.

Heidegger, M. (1971). *On the Way to Language.* New York: Harper & Row.

Hillman, J. (1992). *The Myth of Analysis: Three Essays in Archetypal Psychology.* New York: Harper Perennial.

———— (1996). *The Soul's Code: In Search of Character and Calling.* New York: Warner.

Holquist, M. (1982). The politics of representation. In *Allegory and Representation*, ed. S. J. Greenblatt. Baltimore, MD: Johns Hopkins University Press.

Horney, K. (1987). *Final Lectures.* New York: Norton.

Isay, R. A. (1977). Ambiguity in speech. *Journal of the American Psychoanalytic Association* 25:247–252.

Ivey, G. (1995). Interactional obstacles to empathic relating in the psychotherapy of narcissistic disorders. *American Journal of Psychotherapy* 49:350–370.

Jacobson, E. (1964). *The Self and the Object World.* New York: International Universities Press.

Jaspers, K. (1954). *Way to Wisdom: An Introduction to Philosophy.* New Haven, CT: Yale University Press.

———— (1963). *General Psychopathology.* Chicago: University of Chicago Press.

Johnson, W. (1989). *People in Quandaries.* New York: Harper & Row.

Jung, C. (1933). *Modern Man in Search of a Soul.* New York: Harvest.

———— (1936a). Archetypes and the collective unconscious. In *The Collected Works of C. G. Jung,* pp. 358–407. London: Routledge and Kegan Paul, 1959.

———— (1936b). Psychology of the transference. In *The Collected Works of C. G. Jung,* pp. 495–534. London: Routledge and Kegan Paul, 1959.

Kandel, E. R. (1983). From metapsychology to molecular biology: explorations in the nature of anxiety. *American Journal of Psychiatry* 140:1277–1293.

Karasu, T. B. (1977). Psychotherapies: an overview. *American Journal of Psychiatry* 138:851–863.

———— (1992). *Wisdom in the Practice of Psychotherapy.* New York: Basic Books.

Karasu, T. B., and Skodol, A. E. (1980). VIth axis for *DSM-III:* psychodynamic evaluation. *American Journal of Psychiatry* 137:607–610.

Kemper, J. (1988). Deadlocking and stalemating: primitive defense mechanisms against progression in psychoanalysis. *American Journal of Psychoanalysis* 48:138–155.

Kernberg, O. (1965). Notes on countertransference. *Journal of the American Psychoanalytic Association* 13:38–56.

———— (1975). *Borderline Conditions and Pathological Narcissism.* New York: Jason Aronson.

Kierkegaard, S. (1938). *Journals of Søren Kierkegaard,* ed. and tr. A. Dru. London: Oxford University Press.

Klein, M. (1975). *The Writings of Melanie Klein, vol. 1.* London: Hogarth.

Kohut, H. (1971). *Analysis of the Self: A Systematic Approach to the Psychoanalytic Treatment of Narcissistic Personality Disorder.* New York: International Universities Press.

———— (1977). *The Restoration of the Self.* New York: International Universities Press.

Kohut, H., and Wolf, E. S. (1982). The disorders of the self and their treatment. In *Curative Factors in Dynamic Psychotherapy,* ed. S. Slipp, pp. 44–59. New York: McGraw-Hill.

Korzybski, A. (1941). *Science and Sanity: An Introduction to Non-Aristotelian Systems and General Semantics.* Lancaster, PA: Science Press.

Kovel, J. (1991). *History and Spirit: An Inquiry into the Philosophy of Liberation.* Boston: Beacon.

Kramer, P. (1989). *Moments of Engagement: Intimate Psychotherapy in a Technological Age.* New York: Norton.

Kris, E. (1956). The good analytic hour. *International Journal of Psycho-Analysis* 37:445–455.

Kuhn, T. (1970). *The Structure of Scientific Revolutions.* Chicago: University of Chicago Press.

Kushner, H. (1981). *When Bad Things Happen to Good People.* New York: Avon.

Lacan, J. (1977). *Ecrits: A Selection.* New York: Norton.

Laing, R. D. (1960). *The Divided Self.* New York: Pantheon.

———— (1967). *The Politics of Experience.* New York: Pantheon.

Langer, S. K. (1979). *Philosophy in a New Key: A Study in the Symbolism of Reason, Rite, and Art.* Cambridge, MA: Harvard University Press.

Langs, R. (1973). *The Technique of Psychoanalytic Psychotherapy,* vol. 1. New York: Jason Aronson.

———— (1981). *Resistances and Interventions.* New York: Jason Aronson.

Lasch, C. (1978). *The Culture of Narcissism: American Life in an Age of Diminishing Expectations.* New York: Norton.

Layer, P. (1993). *Time.* Jan. 25, p. 74.

Leighton, A., Prince, R. and May, R. (1968). The therapeutic process in cross-cultural perspective: a symposium. *American Journal of Psychiatry* 124:1171–1183.

Levenson, E. (1976). A holographic model of psychoanalytic change. *Contemporary Psychoanalysis* 12:1–20.

———— (1983). *The Ambiguity of Change*. New York: Basic Books.

London, P. (1964). *The Modes and Morals of Psychotherapy*, 2nd ed. New York: Hemisphere.

Luborsky, L., Singer, B., and Luborsky, L. (1975). Comparative studies of psychotherapies. Is it true that "Everyone has won and all must have prizes?" *Archives of General Psychiatry* 32:995–1008.

Madigan, S.P. (1993). Questions about questions: situating the therapist's curiosity in front of the family. In *Therapeutic Conversations*, ed. S. Gilligan and R. Price. New York: Norton.

Malan, D. H. (1979). *Individual Psychotherapy and the Science of Psychodynamics*. London: Butterworths.

Malcolm, J. (1981). *Psychoanalysis: The Impossible Profession*. New York: Knopf.

Margulies, A. (1984). Toward empathy: the uses of wonder. *American Journal of Psychotherapy* 141:1025–1033.

Maslow, A.H. (1970). Neurosis as a failure of human growth. In *Psychopathology Today: Experimentation, Theory and Research*, ed. W. S. Sahakian, pp. 122–130. Itasca, IL: F. E. Peacock.

Masson, J. M. (1990). *Final Analysis: The Making and Unmaking of a Psychoanalyst*. Reading, MA: Addison-Wesley.

Masterson, J. (1983). *Countertransference and the Psychoanalytic Technique*. New York: Brunner/Mazel.

Maugham, S. (1949). *A Writer's Notebook*. London: Heinemann.

Maurois, A. (1962). *Confession and Autobiography*. New York: Norton Library.

May, R., Angel, E., and Ellenberger, H. (1958). *Existence: A New Dimension in Psychiatry and Psychology*. New York: Basic Books.

Medawar, P. B. (1967). *The Art of the Soluble*. New York: Barnes & Noble.

Menninger, K. (1958). *Theory of Psychoanalytic Technique*. New York: Basic Books.

Merleau-Ponty, M. (1962). *Phenomenology of Perception*, trans. C. Smith. London: Routledge.

Messer, S. B. (1988). Psychoanalytic perspectives on the therapist–client relationship. *Journal of Integrative and Eclectic Psychotherapy* 7:268–277.

Michels, R. (1988). *Psychoanalysts' theories*. Freud Memorial Lecture. University College of London, London, England, January.

Miller, D. L. (1973). *Gods and Games: Toward a Theology of Play*. New York: World.

Modell, A. (1984). *Psychoanalysis in a New Context*. New York: International Universities Press.

——— (1990). *Other Times, Other Realities: Toward a Theory of Psychoanalytic Treatment*. Cambridge, MA: Harvard University Press.

Moltz, H. (1960). Imprinting: empirical basis and theoretical significance. *Psychological Bulletin* 57:291–314.

Moore, T. (1994a). *Care of the Soul: A Guide for Cultivating Depth and Sacredness in Everyday Life*. New York: Harper Perennial.

——— (1994b). *Soul Mates: Honoring the Mysteries of Love and Relationship*. New York: Harper Perennial.

Moszkowski, A. (1971). *Conversations with Einstein*. New York: Horizon.

Ogden, T. (1979). On projective identification. *International Journal of Psycho-Analysis* 60:357–373.

O'Hanlon, W. H. (1993). Possibility therapy. In *Therapeutic Conversations*, ed. S. Gilligan and R. Price, pp. 3–17. New York: Norton.

Orlinsky, D. E., and Howard, K. I. (1987). A generic model of psychotherapy. *Journal of Integrative and Eclectic Psychotherapy* 6:6–27.

Osler, Sir W. (1961). *Aphorisms from His Bedside Teachings and*

Writings, collected by R. B. Bean, ed. W. B. Bean. Springfield, IL: Charles C Thomas.

Parloff, M.B. (1981). *Psychotherapy evidence and reimbursement decisions: Bambi meets Godzilla.* Paper presented at the 12th Annual Meeting of the Society of Psychotherapy Research, Aspen, CO, June.

Parsons, T. (1951). *The Social System.* New York: Free Press.

Perls, F. (1969). *Gestalt Therapy Verbatim.* Moab, UT: Real People Press.

Phillips, A. (1997). *Truth Games: Lies, Money, and Psychoanalysis.* Cambridge, MA: Harvard University Press.

Pine, F. (1990). *Drive, Ego, Object, Self.* New York: Basic Books.

Raimy, V. (1950). *Training in Clinical Psychology.* New York: Prentice Hall.

Redlich, F. and Mollica, R. (1976). Overview: ethical issues in contemporary psychiatry. *American Journal of Psychiatry* 133: 125–126.

Reich, W. (1949). *Character Analysis*, 3rd ed. New York: Noonday.

Reik, T. (1952). *Listening with the Third Ear: The Inner Experience of a Psychoanalyst.* New York: Farrar and Straus.

——— (1956). *The Search Within: The Inner Experiences of a Psychoanalyst.* New York: Farrar, Straus, & Cudahy.

Revel, J. F., Ricard, M. (1998). *The Monk and the Philosopher: A Father and Son Discuss the Meaning of Life.* New York: Schocken.

Ricoeur, P. (1965). On interpretation: an essay on Freud. *JRF Psychoanalysis* 31:499–503.

——— (1977). The question of proof in Freud's psychoanalytic writings. *Journal of the American Psychoanalytic Association* 25:835–871.

——— (1983). *Time and Narrative, vol. 1.* Chicago: University of Chicago Press.

Rilke, R. M. (1903). *Letters to a Young Poet.* New York: Norton, 1994.

Rinpoche, S. (1994). *The Tibetan Book of Living and Dying*. New York: Harper Collins.

Rogers, C. (1961). *On Becoming a Person*. Boston: Houghton-Mifflin.

———— (1965). *Client-Centered Therapy*. Boston: Houghton Mifflin.

Roth, S. (1987). *Psychotherapy: The Art of Wooing Nature*. Northvale, NJ: Jason Aronson.

Sandler, J. (1976). Countertransference and role responsiveness. *International Review of Psycho-Analysis* 3:43–47.

Sartre, J. P. (1957). *Being and Nothingness*, trans. H. Barnes. London: Methuen.

Schacht, T. E. (1991). Can psychotherapy education advance psychotherapy integration? *Journal of Psychotherapy Integration* 1:305–319.

Schacht, T., Binder, J., and Strupp, H. (1984). The dynamic focus. In *Psychotherapy in a New Key: A Guide to Time-Limited Psychotherapy*, ed. H. Strupp and J. Binder, pp. 65–109. New York: Basic Books.

Schafer, R. (1954). *Psychoanalytic Interpretations in Rorschach Testing*. New York: Grune & Stratton.

———— (1970). The psychoanalytic vision of reality. *International Journal of Psycho-Analysis* 51:279–297.

———— (1976). *A New Language for Psychoanalysis*. New Haven, CT: Yale University Press.

———— (1980). Action and narration in psychoanalysis. *New Literary History* 12:61–85.

———— (1983). *The Analytic Attitude*. New York: Basic Books.

Schwaber, E. (1986). Reconstruction and perceptual experience: further thoughts on psychoanalytic listening. *Journal of the American Psychoanalytic Association* 34:911–932.

Searles, H. (1963). The place of neutral therapist responses in psychotherapy with the schizophrenic patient. In *Collected Papers on Schizophrenia and Related Subjects*. London: Hogarth.

Sechehaye, M.A. (1951). *Symbolic Realization*. New York: International Universities Press.

Seguin, C. (1965). *Love and Psychotherapy*. New York: Libra.

Semrad, E. (1980). In *Semrad: The Heart of a Therapist*, ed. S. Rako and H. Mazer. New York: Jason Aronson.

Shane, E. (1987). Varieties of psychoanalytic experience, I. *Psychoanalytic Inquiry* 7:199–206.

Shapiro, D. (1965). *Neurotic Styles*. New York: Basic Books.

Sheikh, A., and Sheikh, K. (1996). *Healing East and West: Ancient Wisdom and Modern Psychology*. New York: Wiley.

Shengold, L. (1995). *Delusions of Everyday Life*. New Haven, CT: Yale University Press.

Sifneos, P. (1973). The prevalence of "alexithymic" characteristics in psychosomatic patients. *Psychotherapy and Psychosomatics* 22:255–262.

Smith, M. L., and Glass, G. V. (1977). Meta-analysis of psychotherapy outcome studies. *American Psychologist* 32:752–760.

Smith, M. L., Glass, G. V., and Miller, T. I. (1981). *The Benefits of Psychotherapy*. Baltimore: Johns Hopkins University Press.

Spence, D. P. (1982). *Narrative Truth and Historical Truth: Meaning and Interpretation in Psychoanalysis*. New York: Norton.

Stern, D. N. (1977). *The First Relationship: Infant and Mother*. Cambridge, MA: Harvard University Press.

——— (1985). *The Interpersonal World of the Infant: A View from Psychoanalysis and Developmental Psychology*. New York: Basic Books.

Storr, A. (1979). *Art of Psychotherapy*. New York: Methuen.

——— (1988). *Solitude: A Return to the Self*. New York: Ballantine.

Strachey, J. (1934). The nature of the therapeutic action of psychoanalysis. *International Journal of Psycho-Analysis* 15:127–159.

Strean, H. (1985). *Resolving Resistances in Psychotherapy*. New York: Wiley-Interscience.

Strupp, H. H. (1960). Nature of psychotherapist's contribution to treatment process: some research results and speculations. *Archives of General Psychiatry* 3:219–321.

Strupp, H. H., Hadley, S. W., and Gomes-Schwartz, B. (1977). *Psychotherapy: For Better or For Worse.* New York: Jason Aronson.

Tarachow, S. (1963). *An Introduction to Psychotherapy.* New York: International Universities Press.

Terman, D. (1984–1985). The self and the Oedipus complex. *Annual of Psychoanalysis* 12/13:87–104.

Tulku, T. (1984). *The Tyranny of the I.* New York: Weather Hill.

Tuttman, S. (1982). Regression: Curative factor or impediment in dynamic psychotherapy? In *Curative Factors in Dynamic Psychotherapy,* ed. S. Slipp, pp. 177–198. New York: McGraw-Hill.

Tyler, S.A. (1990). Eye of newt, toe of frog: post-modernism in the context of theory in family therapy. In *The Systemic Therapist,* ed. B. Keeney, B. Nolan, and W. Madsen. St. Paul, MN: Systemic Therapy.

Waelder, R. (1930). The principle of multiple functioning: observations on over-determination. *Psychoanalytic Quarterly* 5: 45–62, 1936.

Walant, K. B. (1995). *Creating the Capacity for Attachment: Treating Addictions and the Alienated Self.* Northvale, NJ: Jason Aronson.

White, M. (1993). Deconstruction and therapy. In *Therapeutic Conversations,* ed. S. Gilligan and R. Price, pp. 22–61. New York: Norton.

White, M., and Epston, D. (1990). *Narrative Means to Therapeutic Ends.* New York: Norton.

Wiesel, E. (1990). Out of despair. *American Journal of Psychoanalysis* 50:105–114.

Wile, D. B. (1984). Kohut, Kernberg, and accusatory interpretations. *Psychotherapy* 21:18–27.

Wilson, E. O. (1998). *Consilience: The Unity of Knowledge.* New York: Knopf.

Winnicott, D. W. (1971). *Playing and Reality*. Harmondsworth, UK: Penguin.

Wolf, E. S. (1994). Selfobject experiences: development, psychopathology, treatment. In *Mahler and Kohut: Perspectives on Development, Psychopathology and Technique*, ed. S. Kramer and S. Akhtar, pp. 65–116. Northvale, NJ: Jason Aronson.

Wright, K. (1991). *Vision and Separation Between Mother and Baby*. Northvale, NJ: Jason Aronson.

Yalom, I. (1980). *Existential Psychotherapy*. New York: Basic Books.

——— (1989). *Love's Executioner and Other Tales of Psychotherapy*. New York: Basic Books.

Zeligs, M. A. (1961). The psychology of silence. *Journal of the American Psychoanalytic Association* 9:7–43.

Zerubavel, E. (1991). *The Fine Line: Making Distinctions in Everyday Life*. New York: Free Press.

Index

ABOUT THE AUTHOR

T. Byram Karasu is Silverman Professor and the University Chairman of the Department of Psychiatry & Behavioral Sciences of the Albert Einstein College of Medicine. The author or editor of twelve books, author of more than 100 papers, and editorial member of nine journals, Dr. Karasu is the Editor-in-Chief of the *American Journal of Psychotherapy* and a Life Fellow of the American Psychiatric Association. His chairmanship of the APA's Commission of Psychiatric Therapies, and subsequently of its Task Force, produced the renowned 4-volume series, *Treatments of Psychiatric Disorders*. He is Sigmund Freud Laureate and has been the recipient of numerous awards, including the APA's Presidential Commendation.